D1204025

TWAYNE'S WORLD AUTHORS SERIES

A Survey of the World's Literature

Sylvia E. Bowman, Indiana University
GENERAL EDITOR

GREECE

Mary P. Gianos, Detroit Institute of Technology
EDITOR

Clement of Alexandria

(TWAS 289)

TWAYNE'S WORLD AUTHORS SERIES (TWAS)

The purpose of TWAS is to survey the major writers —novelists, dramatists, historians, poets, philosophers, and critics of the nations of the world. Among the national literatures covered are those of Australia, Canada, China, Eastern Europe, France, Germany, Greece, India, Italy, Japan, Latin America, the Netherlands, New Zealand, Poland, Russia, Scandinavia, Spain, and the African nations, as well as Hebrew, Yiddish, and Latin Classical literatures. This survey is complemented by Twayne's United States Authors Series and English Authors Series.

The intent of each volume in these series is to present a critical-analytical study of the works of the writer; to include biographical and historical material that may be necessary for understanding, appreciation, and critical appraisal of the writer; and to present all material in clear, concise English—but not to vitiate the scholarly content of the work by doing so.

Clement of Alexandria

By JOHN FERGUSON

The Open University

Twayne Publishers, Inc.   ::   New York

Library of Congress Cataloging in Publication Data

Ferguson, John, 1921-
    Clement of Alexandria.
    (Twayne's world authors series, TWAS 289)
    Bibliography: p.
    1.   Clemens, Titus Flavius, Alexandrinus. I. Title.
BR1720.C6F4   1974   281'.3'0924 [B]   73-15745
ISBN 0–8057–2231–9

For

CHRISSIE *and* PADDY

Preface

As with my *Aristotle* in the same series, this book is primarily
"What Clement Said." It is an attempt at a detached exposition of
the surviving works, topped and tailed with an introduction, and
an attempt to pull some of the threads together. Such an exposition runs into a number of difficulties from the start. In the first
place it is impossible to be really detached. Clement is an advocate, a passionate advocate, and in reading we are swayed by his
advocacy: "No, that's nonsense" or "Yes, I can accept that." Further, unless we can, either out of conviction, or through imagina-
tion, enter into his world and the things he cared about, we cannot understand him at all. Secondly, any exposition must be
selective, and selection is subjective. How much space to give to
outmoded science or controversies long dead? I have been selective, the exposition is uneven, but I hope that the particular compromise is not gravely misleading. Thirdly, it is impossible to
expound without some sort of commentary, or many of the allusions would be incomprehensible. In this I warmly and thankfully
acknowledge my debt to the French editors of Clement in the
series *Sources Chrétiennes*. Their annotations are thorough and
illuminating; I have accepted their learning, though not, I trust,
slavishly; and this would have been a better exposition if they had
completed their commentary.

I have learned a great deal from the more general books and
articles by the French writers who have been especially diligent
in this field, and in English from the still valuable older work of
Charles Bigg and the more recent work of E. F. Osborn. Three
recent books strike me as of outstanding merit; those of P. R.
Camelot, W. Völker and Salvatore Lilla; all present original insights on the basis of an intensive study of the text. I gladly here
acknowledge my indebtedness to them.

All translations are my own, though I have naturally checked
the versions of others. Clement is particularly difficult to translate
because of his fondness for wordplay. In addition some of his

key terms do not readily go into a single-minded English. I would draw particular attention to the following.

(a) Logos. After considerable thought I decided to retain the Greek word. It means word, speech, or utterance, and is sometimes so used; it may contrast speech with action or theory with practice. It means thought or reason and so the Divine Reason. In *Genesis* God speaks and it is done; the utterance of God is with power. Philo and *John* take up this thought and bring the two strands together. In *John* the Logos is the power behind the universe, revealed in Jesus. For this I have used Logos, but have drawn attention almost tediously to the ambiguities.

(b) Gnostic. This term is used in English most commonly of the heretical sects. Clement uses it most commonly of the Christian who lives in knowledge of God. To avoid ambiguity, except when no error is likely, I have generally spoken of the true Gnostic or the Christian Gnostic. But the root meaning is knowledge, and any term about knowledge is a cross-reference. The Greek had other words for cognition, and I have tried to confine "knowledge" to *gnosis,* but may not always have succeeded.

(c) The Hebrew concept of righteousness, and the Greek concept usually represented by the word "justice" (though this has been influenced by Roman law) are expressed by the same word in Greek, *dikaiosune.* I have discussed the complexities of this in my *Studies in Christian Social Commitment* (London: Independent Press, 1954): enough here to note that I use both English words.

(d) The Greek word *telos* means "end," either in the sense of "goal" or "final point." From this comes the adjective *teleios.* For us in English this is an ambiguous word. It may mean "perfect" or "complete" or "all-embracing" or "fully-grown" "adult" "mature." Sometimes the cognate verb and its nouns are best represented by the idea of fulfillment. The ambiguity is in the New Testament: witness *Mt.* 5,48.

(e) I have discussed in the text the words for love. *Eros* is sexual passion, and I have usually rendered it in some such terms. *Philia* is conventionally friendship or reciprocated love, and I have normally so rendered it. But it also represents natural love within the family, and, by a slightly odd extension, attachment to inanimate or abstract objects as in *philo-sophia,* love of wisdom; here in English, and indeed in the corresponding verb, we can hardly avoid the word "love." *Agape* (three syllables: *a-ga-pe*) is Christian love, the ceaseless seeking of the good of another no matter what his deserts or his response. I have tended to call this "Christian love" except where the simple term is unambiguous.

I have allowed myself some slight repetitions of interpretative material when Clement, as not infrequently, repeats himself. I make no great apology for this. It may be mildly obtrusive to any who are rash enough to read straight through. But I hope that this book will be consulted by those who are interested in particular works, and therefore it is sometimes needful to make the same comment more than once. Also, in summing up in the final chapter, I have deliberately not eschewed the language I have used in the running analysis. On the whole it seemed to me to make the point of the summary clearer. In long years of teaching I have never found it disadvantageous to say the same thing more than once.

Some practical thanks are due: in particular to Professor Mary P. Gianos, the editor of the Greek series, for her kindly and sympathetic encouragement; to Lesley Roff, best of secretaries and friends, whose perfectionism in typing and proof-reading is matched only by her personal interest in the work; to Margaret Bartlett, who has helped the book through its final stages; to my wife, alike for her patience with my preoccupation and for her remarkable skill as an indexer.

Contents

CHAPTER 1

Life and Times

I Clement's Life

OF Clement's early years we know little or nothing. We do not know the date of his birth, though we would guess that it was about A.D. 150. We do not know the place of his birth. Church tradition put it variously at Athens and Alexandria (Epiphanius *Haer.* 32,6). As he was certainly associated with Alexandria in later life his birth there may rest on a faulty deduction, and the tradition of his birth at Athens may rest on an independent and reliable tradition. The name he bears—Titus Flavius Clemens—is Latin not Greek, and we may suppose him to have been a descendant of a freedman attached to the family of T. Flavius Clemens, a relative of the Flavian emperors, and perhaps himself a convert to Christianity.

His parents were not Christians. Clement was a convert, not a birthright Christian. He himself tells us as much (*Paed.* 1,1,1; 2,8,62). So does Eusebius (*D.E.* 2,2,64). But we might have deduced it without explicit evidence from his intimate knowledge of Greek religion. In the second chapter of *The Exhortation* he has an extended and detailed discussion of the several mystery-religions, followed by a rationalizing account of the origin and nature of the Greek gods illustrated with copious examples from mythology. It is plain, as we read, that he has known from the inside the religion which he now mocks, and, if he was indeed born in Athens, it is likely that he was an initiate of Eleusis.

Curiously, he tells us little of his conversion. It was perhaps gradual rather than cataclysmic. Clement was religious-minded. He was seeking God. But God had to satisfy him religiously, intellectually, and morally. He found that the God of the Christians could do this. The gods of the Greeks seemed to him empty of power, philosophically inept, and morally corrupt and corrupting.

So, reluctantly, gradually, thoughtfully, he rejected them, and found among the Christians the God he was seeking.

Almost the only other thing which we know is that he travelled widely in Magna Graecia, the Near East, and Palestine before settling in Egypt. Again we have his own word for it (*Str.* 1,11), His aim, it seems, was to seek instruction in Christianity; we are reminded that the Christian congregations were still small, scattered, and miscellaneous. It is curious that he did not include Rome in his travels. He found some teachers to interest him; he speaks of the clear and animated discourses of blessed and notable men. We cannot be certain who these were. One, an Ionian who taught in Greece, has been plausibly identified with Athenagoras, author of the apologetic *Supplication for the Christians* addressed to the emperor Marcus Aurelius and his son and successor Commodus in the late 170s. Athenagoras had associations with Athens, his favorable attitude to Greek culture is similar to Clement's, and Philip of Side claimed him as Clement's teacher. Melito of Sardis has also been proposed. In Magna Graecia his outstanding teachers were from Coele-Syria and from Egypt; we should only be guessing at their identity. In the East two Christian scholars impressed him, one an Assyrian and the other a Jew. Some have identified the former with Tatian, whose great contribution was a synthesis of the four Gospels entitled *Diatessaron*. Possibly, but Tatian's ferocious attack on Greek civilization seems far from Clement's view, and Tatian considered philosophy no more than a slick scheme for money-making. Bardesanes is another possibility. The Jew might be Theophilus of Caesarea or Theodorus the Gnostic.

Clement's travels brought him to Alexandria in search of further spiritual and intellectual riches. We can discern no intention of settling there. But he met Pantaenus, was conquered, and stayed. Pantaenus is a shadowy figure. He was obviously a great teacher and a magnetic personality. Clement says that, "he, the true, the Sicilian bee, gathering the spoil of the flowers of the prophetic and apostolic meadow, engendered in the souls of his hearer a deathless element of knowledge." From this it has been supposed that he came from Sicily, but this does not follow since Sicilian honey was world-famed, and it may be merely a tribute to the sweetness—and nourishment—derived from his teaching. Philip of Side said that Pantaenus came from Athens, but this is probably only a guess from his philosophical interests. We know nothing of his origins. It seems that he was a convert to Christianity from Stoicism, and that he made a missionary journey to the East, perhaps as far as India; Clement became interested and himself mentions Buddhism (*Str.* 1,15). Clement suggests that Pantaenus was not a writer, and works later attributed to him were presumably suppositious. He was a notable pastor, "a helper to many people," closely identified with his flock, who called him "our Pantaenus." He was a sound expositor of the Bible. Exactly what was the organization of the church in Alexandria is uncertain. Eusebius says that Pantaenus was the first head of the Catechetical School, but this may be hindsight and may suggest a more formal structure than actually existed at the time. But there presumably was some sort of instruction for catechumens or aspirants to membership, and Pantaenus may well have been in charge of this.

It must have been about 180 when Clement came to Alexandria and began to work with Pantaenus. He perhaps shared with him in the teaching of catechumens. But it looks as if the relationship between Pantaenus and Clement may have brought into being something more akin to a philosophical "school." We are not, of course, to think of school buildings in any modern sense; we are not even to think of church buildings. Instruction was in the teacher's private house, and Clement knew what it was to have, as we say, "a full house" for his classes; he also, it seems, knew what it was to be left with a single faithful pupil. Any formal catechetical teaching will have been primarily concerned with, if not confined to, the exposition of the Scriptures; it is hard not to think that Clement ranged more widely at least in providing illustrative parallels from Greek thought, and it has been argued that it was the regular practice of the school to read the philosophers and sift out the good from the bad. Bardy has suggested that we are dealing with a philosophical school rather than a catechetical school. But, as Méhat has pointed out, catechesis is not merely a simple matter of baptismal instruction, and I do not find the two incompatible.

When Clement arrived Agrippinus may have been bishop. He was shortly succeeded by Julian, and it was no doubt Julian who ordained Clement to the office of elder; a later source describes him as priest (*Chron. Pasch.* 7). By the time the combative and long-lived Demetrius reached the bishop's throne Clement was established, and the bishop seems to have done nothing to challenge him. The truth is that we know curiously little about Clement's life in Alexandria. It is clear, alike from his general attitude and from specific references, that he was a shepherd of souls as well as a formal teacher, a minister to the needs of others. The rest is silence. Not even Origen, his greatest pupil, mentions him.

We do not know whether he married, nor, if so, at what stage, nor what happened to his wife. It certainly seems likely that he did. He writes with sympathetic insight of married life, and does in fact at one point associate himself with married men rather than bachelors (*Paed.* 3,11). The man without a home, he says, is missing a lot (*Str.* 7,12), and he writes, as if at first hand, of the wife's concern in times of illness (*Str.* 2,23), of the home-life on a winter night (*Paed.* 2,9–10), of the quiet fellowship of the home (*Str.* 3,9–10). But we are only guessing.

In the persecutions of 202–3, when thousands lost their lives in Egypt and the Thebaid (Eus. *HE* 6,1–3), Clement left Alexandria, never to return. The brilliant, controversial, young Origen took over the teaching. We do not know where Clement went, perhaps to Cappadocia. About 211 he was in touch with the future bishop of Jerusalem (then a bishop in Cappadocia), Alexander, a former pupil of his, and Alexander wrote to commend him to the church at Antioch (Eus. *HE* 6,11,6). The letter concludes with the words: "I am sending this, my dear brethren, by the hand of the blessed elder Clement, a man whose quality has been amply proved. You have heard of him already and will come to know him better. His presence here, through the providential direction of the Master, strengthened and spread the church of the Lord." This implies that Clement had spent some time in Cappadocia, but was not so rooted there that he could not move to Antioch where he was expected to enjoy an extended stay. The persecution had eased, but it does not seem that Demetrius made any effort to recall Clement; he may have felt that Clement went too far in compromising with Greek philosophy. That is all we know, except that by 216 Alexander refers to him in such a way that he must be dead (Eus. *HE* 6,14,8 cf. 6,19,16); he is one of "those blessed men who have trodden the road before us."

We cannot be certain of the dates of his writings, but Méhat

[16]

has suggested a reasonable timetable of the main works as follows: c. 195 *Exhortation;* c. 197 *The Tutor;* c. 198 *Miscellanies* 1; c. 199–201 *Miscellanies* 2–5; c. 203 (after he left Alexandria) *Miscellanies* 6–7; c. 203 *Salvation for the Rich?;* c. 204 *Extracts from the Prophetic Scriptures;* c. 204–10 *Outlines.* This must be there or thereabouts. We can at least be certain of the succession *Exhortation–Tutor–Miscellanies,* which is always assumed (e.g. *Str.* 6.1).

Later Christians did not know very much about him. Eusebius (*HE* 5, 11) describes him as "practised in scripture," Cyril of Alexandria as "fond of learning" and "exceptionally expert in Greek history" (*In Jul.* 7,231; 6,205), Rufinus, who associated him with his own hero Origen, as eminent, catholic in every respect and learned, and, despite his doctrine that the Son was created by God, honoring the glory and eternity of the Trinity, Jerome (*Vir. Ill.* 38) as producing "notable volumes full of learning and eloquence using both scripture and secular literature," Socrates, the ecclesiastical historian (*HE* 2,35), as "full of all wisdom." His works were almost certainly known to pseudo-Dionysius, who calls him "the philosopher," and less certainly to Maximus Confessor who is in some confusion about him. Later, in the ninth century, Photius attacked him for Platonism, Docetism, Subordinationism, and misrepresenting Tradition. The main accusations are that Clement held the eternity of matter, derived a Theory of Forms from scripture, reduced the Son to a creature, believed in transmigration and a plurality of worlds, held that the angels fathered children on women, was a docetist, and held a doctrine of two Logoi. The attack comes from a knowledge of some of Clement's writings, but although it make some valid or genuine points it does not show much real critical understanding. It describes his opinions as "disgusting and outrageous" and the man himself as "burbling and blaspheming." (Phot. *Libr.* 109).

II *Clement's Reading*

Clement was widely read. He cites some 348 authors, and there may be more, from Homer to the obscure Dinon *On Sacrifices.* The citations tend not to be long, and the 25 lines from the Jewish tragedian Ezekiel (*Str.* 1,23,155) is exceptional. The longest quotation from Homer is only seven lines, from Euripides ten, from Plato twelve. The longest extract from the Bible is quite short: *Dan.* 9,24–7. Unfortunately, we cannot be certain that his mention of an author by name implies that he has read him at first hand. There were anthologies and compendia in plenty, and he sometimes no doubt drew on those.

Still, even allowing for an age with fewer distractions, the range of his reading remains impressive. He knew his Bible well, including the part we call the Apocrypha, and those early Christian writings which in the end failed to make the canon. As an Alexandrian he was particularly interested in Philo's synthesis of Greek and Hebrew thought, and many of his attitudes to Platonism, to allegorical interpretation, to the Logos-doctrine, have permeated from Philo. He quotes him freely, often without mentioning him by name. The great allegorical interpretation of the Tabernacle (*Str.* 5,6) draws on Philo, but not exclusively. In the first book of *Miscellanies* he draws on Philo's *Life of Moses*, in the second on his work *On the Virtues*. Alongside Philo he had in his private library a whole range of Gnostic literature, by Valentinus, Basilides, Theodotus and others. It cannot be said of Clement that he quotes his enemies at second hand only. He knew them thoroughly enough to adapt them. Of pagan Greek writers two stand above the others. One is Homer. All Clement's love for Homer does not prevent him from using him as an example of offensive mythology; Plato had done the same before him. But Clement thinks that Homer must have seen through his own anthropomorphism. More often he uses the apt Homeric quotation positively: the Christian's desire for heaven is illustrated by Odysseus's yearning for Ithaca, God's love for man by the mother-bird's care for her fledglings. The other favorite is Plato, and among Plato's works *Phaedo, The Republic, Phaedrus, Timaeus, Theaetetus, Philebus* and *The Laws*, which constitute a solid bulk of reading in themselves. *Parmenides* forms no part of his thought.

For the rest we can be less certain. Hesiod, Pindar, and *The Sibylline Oracles* were probably in his cupboards. About the dramatists we cannot be dogmatic; they are so quotable that quotations may circulate on their own, and the appearance of a text from *Medea* (1078–9) in a similar context in Galen (*De Plac. Hipp. et Plat.* 6), himself citing Chrysippus, and in Clement (*Str.* 2,15) is suspicious. Still, eighty citations from Euripides is a large number; Clement approved of the fact that he cared more for truth than popularity. Menander is also much quoted. There are many parallels with Plutarch, and he had certainly read some Plutarch at first hand. He quotes Herodotus and Thucydides (not Polybius), Isocrates and Demosthenes, Hellanicus and Eratosthenes, and may have possessed some of their works. He is not especially interested in medicine, law, or oratory. The other philosophers he perhaps consulted in the library, or in handbooks. The range of his philosophical reading is not unlike Plutarch's. There is not much Panaetius or Posidonius. Lilla has recently shown convincingly that the sort of synthesis which we find in Clement is found also in Philo and in Middle Platonism, and that therefore we need look no further than these for Clement's sources, Plato always excepted. The premise is well established; the conclusion does not follow irrefragably.

The Bible was of course there, though his citations are interestingly free. There is no part of the Bible which he neglects, but he naturally has his favorite passages. These are *Genesis* 1 (the creation-story), the Decalogue, the Sermon on the Mount, *John* 1 (the coming of the Logos), the hymn to love in the letter to Corinth, *Ephesians* 4. All these are texts which illustrate his theological position. He loves the *Psalms* and the epigrammatic wisdom of *Proverbs*. He is not greatly interested in the historical books. He walks uneasily among the minor prophets, but Isaiah, Jeremiah, and Ezekiel are much in his mind—though, curiously, he never cites the valley of dry bones (*Ez.* 37). He neglects Mark by comparison with the other evangelists, but speaks in a letter of a longer, secret version of *Mark* circulating in Alexandria. Besides the canonical gospels, *The Gospel according to the Hebrews* and *The Gospel according to the Egyptians* were familiar in Alexandria, but Clement accords them a very different status from the others (*Str.* 2,9,45; 3,9,63). He also cites works like *The Shepherd* of Hermas or *The Epistle of Barnabas* which were outside the eventual canon of scripture, but for a long while on the fringe of it.

Clement's use of quotation may be seen in a comparatively short section of *Miscellanies* (1,3). He produces, in quick-fire succession, Democritus, Homer, Solon, *Matthew* 8,20; 1 *Corinthians* 3,19–20, Cratinus, and Iophon; there are only two paragraphs without any quotation at all. It looks more miscellaneous than it is; it is in fact carefully arranged to give the most effective succession. However much he drew on anthologies, such writing would be possible only to a very well-read man.

III *Alexandria* [1]

Alexandria was founded by Alexander the Great. The original citizens were Greeks, but the prosperity of the growing city attracted Egyptians from the countryside as well as Jewish and other immigrants. Already in the third century B.C. it had become a cosmopolis in miniature; one writer calls it "the city of the world," another "a universal nurse." By the first century the free population totalled 300,000; the whole population would be twice as great or more.

Egypt was vital to Rome, negatively as a possible rival, positively for its riches, especially in corn. The emperor became the heir of the Ptolemaic god-kings. He exercised his political authority through a prefect, a member of the middle-class business community, not of the senatorial aristocracy. The chief justice, whose office was in Alexandria, belonged to the same class. The finance-officers also had their center in Alexandria. There was no city-council till the reign of Septimius Severus, despite petitions, and no record of an assembly of the commons. Important magistracies were concerned with education, the draft, food-supply, markets, and religious ceremonies. The Alexandrians had no great reputation outside. Dio of Prusa thought them frivolous. Hadrian (if the letter is authentic) wrote: "The people are mutinous, empty-headed and troublesome; their city is rich, wealthy and prosperous; everyone is busy; their only god is money."

Alexandria's economic prosperity depended on a variety of factors. She was, of course, a notable mart and middleman. But Rostovtzeff argued that a far mightier factor was her natural resources. From the country around came corn; salted meat was also exported, as were wild animals and slaves. Alexandria herself had prosperous light industry: paper-manufacture, linen-weaving, glassware, minor artistic production, high quality metalwork, tapestries, and carpets. When Augustus rewarded the flattery of some Alexandrian sailors he made them promise to use the money on Alexandrian goods (Suet. *Aug.* 98,2). The main imports were timber, metals, wine, olive oil, pickled fish, fruit, cheese, slaves, and horses.

The city was built on a typical Hellenistic grid-pattern. There were at least eleven important streets running east and west, and seven north and south. The main streets were as much as a hundred feet wide, with elaborate street-lighting. The houses were multi-storey, well-built with more stone than wood in the structure and so exceptionally fire-proof. The city was divided into five districts named after letters of the Greek alphabet: the Jews had a walled ghetto in Delta. The water-supply was secured by an astonishing series of vaulted reservoirs, seven hundred of which were still in use in the nineteenth century. Among general buildings we know of a Forum of Augustus, docks, warehouses, theaters, baths, gymnasia, athletic stadia, and a hippodrome. Even greater were the palace, built of alabaster and polychrome marble, and laid out with splendid mosaic floors and luxurious carpets, and containing Alexander's mausoleum, called the Sema (Tomb) or Soma (Body); the Museum or University, a center of scholarship, scientific research and literary culture, founded about 290 B.C., and containing a zoo, botanical garden, and library of three-quarters of a million volumes; and the lighthouse which rose over four hundred feet in the air with three tiers, the bottom square, the next octagonal, and the top round, with its hydraulic lift and its curved metal mirror projecting the light twenty miles out to sea.

The Egyptian gods were naturally prominent in worship: especially Zeus Sarapis (as he was known to the Greeks). There are dedications to Isis, Osiris and Anubis, and most of the Egyptian deities are represented, including a local *daemon* named Cnephis. Among the Greek gods Zeus came first; he hospitably identified himself with various Egyptian powers. Poseidon was naturally prominent in a port, and Demeter for the corn-harvest; there were parallels with the myth of Isis, and we have an elaborate account of a festival of Kore, the maid (Epiphan. *Panarion* 51,22,9–11), which has some Gnostic phrases. Apollo, Hermes, Heracles, Aphrodite, Hera, Dionysus (with whom Antony was identified as consort of Cleopatra-Isis), Hygieia (Health), Tyche (Fortune), and many others are found. Foreign cults also penetrated, Bendis from Thrace, and Adonis from Palestine, for instance. And there was of course ruler-cult. There was an elaborate temple called the Caesareum or Sebasteum (from the Greek name for Augustus), described in superlatives by the Jewish Philo (*Leg.* 22).

The Jews were present in large numbers from early days. They occupied their own quarter of the city and had their own administration. They enjoyed equal rights with the Greeks (Jos. *BJ* 2,18,7). Alexandria was a center of liberal Judaism. Here the Old Testament scriptures were translated into Greek; the legend is fantastic, but the fact certain. Here developed the attempt to co-ordinate the Jewish faith with the philosophies of Plato and Zeno, associated above all with the name of Philo. The degree of hellenization was remarkable. Hebrew and Aramaic soon died out, and the Jews even wanted to participate in athletics. According to the Talmud there were four hundred twenty-five synagogues in Alexandria. But trouble was stirring. First a persecution under Caligula. Then a pogrom during the Jewish War of A.D. 66–70, in which 50,000 lost their lives before the prefect, Tiberius Julius Alexander, himself a lapsed Jew, could restore order. Then more trouble under Trajan and Hadrian. By the time of Clement the Jews, though still numerically significant, had ceased to be a political force of any weight.

Dwellers in Egypt were present at Pentecost (*Acts* 2,10), and the Christians found an important convert in Apollos, a Jew from Alexandria, "mighty in the scriptures" (*Acts* 18,24); he may even have studied at the Museum. *Hebrews* is characteristic of the whole Alexandrian approach, though perhaps due to Apollos's friends Priscilla and Aquila rather than to himself. But even the liberal Jews of Alexandria did not welcome the new religion, and it was the synagogue of Alexandrians in Jerusalem which so bitterly opposed Stephen (*Acts* 6,9). How Christianity reached Alexandria we do not know. Eusebius records a tradition that Mark was sent to Egypt to preach the gospel he had written, and established churches in Alexandria, where the Christians combined asceticism with philosophy (Eus. *HE* 2, 16). The tradition is improbable, simply because neither Clement nor Origen mentions it. Eusebius also records a shadowy succession of bishops: Annianus, who laid down in office in 83–84, Abilius, who lasted till 96–97, Cerdo, who died in 108–09, and Primus (*HE* 3,21; 4, 1). All we can be certain of is that Christianity almost certainly reached the city in the first century, since there was a flourishing Christian community in Egypt early in the second. But we can project back from Clement something of the growth of the church; he claims that it had spread to every tribe, village, and township in Egypt (*Str.* 6,18,167), and Eusebius speaks of large numbers of martyrs (Eus. *HE* 6,1–3). We can see that it spread among all classes; that its orders included presbyters, deacons, and widows; that there was a powerful concern for education; that there was an effulgence of the written word, understandable in a university town (an Alexandrian origin has been claimed for *The Gospel according to the Egyptians, The Epistle of Barnabas, 2 Peter, The Didache, The Preaching of Peter, The Apostolic Canons* and other writings as well as *Hebrews*); that there were links with the churches of Palestine; that there was intellectual division and heresy, and particularly the growth of Gnostic sects; and that there was a firm faith exemplified in the bearing of the martyrs, not least the women, and the devoted service to others.

R. B. Tollinton, more than half a century ago, in the fullest and best account of Clement available in English, identified some aspects of Clement's writing which may plausibly be attributed to his environment in Alexandria. Thus Alexandria was one of the greatest ports of the ancient world, and Clement is particularly fond of the images of the Divine Pilot, and what Gerard Manley Hopkins was to call Heaven-Haven. The image is not original with Clement, but it is strongly persistent. Again, one of the most striking features of the scene at Alexandria was the sanctuary of Pan, a tower in the shape of a cone, with a spiral staircase, whose summit commanded an extensive view over the city (Strabo 17,1, 10). Clement, in borrowing a phrase from Plato (*Pol.* 272E; Clem. *Str.* 7,2,5,) about the "look-out point" occupied by the Son of God, may well have had this tower in mind. Sometimes his references are direct: to the statue of Sarapis, to the great library with its innumerable volumes, to the crowds in the theater or sportsfield, to the city's idle distractions. Sometimes they are more allusive. The name of Savior, *Soter*, as applied to Jesus, is natural enough; yet it had peculiar appositeness in the former capital of Ptolemy Soter, where the lighthouse bore the inscription "To the Savior Gods." Again it was natural to give to Jesus the soubriquet of "The Good Physician"; he had healed diseases of body and soul alike, and his followers continued to do so in his name. But it was a doubly appropriate title in a city with a great medical school. Yet again, Alexandria was a noted musical center. At the beginning of *The Exhortation* Clement has an extended passage of musical imagery, highly relevant in the context of Alexandria. Elsewhere too he likes to use the figure of the harmony of the cosmos. The language of athletics, though borrowed from Paul, would have an immediate appeal in Alexandria.

IV A *Sketch of the Times*

By the first century A.D. the broad picture of Roman imperial power was complete. This was the era of the "immense majesty of the peace of Rome" (as Pliny called it). There might be frontier wars, but a larger area of the earth's surface knew a longer period of untroubled peace than at any time in the history of man either before or since.

Roman power was established by a ruthless imperialism. There was military massacre and enslavement. But, once established, the Romans governed by consent. One example will suffice. The whole of North Africa, from the borders of Egypt to the Atlantic, was policed by a single legion based at Lambaesis in present-day Algeria. When one reflects what the disaffected Algerian guerrillas were able to do against the power of the French in a very small part of that area, we realize that Roman rule was accepted. Recent studies have shown that in this same area there was no question of a small, immigrant, alien ruling-class dominating the indigenes, but that there was interaction and intermarriage and the sharing of power. Rome brought material benefits. Pirates by sea and brigands by land were brought under control. Finely paved roads spanned the empire, and made sixty miles a day a regular journey, and two hundred miles a day possible in emergency. There were no passports, no visas, no forms to fill. Alongside the roads, and of greater importance, was the provision of water. Aqueducts marched across the plains bringing fresh supplies from the hills to the cities and towns. Hygienic public lavatories were available. Timgad (Thamugadi), not far from the north edge of the Sahara desert, had twelve public baths, some of considerable size. In the village of Djemaa n' Saharij (Bida) in the Kabylie, the villagers wash their clothes at a washing-place which goes back to Roman times. "Cleanliness," said John Wesley "is, after all, next to godliness." So is literacy. Tacitus writes of Agricola's governorship of Britain: "He trained the sons of the chiefs in the liberal arts and expressed a preference for British natural ability over the trained skill of the Gauls. The result was that in place of a distaste for the Latin language came a passion to command it." Timgad had a public library with a capacity of

23,000 books. More broadly on the cultural side, Martin Charles-worth in his Gregynog lectures, *The Lost Province,* used the evidence of the Welsh language to suggest that where the Welsh word is derived from the Latin the thing it stands for was some-thing new, and that we can thus get a summary view of Roman cultural achievement. He instanced words connected with ship-ping (anchor, oar, port, ship), with building (wall, partition-wall, door-post, gate, transom, window, step), with country-work (pitchfork, bridle, halter, saddle, manger, mill, well), with inns and shops, with vegetables, fruit and trees, with eating and drink-ing (kitchen, cooking, platter, knife, pan, cake, oven), with writ-ing, with washing (soap and sponge). Alongside these material things should be added Roman law, enriched and humanized by the Stoics. Besides, there was remarkable tolerance. There was real local responsibility: the Roman empire was the great period of the *municipium,* the self-contained, self-governing, genuinely local township. At the same time there was unity: it was the boast of Rome to have made of the world (*orbem*) a single city (*urbem*). This unity fostered the spread of Christianity.

Egypt was an area of peculiar importance to the Roman empire. Its position was anomalous, indeed unique. On the whole the Romans despised the Egyptians; it is an exception to their usual tolerance. They were not allowed to become citizens of Rome, not allowed to enlist in the army. The value of Egypt to Rome was material, and that was immense. Egypt was the granary of Rome. She provided corn, and (though of less immediate importance) papyrus. Here alone the emperor, who at Rome bore the title "first citizen," was a divine king. The province was too rich and im-portant for Augustus to entrust it to a senator to govern; there would be too many temptations to independence and disaffection; the governor here alone was appointed from the middle-class businessmen, the "knights." The Romans inherited and maintained the ruthlessly efficient totalitarian bureaucracy established by the Ptolemies, and they applied to it a system of compulsory public service. Egypt then was a province of exceptional economic im-portance, and this involved an exceptional political structure.

For a century the supreme power lay within the extended family of the first emperor. Then the excesses of Nero led to re-bellion, and some months of chaos. Out of this a new dynasty, the Flavian, emerged. But the third Flavian emperor, Domitian, again degenerated into tyranny, and there was assassination and more turmoil. From this followed nearly a century of high-quality paternalistic government from Nerva, Trajan, Hadrian, Antoninus Pius, and Marcus Aurelius. Whether by an accident of childlessness or by deliberate policy, the dynastic succession was abandoned and the principle established that each emperor adopted as his heir the man best fitted to succeed him. It is one of the ironies of history that the period of prosperity should end when Marcus Aurelius, a Stoic philosopher on the throne of the world, should restore the dynastic principle in favor of his worthless son Commodus. Clement was born into this period of relative tranquility.

But Clement was to live through sadder days for the empire. The reign of Marcus Aurelius had seen a disastrous plague, the cracking of the frontier on the Danube and elsewhere, economic crisis, and the depreciation of the currency. After his death the stability had gone. In the next one hundred four years there were twenty-nine emperors and countless pretenders; they came from all parts of the empire and all classes of society, from Africa to Arabia, from peasants to princes. Commodus was a disaster; he was garroted in A.D. 192. His successor, Pertinax, was a man of wise policy but the troops were now out of hand; he was murdered, and the empire was put up for auction to the highest bidder; the foolish millionaire who bought it paid with his life within weeks. There were pretenders all over the empire. A ruthless soldier from Africa, Septimius Severus, won, though it was some time before he had suppressed all rivals. He restored military discipline, re-established frontier security, cut back the power of the senate and encouraged the middle-class, developed the legal system, benefited his native Africa, and restored the economy. He died in 211. Clement lived to witness the falling out of his two sons, and the remarkable constitutional move whereby in 212 virtually every citizen of any part of the empire became a citizen of Rome, but before he was dead things fell apart again, and the restoration was completed only a century later with the egocentric military autocracy of the ruthless Constantine, who succeeded in achieving a synthesis between the sun-worship which had become the official religion of Rome and the new power of Christianity. Clement's faith was such that he would not have been surprised to see the dominance of Christianity; but what his gentle pacifism would have made of Constantine's brutal, power-seeking militarism is quite another matter.

V *The Church*

Clement tells us surprisingly little about the church of his day. The church is for him a body, a body which God puts on. He likes to speak of the church as Mother. In its true self it is one, and stands in line from Christ and the apostles. Yet it is only a dim reflection on earth of the invisible church, the heavenly city.

Members of the church at Alexandria were mixed in background, education, nationality, wealth, social standing. They seem to have met in a place set aside for worship, though this was perhaps only a room kept for this purpose by one of the wealthier members.

The main sacraments of baptism and the Eucharist were observed. Baptism was the total immersion of adults on profession of faith; immediately after, they were fed on milk and honey. The whole ritual is focused on cleansing and rebirth; Clement likes to speak of illumination, a word borrowed from initiation into the mystery-religions. The Eucharistic service included scripture-readings and a homily, the offering of bread and wine and their distribution, prayer, a hymn, and at some point the kiss of peace. It is not clear whether the regular practice was to celebrate the Eucharist in the context of the Agape or Love-Feast, but it is clear that this last was a valued part of the common life of Christians.

Eusebius, as we have seen, records a succession of bishops stretching back into the first century. They are all names and no more until Demetrius takes office in A.D. 190, that is to say, until the lifetime of Clement, and it seems as if Demetrius was the first effective bishop, if not effectively the first bishop. We must not project too systematic an organizational structure too early. There is a curious phrase in a letter attributed to Hadrian which charges the "bishops of Christ" with being devotees of Sarapis. This may mean that there was more than one church, or grouping of churches, each with its own superintendent minister, or it may mean that the term was more loosely used—or it may not be authentic at all. The same document speaks of elders or presbyters; Clement too speaks of them and belonged to their number. We know from him also of an order of deacons. But exactly what the distinction was at this time in Alexandria we do not know. Later legend depicts an authoritarian bishop, like the later patriarch; a council of bishops or elders; deacons as a separate order with no line to the bishopric; and a congregation with no powers of independency. But this may be a projection back. The monarchical bishopric, however, had been a formulated idea since the time of Ignatius. It would be just to say that the strength of the church in controversy and martyrdom, and indeed in the fellowship of the common life, was due in part to a structure in which there was clear leadership while at the same time each church member felt that in the most sacred sense everything depended on him.

Alongside the worship and the organization was the importance of the scriptures. The Christians had inherited the canon of the Old Testament. For a hundred and fifty years the fundamental authority alongside this was the words of the Lord handed down orally. Clement's older contemporary Irenaeus can still count this as independent of the written gospels. But controversy demanded authority, and through the second century the canon of the New Testament was formed. The Muratorian Canon in fact dates from about A.D. 200 and lies right in Clement's lifetime. However doubtful some may be about some of the lesser writings, 2 *Peter* say, a glance at the Apocryphal New Testament will leave no doubt of the general good sense of the church in their choice of gospels. Compared with the excluded writings, the canonical gospels show a remarkable freedom from fantasy, extravagance, and superstition. It was important to have an authoritative body of writings; yet it was also important that they should be seen as a living witness to Jesus, not as a newly ossified Torah to replace the old in like kind. On the whole this is true of Clement's attitude. He treats the New Testament with loving respect. He does not allegorize it as he does the Torah: this is alone enough to show that he sees it as the source of a living faith. And it is for him a liberation not a new imprisonment. Jesus and his teaching are for Clement primary, not the book that encapsulates them.

Irenaeus and Tertullian speak also of the Rule of Faith. Clement, I think, does not. There are two important aspects of the Rule of Faith which are, however, clearly critical for Clement's thought. Firstly, the Rule of Faith is derived from two sources, scripture and tradition. Tradition is important in Clement; indeed he links it with the concept of Christianity as a mystery-religion. Secondly, the Rule of Faith is not yet a creed; not unless we can call such sentences as "God is Lord of all" a creed. But it is moving in that direction. It is, through tradition and scripture, sifting speculative opinions, and approving them or declaring them wanting. It is the basis of the distinction between orthodoxy and heresy. There were already such problems in the first century; they are reflected in Paul's letters. They begin to assume greater importance in the second century. It was part of the work of preserving the church from losing the gospel in mists of speculation. It preserved what across the centuries the majority of Christians have believed about Jesus, that he was fully human, and yet at the same time a full revelation of God, from beliefs which in denying his humanity made of his life an unreal fairytale or in denying his divinity weakened his claims on the allegiance of his followers. But though something was preserved, something was in the end lost. Intellectual assent to a series of propositions became more important than right living, even than faith. And in the controversies which emerged the pagans who had once spoken the words "How these Christians love one another!" with admiring, envious respect, came to spit them out with savage sarcasm. Clement is at a point of transition. He is concerned to combat error. But truth for him is not formulated and formalized. It is lived in faith and love.

VI   *Church and State*

The Romans were in general tolerant, though Jewish intolerance was difficult to swallow. As Christians and Jews came into conflict it became clear that the Christians were a separate sect, on the face of it politically dangerous, since their founder had been executed for sedition (crucifixion was a political penalty). If Judaism was, reluctantly, an authorized religion (*religio licita*), and Christianity was not Judaism, then Christianity was an unauthorized religion. Further, there were suspicions of immorality, incest, and cannibalism; the Christians called one another brother and sister, greeted one another with a kiss, accorded women a freedom and equality (for example in sharing common meals) unfamiliar to others, and spoke of eating the body and drinking the blood of Jesus. So political and popular suspicion walked hand in hand.

The first clash was almost accidental. The great fire of Rome in A.D. 64 had itself been an accident. But Nero saw the opportunity of grandiose rebuilding, and, once evacuation was complete, he relit the flames. He was accused of starting the fire in the first place. He looked for scapegoats and found them in the Christians. But—inevitably in the circumstances—the investigating magistrates looked for evidence of Christianity, not of arson.

There are signs of continuing pressure. The next explosion was in the reign of Domitian. He, a younger son, uncertain of himself, became assertive in office. He demanded to be honored as "Lord and God." The Christians refused. The author of *The Gospel according to John* showed that for him Jesus alone could have those names (*Jn.* 20,28); the author of *Revelation* portrayed Rome as a scarlet woman drunk with the blood of saints and martyrs (*Rev.* 17,6). At Rome Flavius Clemens and his wife Domitilla were executed.

In A.D. 112 the younger Pliny was governor of Bithynia. Christianity was spreading in town and countryside: temples were empty, sacrificial meat unsold. Pliny executed some Christians who were not Roman citizens, and held others for enquiry. He knew that Christians had been executed; he was not clear whether the offense was Christianity itself or associated crimes, but he gave the Christians a chance to recant, and was puzzled to find nothing criminal in their normal activities. He reported fully to the emperor, who approved his action, and told him to avoid witch-hunts but punish any Christians he found. Tertullian, Clement's contemporary, later made great play with this: if they were guilty, they should be hunted down; if innocent, they should not be punished (Tert. *Apol.* 2).

Christianity remained a capital charge, but the charge was pressed home only in exceptional circumstances or on exceptional individuals. The mob were always ready to blame natural disasters on the anger of the gods with the Christians: "If the Tiber floods its banks, if the Nile fails to flood its banks, if the sky fails to open, if the earth opens, if there is famine or pestilence, the shout goes up immediately 'The Christians to the lion'" (Tert. *Apol.* 40). There were ugly scenes in Greece and Asia in the 150s, at Rome in about 165, in Lyons and Vienne in 177, in Carthage in 180, in Carthage again and Alexandria in the early years of the third century. The most systematic of all the persecutions lay later. In 250 Decius ordered all citizens to show a certificate that they had sacrificed to the gods of the state; fifty years later, in

302, Galerius began a systematic persecution. Yet through all these the blood of Christians was seed, and the church strengthened.

Why were the Romans intolerant of the Christians? There is no easy answer. There was immediate political suspicion of anything which savored of a secret society. Trajan would not permit a fire-brigade in Nicomedia for this reason. When the founder of the sect had been executed for setting himself up as king, it looked very suspicious (*Acts* 17,7). There was the refusal to take part in public affairs and political office, or in military service; the Christians were implacably opposed alike to idolatry and the taking of life. The reasons were ethical and religious but it looked like disaffection. There was the refusal to support the gods of the state and in political crisis this looked like a rejection of the state itself. If a Roman emperor could put Jesus in his private chapel alongside Orpheus, Pythagoras, and others, why could the Christians not honor Jupiter, or the emperor, or the Unconquered Sun, alongside their Jesus?

VII *Greek Philosophy*

At the time when Clement was growing up there were four main schools of Greek philosophy, Platonist, Aristotelian or Peripatetic, Stoic, and Epicurean; Marcus Aurelius had established chairs of these four in Athens.

Behind all four, however, lay the tradition of Ionian natural philosophy. This began with a group in Miletus somewhere about 600 B.C. Mythical elements remained in their work, but fundamentally they were asking new questions and giving a new sort of answer. They were examining the natural world, trying to reduce it to its simplest terms, to understand its structure, and the process of change by which presumably simple elements might produce the extraordinarily varied and complex world we know. Clement perhaps knew their work only or mainly at second hand. So do we, and Clement remains one of our more important sources for these early thinkers. Their answers moved from the simple to the complex, from the isolation of a single element such as water, to a fully fledged atomic theory, though on speculative rather than on experimental grounds. In between had appeared two towering figures, Parmenides and Heraclitus. Clement is aware of Parmenides, but scarcely of his thought (*Protr.* 5).

Parmenides was a ruthless rationalist who carried reason to the extent of asserting that change is impossible, since it involves an object in *not being* what it was before or *not being* before what it is now, and we may not say that not-being exists. What is has no past or future; it is entire, immovable, without end; it is one. To Parmenides ultimately is to be traced back the concept of God as the One. At the other extreme stood Heraclitus. He started from the material world, and showed it was forever changing. Everything is in flux. Yet there is a principle of permanence. It is found in the equilibrium of tensions. Behind this lies a principle of balance. Heraclitus calls this the Logos. We shall be meeting the term frequently in Clement. The root-meaning is perhaps something to do with picking up, but the three main usages are for counting, speaking, and thinking. (For the connection between the first two compare our "telling," or "counting" and "recounting": for the last, language and thought are plainly interconnected.) In Heraclitus the word does not translate simply into English, but this merely means that our categories of thought are different. It is a rational principle which lies behind the universe and manifests itself in the proportioned and orderly arrangement of things and in rational discourse. This concept was taken over by the Stoics. Also in the background of later thought, influential on Plato, is Pythagoras, a shadowy figure, whose thought has affinities with Hinduism, and whose followers combined mathematics, metaphysics, and mysticism, taking number as the root of the universe, teaching the transmigration of souls, and intervening in politics with a sometimes reactionary puritanism.[2]

At the end of the fifth century came Socrates. He was a charismatic personality, more important for what he was than for anything he taught. Indeed, he claimed not to teach, but to be an intellectual midwife, helping others to give birth to the thoughts that were in them, and the diversity of views held by his associates makes it difficult to believe that he was a dogmatic adherent of, say, either Platonic metaphysics, or Antisthenes's rejection of them, a philosophy of pleasure or a philosophy of asceticism. Socrates's charisma long survived him, and the later schools of philosophy invented spiritual family-trees with Socrates as the root. He became, for example, the ideal Stoic sage.[3]

The fourth century saw the emergence of two of the greatest minds ever to touch the study of philosophy. Their influence and the schools they founded were to last for more than eight centuries. Plato was an associate of Socrates, though not perhaps a very intimate one. On the foundation of Socrates's definition by generalization he built the metaphysical skyscraper of his Theory of Forms. He agreed with Heraclitus and Cratylus that the material world was ever changing, with Parmenides that true reality cannot change, with Socrates that we need ethical definition, norms, and standards. The Pythagoreans gave him the key. Mathematical theorems are perfect truths about a world known only to the mind. It is never more than approximately true that in the circle I draw the angle subtended by the diameter at a point on the circumference is a right angle, but it is absolutely true of the circle I can think but cannot see. So, said Plato, beautiful objects are imperfect manifestations of the perfect Form of Beauty, courageous acts are imperfect manifestations of the perfect Form of Courage—yes, and even the loveliest Attic drinking-cup is an imperfect manifestation of the perfect Form of Drinking-cup. God— or, as Plato calls him, the Craftsman—makes the world we know by realizing the blueprint of the Forms in incoherent matter within the receptacle of space. But true reality is in the immaterial Forms, known not with the senses but the mind or soul. They are eternal and the mind or soul that knows them must be correspondingly eternal. Our bodies perish but our souls live on. And beyond even the Forms, beyond being, beyond reality, is the Form of the Good, which gives to everything its meaning. Intellectually, Plato's thought is dualistic, and this affects the emergence of Gnosticism. The vision of perfect beauty in *The Symposium* (211 D), the elimination of false gods in *The Republic* (2,377 D ff.), the doctrine of the tripartite soul in *Phaedrus* (246 A ff.), Reason the Charioteer controlling the more or less unruly horses of Temper and Desire), the assimilation to God in *Theaetetus* (176B), and the account of creation in *Timaeus* were more widely influential on religious thought.

Plato taught in an area of Athens known as the Academy, and the name stuck to the school. For a century and a half they were engaged in working out the implications of this philosophy. Then came a curious interlude when there was an intense concentration on epistemology. The Platonists of this period replaced their founder's dogmatism with an extreme scepticism, directed in no small measure against the rival dogmatism of the Stoics. However, they retained their basic beliefs in other ways, defending them as probable rather than assured. Under Rome a new group of thinkers emerged whom we call the Middle Platonists. They include Maximus of Tyre with his mystical vision of God and the great gulf between God and the world; Albinus, who blends in with his Platonism some Stoic theories, and accepts three first principles: matter, the Forms, and the transcendent God who thinks the Forms; and Numenius, who shakes together Plato, Aristotle, and Pythagoras, and who believed in an ultimate god, identified with the monad of Pythagoras, the Form of the Good in Plato, and Aristotle's Unmoved Mover, who is himself the Form of the second god, Plato's Craftsman—and so through a whole chain we pass down to matter, which is evil. It is important to see that Clement and Origen belong to this group; only they blend in Christianity where the others blend in other philosophies. All alike point forward to the Neo-Platonism of Plotinus, with his exalted vision of God as the One.

Aristotle was a doctor's son who spent twenty years with Plato before breaking off on his own. The doctors were the real scientists of Greece; they observed, recorded, drew generalizations from their records, and tested them. The Peripatetic school, as the Aristotelians came to be called, stood for just this. They collected data, and generalized from these. This principle was applied in many fields: a collection of plays would be the basis for literary criticism; a collection of constitutions for political theory. This tradition continued at Athens; equally important, it was transferred to Alexandria, where the Museum was founded under the Aristotelian guidance of Demetrius of Phalerum, and the zoo, botanical garden, and library show the passion for facts as the foundation of theory.

Two aspects of Aristotle's philosophy remained of particular importance. One is his vision of a kind of ladder of being with God at the top, who is pure Form, pure Actuality, the Unmoved Mover, engaged eternally in abstract thought, and at the bottom (as we may deduce, since it is by definition unknowable) pure matter, mere potentiality without any actuality. The other important point is his ethical theory. In this later generations were fascinated by the doctrine of the mean. Thus courage is a mean (not an exact middle-point) between rashness and cowardice, generosity between extravagance and stinginess, truthfulness between exaggeration and understatement. It is to be noticed that Aristotle insists that though virtue is in essence and definition a mean, in value it is a peak.

By the time of Clement the impulse to original research had expended itself among the professed Aristotelians. Even this needs some qualification. Clement's older contemporary Galen might not have called himself an Aristotelian; his first loves were Hippocrates and Plato. But he wrote commentaries on *Categories* and *Analytics*. At the same time his medical researches, combined with his polymathy, are very Aristotelian. More purely Aristotelian were the commentaries of Aspasius, who flourished in the middle of the second century and wrote on *Physics, Metaphysics, Ethics* and *Categories* among other things, and the works of his contemporaries, Aristocles of Messana, and Herminus, who also wrote original works structured along Aristotelian lines. The greatest of all Aristotelian commentators, Alexander of Aphrodisias, began teaching in Athens at much the same time that Clement was leaving Alexandria. For the Platonists, then, there were new developments; for the Aristotelians consolidation.

The other two schools were formed at the beginning of the period of Macedonian dominance, and spoke to "the failure of nerve." Plato and Aristotle were interested in the truth about the universe, and so in man's place within it. But Epicureans and Stoics were interested in how men and women can find their real selves in an insecure world, and the understanding of the universe is a means to that end. All the philosophies of the Hellenistic Age pursue *autarky*, self-sufficiency, that which Aldous Huxley calls "non-attachment."

Epicurus was an Athenian, born in the land of Samos in about 342 B.C. In 306 he settled in Athens, purchasing a house with a garden, where he and his followers could be out of the hurly-burly of the outside world, and enjoy the communal study of philosophy. Epicurus asserted that the highest good was pleasure, and that pleasure had its origins in physical satisfaction. From this came the malign abuse which treated him as a profligate. But in fact Epicurus believed in the hedonistic calculus—that we should choose the course which involves the greatest excess of pleasure over pain, or the least excess of pain over pleasure. Pleasure in fact is found in tranquility, freedom from disturbance. For this we must free ourselves from the tyranny of desire and fear. Desires are natural and necessary (as for food), natural but un-necessary (as for good food), unnatural and unnecessary (as for fame, position, wealth). The first should be accepted, the second controlled, the third eliminated. So pleasure is found in the simple life lived in retirement. The principal fears are fear of the gods, fear of death, fear of the unknown. Fear of the gods may be eliminated by a sound theology. Epicurus is often accused of atheism, but he was not an atheist. He did not believe in popular superstitions. He believed in gods who do not interfere in the world; but those whose lives are right and who are therefore in tune with the infinite can pick up helpful emanations from them. Fear of death may be eliminated by the realization that death is annihilation, the dispersal of the atoms of body and soul alike, no more to be feared than a dreamless sleep. Fear of the unknown may be eliminated by a scientific understanding of the universe, which Epicurus interpreted in terms of atoms and void. Epicurus believed firmly in free will, in the joy of friendship, and in fellow-ship between men and women.

Epicureanism was somewhat disreputable, and therefore the extent of Epicurean influence has been underestimated. In fact the second century A.D. was the great period of Epicureanism. Clement grew up in a world of Epicurean missionary endeavor. His references are mostly hostile, but occasionally approbatory. There is some evidence of Epicurean influence on the develop-ment of Christianity, for example in the form of Christian writ-ings, or the assimilation of portraits of Christ, once these emerge, to the type of Epicurus. Certainly in the third and fourth cen-turies there are plenty of records of Epicureans joining the church.[4]

Stoic views were generally less repugnant to the establishment at Rome, and in Marcus Aurelius, we can see a Stoic, though a sin-gularly agnostic one, on the throne. Some aspects of Stoic philoso-phy, especially an outlook permeated with religion, and some of the ethics, were acceptable to Christians, as to the Platonists of the period. Stoicism is a religious philosophy; the Stoics were pantheists. God might be called fate, or providence, or nature, or universe. Another term for God, taken over from Heraclitus, is Logos, the divine Reason at the root of the universe. It follows that all is for the best in the best of all possible worlds, that our lives are ordained under providence.

The soul of man is a particle of the divine spirit, interpenetrating our whole frame. Our *ruling principle* is the heart, which is the seat of the mind. The operations of the ruling principle consist in response to the world around us. They are five: *sensation, presentation, assent, desire,* and *thought.* A presence leads to a presentation which leads to an attitude of mind. Desire or will comes from an interpretation of a judgment made by the ruling principle. We have *impulses* and *aversions* naturally within us; only when governed by reason do they become *right impulses.* At birth the mind is a *tabula rasa;* our first impressions come from the senses and are preserved by memory. General notions arise in two ways: from *preconceptions* (the Epicureans use the same term), which seem to be common to all men, and from rational reflection and instinction. Ultimately, the criterion of truth is the Logos, the divine Reason working through human reason. The Stoics came to speak of *an apprehensive presentation:* it is not quite clear whether this means a presentation which the mind grasps, or a presentation which grasps the mind. The consequence is the same. The wise man (the Stoic ideal, a cross between sage and saint) is like a carpenter using a rule, or a man using a balance. He brings his faculties to bear, and if his organs are healthy and the object real, the presentation is apprehensive. Zeno, lecturing, would hold his hand out flat: "There is presentation." He would then incline his fingers: "There is assent." Then he would clench his fist. "There is apprehension." And, finally, as he smashed his closed fist into the palm of the other hand: "There is knowledge."

Ethically, the aim of man is to follow nature and reason. Virtue is a permanent disposition to be chosen for its own sake; the virtues are different manifestations of this, and it is impossible to possess one without possessing them all. Anything which falls short is equally sin; he who offends in one point is guilty of the whole law; you are drowned one foot below the water's surface as surely as full fathom five. (This paradox was too much for the Romans, who developed the concept of progress. It is true that, whether you are in Tokyo or Newark, you are not in New York, but if you are in Newark you can more readily get there.) There is nothing evil but vice, nothing good but virtue. All else—wealth and poverty, life and death—is *indifferent.* But, other things being equal, among indifferent things some are *preferred:* mental qualities such as skill, physical qualities such as health and strength, and *external things,* such as wealth and fame. The wise man will seek the *appropriate* action; this is a semi-ethical concept; it is appropriate to restore a deposit or to honor parents, but it becomes virtuous only through the motive behind it.

> Who sweeps a room, as for thy laws,
> Makes that and th'action fine.[5]

Unreasoning impulse leads to *passion.* The word is a difficult one; we have no real English equivalent. Cicero in Latin rendered it as "perturbation of the mind"; sometimes it is called an "affection." Anger and fear are obvious examples. The Stoic wise man enjoyed *freedom from passion (apatheia),* and this ideal, which hardly seems Christian unless carefully restricted, misled Clement. The later Stoics were not happy with it, and some of them substituted a *right use of passion.* These technical terms are important; they recur in Clement.

VIII   *Gnosticism*

It is difficult to say anything about Gnosticism [6] in a small compass, but it was a vital part of the thought-world of Clement; much of his writing was polemic against it, and at the same time it influenced his categories of thought. Our task is complicated by a number of factors, of which two predominate. The first is that there was no such thing as a Gnostic religion or school or sect. The word "Gnostic" is applied to a wide variety of groups. Gnosticism is thus to be seen as a trend or tendency rather than as a well-defined philosophical or religious stance. As such it can be seen at least embryonically in the background to some of Paul's letters; plainly there was a group at Corinth who exalted the idea of knowledge, and Paul counters this with his hymn to love (1 *Cor.* 13,2). But the main systems associated with the name emerged rather later. Indefiniteness then is the first problem. The other is the fact that though with the Nag-Hammadi finds our primary documentation is greatly enhanced, we still rely to an unreasonable extent on critics and opponents such as Irenaeus, Clement, and later Epiphanius and others.

There are certain trends. In the first place, the very name Gnostic implies the centrality of *gnosis,* knowledge. It is knowledge, not faith or love, which matters. But knowledge of what? Clement tells us in relation to one system (*Exc. ex Theod.* 78) that it consists of "who we were, what we have become (or been born as); where we were, or where we had been thrown (or made to fall); where we are hurrying to, from where we are being redeemed; what are birth and rebirth." Much of this can be summed up as, in the deepest sense, self-knowledge. It is the old Delphic commandment "Know yourself."

Certain other things follow which may serve as reasonable generalizations. In the second place, the knowledge is redemptive. One definition of *gnosis* describes it as "redemption of the inner spiritual man" (Iren. *Adv. Haer.* 1,21,4). Gnosticism is a religion of redemption: it portrays man as in a predicament from which the particular system offers an escape. Third, this very definition shows another feature of most Gnostic systems. Redemption is for the spirit, not for the body or even the soul. The Gnostics see mankind as spiritual beings from another world who have fallen or been thrown down into this material world and are compelled to inhabit bodies and souls. Knowledge enables them to hurry back to the world from which they came. The questions listed by Clement from Theodotus are in fact loaded questions; they imply certain answers. There is a splendid passage in *The Gospel of Truth* (22,3-19): "He who knows is a being from above. If he is called, he hears, he replies, he turns to the one who calls him, in order to return to him. And he knows what he is called. Possessing knowledge, he carries out the will of the one who has called him; he desires to do what pleases him. He receives rest. He who in this way possesses knowledge knows where he has come from and where he is going to. He knows, like a man who has been drunk and awakens from the drunken stupor in which he was, returning to himself and restoring what belongs to him." Gnosticism thus takes an optimistic view of man's fundamental nature, but a pessimistic view of his present state.

Finally, we may notice a tendency of the Gnostics to build inordinately complex systems of spiritual beings. The closest parallel in recent centuries is perhaps William Blake. It is possible to argue about both Valentinus and Blake that they are trying to do justice to the enormously complex combination of contending forces within the human psyche, and applaud them for this.

At the same time it is hard to think that we know quite as much about the spiritual world as the Gnostics seem to claim.

It will be useful to give one or two examples of Gnostic writings or systems. First, there is *The Song of the Apostle Judas Thomas in the Land of the Indians*, which is its proper title; modern editors call it *The Hymn of the Pearl*. This is a charming, tender verse-narrative. It begins

> When I was a little child
> and lived in the kingdom of my Father's house,
> I took joy in the riches
> and splendor of those who looked after me.

The parents take off his fine clothes and send him on a journey down into Egypt along a dangerous road to fetch the single pearl which is guarded by a snake. He goes, and waits for the snake to sleep. He dresses like the Egyptians, but they recognize him as alien and drug him with their food and drink, and he forgets the pearl. His parents send him an admonitory letter which reaches him in the form of an eagle and brings him to himself.

> I remembered that I was a son of kings,
> and my freeborn soul longed for its own kind.

He charmed the snake with his father's and mother's names, seized the pearl, and set off home, taking off his Egyptian clothing. When he reached a key point in his journey, his father sent him his fine clothes of before, and wearing these he suddenly found his real self.

> I bowed my head and did homage
> to the majesty of my father who had sent it to me,
> for I had fulfilled his commands,
> and he had done what he had promised. . . .
> And he promised that I should go with him
> to the court of the King of kings,
> and bringing my pearl as a gift,
> should appear with him before the King.

Plainly the father's house is the original heavenly home, and Egypt the material world (note that the journey is down). The heavenly clothes are his true spiritual self, the ugly, dirty Egyptian clothes are his body. The snake is the evil principle of the material world. What is the pearl? It is a common image for the soul, not as part of the material integument, but the very being of a man. Here surely the Prince is the Son, the Savior, who puts on flesh in order to rescue the pearl, which must be a generalized picture of mankind. The period of sleep will be the thirty "hidden" years of Jesus's life; the eagle will be the Holy Spirit at the moment of John's baptism of him. This then is a fairly straightforward and only mildly unorthodox (but note that the Passion is absent) mythical account of the coming of Christ.

Alongside this, look at the system of Valentinus, though it is exceedingly difficult to summarize concisely and intelligibly. "Indestructible Spirit greets the indestructible one! To you I speak of secrets, nameless, ineffable, supercelestial, incomprehensible to the Dominions, Powers, inferior beings and to the whole Amalgam, revealed to the Intelligence of the Immutable alone" (Epiph. *Haer.* 31,5,1). We are already in a very different world. Before the beginning was an Aeon called the Abyss or Forefather, and with him the female principle of Intelligence or Silence. The Abyss ejaculated the seed of the Beginning or First Principle into his partner, and from this union came the male offspring Mind, Only-begotten, Father, First Principle, and the female offspring Truth. From them came the male Logos (Word, Reason) and the female Life, and from them the male Man and female Church. These are the original Ogdoad of Aeons. Logos and Life produced ten more Aeons, Man and Church produced twelve, and these fifteen pairs compose the Pleroma or Fullness. This is the divine hierarchy: hierarchy it is: only the Only-begotten Mind can know the Forefather. Of the other Aeons we need note only that the last born was the female Sophia or Wisdom.

The other Aeons wanted to see the Forefather. Sophia in particular fell into a passionate yearning, which was not directed to her true mate, and began to explore the depths of the infinite Abyss, where she encountered the barrier of Limit (or Cross). This persuaded her that the Forefather is not to be known, but in the search she had conceived and given birth to a formless being, conceived in ignorance, anguish, and fear. Error thus finds being, and from it the world of matter arises. Limit, which separates the Forefather from the rest of the Pleroma, also separates the Pleroma from the cosmos. The balance and order of the Pleroma has thus been upset, and there is no existence outside the Pleroma. This is countered by the emergence of two new Aeons, the male Christ and female Holy Spirit, whose task is to restore the Pleroma and give form to the formless being outside. To restore the Pleroma they bring them knowledge (not personified). Out of their new unity the whole Pleroma conspire to produce a single new Aeon, Jesus, "the perfect fruit of the Pleroma," who is as Savior to bring the Fullness out into the Emptiness outside.

From Sophia's passion had come formless being, and Christ had been assigned the task of looking after this. Sophia's Desire survives outside the Pleroma as a lower wisdom named Achamoth, from the Hebrew. Christ reaches out to her over the Limit which is also the Cross, and gives her first shape. She makes for the light, but Limit stands in the way, and she becomes absorbed in sufferings of all kinds, which become the material from which the world is formed—in one version, grief, fear, shock, ignorance—and also conversion or supplication. Jesus is now sent from the Pleroma to find his partner in Achamoth. He frees her from her passions, and turns them into matter. Matter thus has in it bad elements (from the undesirable passions), and good elements (from conversion or supplication): earth comes from shock, water from fear, air from grief, and fire from ignorance: from conversion comes soul. From this last substance Achamoth forms the ruler of the lower world, the Demiurge or creator-craftsman, who creates the seven heavens and the world we know. The creator of our world is thus a very inferior being; even to Achamoth he stands as "soul" to the superior "spirit." He is ignorant, and in his ignorance presumptuous, believing himself to be the Almighty. The Torah is his rule. To counter it the Aeons Christ and Jesus are incarnated in the historic Jesus at his baptism, and bring the redemptive knowledge. Some Valentinians declared that the Aeons left before the Crucifixion, but Valentinus, himself in *The Gospel of Truth* recognized and honored the suffering of Jesus.[7]

Valentinus saw himself as a Christian. He is steeped in the New Testament and especially in *The Gospel of John.* His speculations are not so very different from those to be found in *The Shepherd* of Hermas. Nonetheless his system, and still more the systems of his followers, do seem inordinately complex. It is not this complexity which puts off the orthodox Christians; rather does it fascinate them. They are concerned with such matters as the severance of the Old Testament from the New (particularly strongly asserted by Marcion), the complete elimination of faith from the scheme of salvation, the idea that the world of matter is evil (this was very strong among the Manichaeans). They react too against some of the practical and ethical conclusions drawn from the severance of the two worlds, or indeed of the two Covenants. If the Old Covenant is the word of a fallen god, then it must be virtue to break the Commandments. Or, by contrast, if matter is evil, all to do with matter (e.g., sex) must be avoided. The one might lead to licence; the other to an unnatural asceticism. In general, the Gnostic systems, even at their simplest, seem a far cry from the synoptic gospels, and it is significant that the Gnostics find little to their purpose among them, and then they are forced to allegorical interpretation; it is significant also that Clement refuses to allegorize the New Testament. But there are parts of the New Testament which are wide open to Gnostic interpretations, notably *John* and *Ephesians*. Yet at the same time, if we compare the opening verses of *John* with the system just outlined, we can see that the Gnostics have created an impossible fantasy which was in the end distracting from the nature of the Christian religion.

CHAPTER 2

The Exhortation to the Greeks

Introduction

*P*ROTREPTIKOS is short for *protreptikos logos,* an exhortatory discourse. The exhortatory discourse was a familiar literary genre. Usually they were exhortations to the study of philosophy. Aristotle's was one of the most famous in antiquity; it was here that he produced his celebrated defense of philosophy. Cicero's *Hortensius* was another. It was this work which, two hundred years after Clement, was to help Augustine of Hippo to find stability and a purpose in life. In using this title Clement was well aware of its appeal. But the title itself implies a certain ambivalence. We expect an exhortation to the study of philosophy. Is our expectation fulfilled? Is Clement deliberately using the term associated with the appeal of philosophy and transferring it to an invitation to Christianity? Is he calling the Greeks to philosophy, seeing philosophy as a forerunner of Christ, leading men to Christ? Or is he arguing that the Christian religion is the true inheritor of Greek philosophy?

H. Steneker has recently made a careful study of the language and style of Clement's *Exhortation*. He begins by pointing to a notable ambiguity which extends to the very title. The title was familiar: it is a well-known literary genre. In its full form it would appear as *The Exhortatory word*. If we reverse the capitals we see a kind of Christian pun—*The exhortatory Word*. The pun is hidden, rather as George Herbert's "Love bade me enter" might have been called *The Host*, which would have given a pun between the host inviting the guest and the communion host; the pun is unexpressed. In his very title Clement is suggesting that Christ, the Word of God, calls us to the true philosophy. This warns us to look carefully at the word *logos*, and we do well to do so. At 10,3 "the gates of *logos* are governed by *logos*"; shall we translate "reason" or "the Word"? At 68,4 the knowledge of the true God is said to depend on "the health-giving—or healthy—*logos*, the sun of the soul"; shall we translate "reason" or "the Word"? At 93,3 there is a clear play on words: *philologos*, "concerned with language" or "with reason" is used to mean "devoted to the Word." At 99,1, the non-Christians are reproached with being irrational—or rejecting the Word (*alogos*). At 99,3 the curious phrase "logical water" is plainly water blessed by the Logos for baptism.

Clement is on the watch for bridges of this kind. *Pneuma* may mean wind, breath, spirit, or Spirit; John had already built the complex image into the conversation between Jesus and Nicodemus. At 5,3 Clement uses the ambiguity between the Holy Spirit and the breath of man; and at 118,3 he promises Odysseus "a wind from heaven" to carry him past the sirens—but the words can mean, and are intended to mean "heavenly Spirit." Other words ambiguously used are *daemon*, pagan god and evil spirit (40,1; 42,9; 55,4); *eidolon*, wraith and idol (55,4–5); *hypocrites*, interpreter and hypocrite (1,3; 2,2; 4,3; 108,1). In all these we can trace the change of meaning. It is a sheer pun when he passes from the cry of the maenads *Evan* to the name of Eve.

Similar to these are ambiguities of image. We may single out two in particular. One is the snake, which played a significant part in pagan mythology and religion. But the snake was the tempter in the Christian myth of the Fall, and Clement does not hesitate to suggest that Zeus appearing in the form of a snake is the Tempter himself (7,5;16,1). The other ambiguous image is fire: Clement does not allude to fire in pagan myth without some underlying thought of the fire of hell (22,1; 43,3–4; 53,1–3; 118,2).

II Introduction: The New Song of the Lord (1)

The first words of Clement's great sermon—for such we must call it—are characteristic but at first sight surprising: "Amphion of Thebes and Arion of Methymna. . . ." Clement does not start his his appeal for Christ with Christ. He starts with names familiar to his hearers and promptly dismisses them: ". . . were both musicians—and both myths." It is strange that some modern historians have suggested that the historicity of Christ was no part of Christian apologetic; the Christian apologists continually attack the mythical quality of Greek religion, as Clement does here. He assails other legendary figures, as Orpheus and Eunomus.

Pagan cults and pagan hymns celebrate sacred mountains, Cithaeron, Helicon, the ranges of Thrace, where Apollo, the Muses, and Dionysus were honored. The poets who write of them should be banished to those mountains! And now Clement—in the words of the Negro preacher—"switches on the rousements." "Let us bring Truth down from the heavens above, attended by Wisdom in all her splendor, and set her on God's holy mountain amid the holy chorus of prophets. Let Truth project her shining rays to the utmost distance, illuminating on all sides those who are wallowing in darkness, and rescuing human beings from error, reaching out with understanding, which is her strong right hand, to lead them to salvation. Let them respond by gazing upwards, abandoning Helicon and Cithaeron, and making their home in Sion." "Wisdom in all her splendor." The phrase is adapted from Plato (*Philebus* 16 C), but Clement speaks of a revelation beyond that which Plato would allow.

Clement offers his hearers a new song, the song of the Word, which he calls, in an Epicurean phrase, "a medicine against grief." The Word has accomplished those things claimed for other singers. He has tamed the least manageable of all wild animals—man. He has tamed birds in flighty men, reptiles in crooked men, lions in men of strong passions, pigs in pleasure-seekers, wolves in men of rapacity, stocks and stones in men of folly. Yes, and it was this new song which made a melodious composition out of the universe, with the Holy Spirit providing instrumental accompaniment. Here Clement, starting from the Jewish philosopher, Philo, anticipates the writers of odes or hymns to St. Cecilia, who later became the patron saint of music, and borrows his account of the order and harmony of the universe from a philosophical tradition going back at least to Socrates and especially strong among the Stoics.

And now Clement comes to one of the great words of Christian affirmation as he speaks of God's *philanthropy*, his love for mankind. This had been a catchword of the fourth-century orators in Greece; in the Hellenistic age it was applied particularly to monarchs, and attracted an aura of condescension which is not implicit in its root-meaning. Yet this made it particularly appropri-

ate for the Christians to apply to their God, and from *Titus* on-
wards it was so applied.

The Word (Logos)—and we must never forget that the same
word was used by the Stoics of the Divine Reason—was in the
beginning (*John* 1,1). But he only recently manifested himself to
men in person. He is thus both God and man: this is the first
explicit statement of a dogma which was later to split the church.
He is our Teacher; so Clement anticipates the final and unful-
filled portion of his projected trilogy. From him we learn thoroughly how to live well (the thought is from Aristotle), and so
are brought on our way to eternal life. He is our savior; he exhorts
us to salvation. Like a good doctor he offers different treatment
for different patients; from poulticing to amputation, from lam-
entation to threatening. In the prophets the Divine Reason ap-
peals through reason (a slightly odd evaluation of those often
obscure poets, but Clement cannot resist the pun).

And now at last Clement pours out the evidence of Christian
scripture to the faith which he holds. The angel's voice to Eliza-
beth and John the Baptist's voice, "Make straight the ways of the
Lord," refer enigmatically to the salvation to come. And Clement
cites *Matthew* and *Luke* and *John*, bringing them together in a
single synthesis; he cites the epistles, *Philippians* and *Ephesians*
and *Titus*; he cites from some other Christian source a tradition
that John "exhorted" us to recognize the farmer and seek out the
husband; and, characteristically, he mixes in snippets of Homer—
all to show the door of life.

III   *The Gods of the Greeks (2–3)*

After this affirmation of faith Clement turns to the offensive.
He begins with a general warning against meddling with sanctu-
aries, divination, oracles. They are all in decay anyway: "The
spring of Castalia is silent; so is the spring of Colophon." He is
sarcastic about divination by flour, the production of mediumistic
voices, the training of animals for allegedly prophetic purposes,
and reinforces his scepticism by a couple of violent puns. *Mantike*
is *manike* (prophecy is madness) and *chresteria* are *achresta*
(oracles are useless): as we might say that prophets are un-
profitable, and their pronouncements to be denounced.

He goes on to the Mysteries, expressing his distaste for the
rending and eating of a live animal which was the climax of the

Mysteries of Dionysus, and the rape of Kore, the Maiden, celebrated at Eleusis. Again his attack is associated with vigorous
wordplay. The Bacchants cried in their ecstasy "*Evan!*" and
Clement pretends that it is the name of that Eve through whom
transgression has dogged our steps; he makes a double-play in
deriving this (wrongly) from the Hebrew word for a snake. Then
he derives "orgy" from the Greek word for anger (*orge*) and
"mystery" from the Greek word for pollution (*mysos*) or else
with an alternative wordplay *mysteria* are *mytheria*, fictions (but
there is a pun on *theria*, wild animals).

Clement shows considerable knowledge of the Mysteries which
he attacks. Some of his accusations, being made from outside, may
be as groundless as the pagan charges of promiscuity, incest, and
cannibalism against the Christians. But much ancient religion had
its roots in fertility ritual: Aphrodite did have her sacred prostitutes, and there was much to shock the puritan.

There is much of interest to the student of Greek religion.
Initiates of Aphrodite receive the gift of a cake of salt and a
model phallus and give a coin in return. Initiates in the Mysteries
of the Corybantes proclaim: "I ate from the drum; I drank from
the cymbal; I carried the holy plate; I crept into the bridal bed."
The ritual includes a taboo on wild celery. The priests are called
"Celebrants of the Sovereigns." Initiates of Sabazios have a snake
tattooed on their chest. The ritual of Dionysus involves knuckle-
bones, balls, tops, apples, wheels, mirrors, and a fleece. The affirmation of the Eleusinian Mysteries runs: "I fasted, I drank the
potion; I took from the chest; I tasted; I transferred to the basket,
and from the basket back to the chest." Clement uses the name
of Demeter, literally Earth-Mother, but to him Mother Deo, to
play on the idea of Zeus having intercourse with his mother. The
Thesmophoria involves a taboo on pomegranates. The mystic
symbols of Ge Themis are marjoram, a lamp, a sword, and a
woman's "comb" (a euphemism, says Clement, for her sex-
organs). The contents of the mystic chests, Clement continues,
revealing, as he claims, holy secrets, are cakes of sesame, cakes in
the form of pyramids, doughnuts, cakes with holes in them like
navels, salt cakes, a snake, pomegranates, branches from fig trees,
stalks of fennel, ivy leaves, round cakes, and poppies. Once again
Clement bursts into rhetoric as he dwells on the thought of all
that he regards as immorality and triviality: "Put out the fire, of-

ficiant. Feel awe before the torches, torchbearer. The very light convicts your Iacchus. Assign your Mysteries to the night to cover. Let your orgies be judged by the darkness. The fire is not on the stage; it has instructions to convict and punish."

The Greeks called the Christians godless, because they did not recognize the gods of the Greeks. Clement flings the epithet back in their teeth. It is the Greeks who are godless in not recognizing the true God, and in giving the name of gods to beings who do not exist. An interesting parenthesis lists some of those rationalists who had attracted the title of godless, Euhemerus, Nicanor, Diagoras, Hippo, Theodorus, and others. Clement comments that they may not have understood the truth but they at least suspected the error, and that was enough to kindle a seed of wisdom. Atheism and superstition are the poles of folly; the argument is very Aristotelian. Clement claims that men have an innate fellowship with heaven, and cites Euripides to prove his point.

He now turns to identify seven causes of idolatry. These are:
1. The deification of the heavenly bodies,
2. The deification of the fruits of the earth,
3. The invention of gods to explain disaster in terms of punishment,
4. The representation of emotions as gods,
5. The derivation of gods from the texture of human life,
6. The twelve gods of Hesiod and Homer,
7. The invention of savior-gods to explain the blessings received from the true God.

With citations from the philosopher Empedocles and the so-called *Sibylline Oracles* Clement calls his hearers to renounce error. He goes on to point to the number and variety of gods of the same name, three Zeuses, five Athenes, six or more Apollos, and he draws the conclusion that the gods were originally human beings. He does not here mention the name of Euhemerus, the author of a romance which included a cosmopolitan Utopia and this theory of the origin of the gods, though he knew of his work, as we have noted above; we still call this theory Euhemerism. Clement adduces in evidence: Ares; Hephaestus, a smith; Asclepius, a doctor; Poseidon, also known as a doctor; the Dioscuri, even in myth subject to death; Heracles, described by Homer as a man (Hom. *Od.* 21,6); the Muses, who were really (says Clement, fascinated by the relation between words) Mysian girls.

He goes on to an extended study of the immorality of the gods; with Freud behind us we may suspect what lies subconsciously behind such vehement moralizing about "astonishing tales of incontinence, wounds, fetters, uproarious laughter, battles, servitude, drinking-parties, embraces, tears, emotions, lustful pleasures." Clement is not without humor. He quotes some of Homer's most majestic lines in description of Zeus (Hom. *Il.* 528–30) and goes on: "Homer, that's an awesome Zeus you're painting. You endow him with a nod which calls for reverence. But just show him a woman's waist, my dear man, and your Zeus is seen for what he is." What are we doing? Educating the young in fornication?

So Clement piles on the evidence: the trivial origins of the great athletic festivals; the phalluses consecrated to Dionysus; the stories of gods serving as slaves; the myths portraying the gods as all too human, cowardly, hungry, strongly sexed—and dead; and some of their odder titles (a fascinating section for the student of ancient religion): Zeus Agamemnon, Artemis the Hanged Goddess, Gouty Artemis, Yawning Apollo, Guzzling Apollo, Zeus the Fly-swatter, Aphrodite the Tomb-robber, Coughing Artemis, Bald Zeus, Avenging Zeus, Spread-eagled Aphrodite, Aphrodite the Courtesan, Aphrodite of the Beautiful Buttocks or Beautiful Bottom, Dionysus the Eunuch. Better the Egyptian animal-gods than these. And the Greeks have animal-gods too.

But perhaps these gods are daemons, second-class divinities. The word is an interesting one. Its root is uncertain, possibly giving the meaning "brilliant." In early usage *daimon* is virtually indistinguisable from *theos* (god), except that it is generally used of god in relation to men. But as the gods, and in advanced circles the single god, came to be separated from other spiritual powers, the word *daimon* was increasingly applied to these other, intermediate beings. It is a commonplace of Christian apologetic to say to the pagan, as G. K. Chesterton said to the Spiritualists: "The powers in which you believe exist, but they are evil." Hence *daimon* from meaning a daemon, a spiritual power *pur sang*, comes to mean a demon. This is the gravamen of Clement's attack, and by interpreting *daimon* in Hesiod in terms of the vocabulary of his own day he makes a good debating-point. Clement has claimed that his God is *philanthropos*, loves mankind. The daemons, he says, are *apanthropoi* and *misanthropoi*, alien to mankind and hostile to mankind. Human sacrifice is but one example; it is interesting to note that Clement cites (from a Greek historian) a case from Roman history, of Marius sacrificing his own daughter. Men show love of mankind more than these gods. Apollo, in the famous story (Hdt. 1,30; 85–8), let Croesus down; Cyrus spared him. And Clement, who does not mind about the consistency of his attacks, goes back to Euhemerism, and says that the temples are really tombs, anyway.

IV   *Idolatry (4)*

An extended section follows on the evils of idolatry. Here we are aware of the Jewish background of Christianity, and towards the end of the section Clement does indeed quote the prohibition on image-making from the Torah (*Ex.* 20,4; *Deut.* 5,8). But for the most part his exposition is not Judaic. For, in the first place, his arguments are reasoned and philosophical, not *ex cathedra*, and, in the second, he shows a rich appreciation of the work of sculptors and artists; even if it is villainy, it is fair-faced.

The earliest objects of worship were rivers, blocks of stone (an interesting reference to the Ka'aba at Mecca), unhewn wood and the like, and it was out of such blocks of stone and wood that the more sophisticated statues were carved. And they were carved by men; Clement lists some cult-statues by known artists, and gives his sources. This leads him to an account of the origin of the Egyptian god Sarapis (who by this time was widely worshipped and identified with Zeus in a virtually monotheistic cult: "Zeus Sarapis is the One God"); he calls Sarapis "the great daemon." Sarapis had a title "Not made with hands." Clement gives various versions of his origin, and argues that he and his statue were alike human creations, a fusion of Osiris and Apis. He is right in that Sarapis was a political creation of the Ptolemies to provide a religion for their new régime.

This leads Clement to a digression away from the idols along the lines of the consecration of new divinities. The emperor Hadrian deified his handsome young favorite Antinous. Clement is eloquent and Platonic in comment: "Why do you dilate at such length on his beauty? Beauty becomes ugly when it is consumed by outrage. Mortal, do not play the tyrant over beauty. Do not commit outrage against the bloom of youth. If you want beauty to be beautiful, keep it pure. Be a constitutional sovereign, not a tyrant towards beauty. Let it remain free. When you have kept its likeness pure, then and only then will I acknowledge your beauty. When beauty is the true archetype of all that is beauty, then and only then will I accord it worship." It is a fine passage.

Clement returns to his theme. The philosopher Heraclitus rebuked the statues for their want of feeling. Hermes is treated as a janitor. The Romans show what they think of Fortune, their principal deity, by erecting her statue in the public lavatories (a fascinating passage on all counts). Statues have no sensation at all; they are lifeless; they allow themselves to be mauled around by the craftsmen who make them; they are subject to the depredations of dictators, defilement from birds, burglary, destruction by fire and earthquake; we happen to know that the temple of Sarapis in Alexandria was destroyed by fire in A.D. 181. In the middle of this passage comes another epigram of pellucid Platonism: "God, the only true God, is perceived with the mind, not with the senses."

Sculptors use human models for the statues of the gods. The famous courtesan Phryne was much in demand for Aphrodite; Alcibiades in his heyday served as a model for Hermes (another interesting piece of information since Alcibiades was accused of mutilating the statues of Hermes). This leads Clement back to the thought of human divinities. Kings have proclaimed themselves divine; so have commoners. "Those whom you worship were born human and later died." Clement has a complex treble pun. The Greeks, he suggests, were right in calling their gods idols and daemons. There is a pun in the word for "right" (*eikotos*), which is connected with the word for "likeness" (*eikon*, compare "icon"). There is a pun in the word "idol" (*eidolon*), which can mean "image" or "insubstantial being." There is the now familiar pun in "daemon" between "divinity" and "demon." These gods are insubstantial shadows, "shadowy apparitions" (Hom. *Il.* 9,502–3) "haunting tombs and memorials" (Plat. *Phaed.* 81 C-D). If the Devil can quote scripture to his purpose, Clement can draw on vast reading in pagan literature to turn against the pagans.

The statues, he goes on, are of the earth, earthy; Platonic immaterialism raises its head again. Some of the statues are crude; others are brilliantly deceitful. In the fascinating passage which follows Clement begins to sketch a theory of art. First, technique may be praised in its own right. Second, art can create illusion, but it can never create life, and cannot take in a rational being (Clement uses strongly Stoic language here). And then, in spite of his obvious admiration, Clement does not develop his theories constructively. He is obsessed with Plato's view of art as illusion and dismisses the products of the artists as "deadly toys."

The thought of Plato leads him to echo Plato's attack (in *The Republic* (2,377 D ff.)) on the immoral stories about the gods, and this leads him to a repressed and repressive attack on immodest paintings and statues. The pagans have turned their backs on the better and chosen the worst, mere spectators of good, competitors in evil. Christians are forbidden by the Mosaic Law to make graven images. Clement, as so often, ends with a passage of real eloquence: "Do not any of you worship the sun; set your hearts on the sun's maker." We recall how Tertullian, at much this same period, shows an appreciation of natural beauty rare in the ancient world, and looks behind the creation to the creator. A flower in the hedgerow, a seashell, a feather from a moorfowl, a spider's web speak of a creative artist. "If I offer you a rose, you will not scorn its creator" (*Adv. Marc.* 1,13–4). We recall too how Augustine two centuries later went to adore the forces of nature, the sun, moon, and stars, and heard all of them cry, "Not us, but him that made us." (Aug. *Conf.* 10,6). So Clement comes to his conclusion: "Do not any of you make a god of the universe; search for the craftsman" (a Platonic word) "who made the universe. After all, it seems, the only refuge for the man who purposes to reach the gates of salvation is divine wisdom. From there, as from a sacred sanctuary, no daemon can now carry him off. He is speeding on his way to salvation."

A hundred years before, Dio of Prusa had used Phidias's statue of Zeus as the basis for a defense of images (Dio. Chr. 12,59–61). No man can portray abstract thought, pure spirit. But we use the human form, itself a vessel of thought and reason, as a symbol and reminder of that which we cannot represent directly. Again the second-century Platonist, Maximus of Tyre, has an eloquent apology for images (Max. Tyr. 2,1–2). It is natural, says Maximus, in men to seek visual representations of the gods to show gratitude for benefits received. The Divine Being does not stand in need of images. It is humanity in its weakness which needs symbols. Again the body of writing associated with the name of the divinity Hermes the Thrice-Greatest, miscellaneous and of varied date, contains a number of defenses of images. One, in the treatise called *Asclepius*, suggests that man cannot help imitating the divine, and as the one God makes the lesser gods, so man makes gods in his own image. Another argument, in the seventeenth *Tractate*, asserts, much as later Christians did about sacraments, that the Divine is revealed through the definite not the indefinite, and that images contain the visible forms of the intelligible world. In fact, by the time of Clement Christians were already familiar with the image of Christ as the Good Shepherd, and as time went on they were increasingly to take over these arguments; thus, Basil of Caesarea says that the homage passes through the symbol to the person, and Pope Gregory I, while deploring the veneration offered to images, justifies them in the name of tradition, and as the books of the illiterate. The whole matter of images occasioned a major controversy in the Byzantine church. In the meantime it is interesting to reflect on the *volte-face* across the centuries; there is no trace of such tolerance in Clement.

V   The Philosophers and God (5-6)

So far the critique has been almost entirely negative. Clement now turns to the philosophers and arouses the expectation that while some of their views will be seen as empty materialism, others have glimpsed the truth as in a dream. Clement has little appreciation of the achievement of Thales and the Ionian monists or of the pluralists who succeeded them in helping to separate science from superstition. He regards them as atheists in their exaltation of matter. As well honor Poseidon as honor water; Clement digresses to derive Poseidon from *posis*, drink, and (following Chrysippus, the voluminous Stoic) Ares from *anairesis*, destruction. Clement, like Socrates in Plato's *Phaedo*, is interested in the why not in the how. His summary is good and clear. He is right in seeing a residual religious mythology in these early philosophers, and his insistence that they were seeking the material substrate of the universe is strong against the view of some modern critics that their prime concern was with the problem of change. It is, however, odd to find Parmenides listed as a materialist and a dualist, and whatever that strange man did, he did not introduce fire and earth as gods.[1] Clement goes on to suggest (rightly) that fire-worship was found in Persia long before Hippasus or Heraclitus. Paul calls the elements "weak and beggarly" (*Gal.* 4,9); the philosophers failed to discern the creator of the elements.

Others aimed higher in an interfering kind of way: Anaximander with his Infinite, Anaxagoras with his Mind, the Atomists with their Fullness and Void. Some saw divinity in the stars; the Stoics shamefully suggested that the Divine permeates all nature. Clement is particularly interesting on Aristotle. He makes a joke about the father of the Peripatetics being ignorant of the Father of all. Aristotle calls his highest principle the soul of the universe, but he does not allow the divine to extend into the sublunary sphere, and so contradicts himself.

Critical though Clement has been, he evidently considers the views of all these thinkers worth recording. Epicurus alone he banishes from memory. This is slightly ironical, as Christianity owed some debt to Epicureanism, and it was Epicureans and Christians who a few years earlier had combined to attack the fraudulent Alexander of Abonuteichos when Stoics and Platonists had been his gulls.[2]

The philosophers, says Clement, are scaring us with ghosties and ghoulies, with their flux, locomotion, and unplanned vortices. It is idolatry to worship winds, air, fire, earth, stones, stocks, iron, the very world. Their astronomy is astrology; Clement's language echoes the words used of Socrates by his critics. He goes on: "I yearn for the Lord of the winds, the Lord of fire, the Craftsman who made the universe, the Kindler of the sun."

But some have glimpsed the Truth. Plato, for example. Clement shows an assimilated knowledge by bringing together a passage from *Timaeus* (28 C), a passage from the seventh *Letter* (341 C) and a passage from *Phaedrus* (247 C) to present Plato's view of the ineffability of God. Euripides too:

> Tell me—how ought we to think of God?
> As one who sees all and remains unseen.
>
> (fr. 1129 N)

God is the measure of the truth of all things: Clement's assertion is a counter to Protagoras's famous "Man is the measure of all things." It is Plato above all who grasped the truth. Elsewhere,

Plato pays tribute to the debt of civilization to non-Greeks; Clement suggests that he may himself owe a debt to the Hebrews. It was at much this time that Numenius, astoundingly, called Plato "Moses speaking Attic Greek."

Others too laid hold of the truth—Antisthenes, and Xenophon, and Cleanthes, and the Pythagoreans. Clement makes a curious mistake over Cleanthes by ascribing to God a description of the *summum bonum.* But his general approach is interesting. He is not afraid to assert that the Pythagoreans were writing under God's direct inspiration.

VI   *Poetry and God (7)*

What then of poetry? It is of course concerned with fiction; we must remember that the Greek *poietike* which we translate "poetry" means "creation" or "creative writing." Will it be brought to bear reluctant witness to the truth? Will it confess that it has taken the wrong path, the path of superstitious fable?

Clement quotes with approval passages from Aratus the Stoic, Hesiod, and (surprisingly) Euripides, since the last passage suggests that the upper air and sky are God, which one would expect him to condemn as materialistic atheism. Next follows a passage which he oddly attributes to Sophocles. The lines, beginning "One in all truth, God is one," are favorites with Christian writers. We do not know their source, but the attack on idolatry suggests a Jewish writer; they can hardly be by Sophocles, and it is not easy to see by what process they were fathered on him. Then follow passages from the Orphic writings proclaiming that God is one. So Clement accords the Greek poets credit for grasping some glimmerings of the divine Word; the double meaning is clear.

But their witness is negative as well as positive. Menander is not afraid to attack the gods of the Greeks. Homer treats them with human scorn. Euripides openly attacks Apollo in *Orestes* (and, we may add, elsewhere) and paints a singularly unflattering picture of Heracles. Clement ends this brief but telling section with a familiar passage from Euripides's *Ion* (422–7):

> How is this just? You prescribe laws
> for men and yourselves are guilty of injustice.
> But if—it won't happen, but I'll offer the hypothesis—
> if you were fined before men for all your rapes,

you, Apollo, and Poseidon, and Zeus, the lord of heaven,
you'd empty your temples in atoning your injustices.

What is so interesting about this section is not so much what
Clement puts in as what he leaves out. He is well-read in Greek
literature, and not insensitive; he realizes, as not all modern editors have realized, that a Greek play was meant to be staged, not
read. He knows his Homer well, and can quote relevantly, and
generalize fairly about him. But Pindar is notably absent. Among
the tragedians, he has a thorough knowledge of Euripides. But
Aeschylus has some exalted theology much to his purpose; equally
Prometheus offered him weapons for his aggression; neither is
used. Sophocles is wrongly cited, but the passage in *Antigone*
about the immutable laws of heaven does not appear. Callimachus offered a storehouse of myth for him to attack, and one
might have expected Clement to adduce the poet of Alexandria
in evidence, but he does not do so. In short, Clement's main familiarity is with the three poets most popular in his generation, as
the papyri found in Egypt remind us: Homer, Euripides, and
Menander. This is not unexpected. Clement, though having the
courage to stand as a Christian, is essentially a middle-of-the-
road man.

VII   *The Scriptures and God (8–9)*

He now turns to what is for him the real thing, the prophetic
scriptures, whose oracular utterances hold before us in the clearest
possible light the direction towards piety, and so lay the founda-
tion-stone of truth. It is of particular interest that Clement does
not start from one of the Hebrew prophets, but from a passage
from *The Sibylline Oracles*. The passage, with its exaltation of the
One True God, clearly belongs to the Judaeo-Christian strands in
this curious amalgam; Clement, however, from what he says elsewhere, believes in the high antiquity of these oracles. He goes on
to quote Jeremiah, Isaiah, "Moses" (in *Deuteronomy*), Amos,
"Solomon" (i.e., *Proverbs*), "David" (i.e., *Psalms*), about the
power of God and his rejection of idolatry. He quotes, as we
should expect, from the Septuagint, the Greek version, not the
Hebrew original. At two points he makes false attributions. He
quotes Isaiah freely and accurately, but in the middle attributes
to him a catena of passages taken from Jeremiah. And, as we have

noted, he quotes Amos, but he in fact attributes the passage to Hosea. Such errors are easy to make; they show that Clement is quoting from a well-stored memory, and does not always follow Dr. Routh's maxim "Verify your references." Our generation is better equipped with tools of reference than Clement's; Clement antedates Alexander Cruden by one and a half millennia, and relied on his memory more than we do. This makes his assimilated knowledge the more impressive.

He turns next to the New Testament and can still startle us by throwing in a phrase from Homer in the middle of his scriptural citations. God shows supreme love of mankind. He does not behave like a teacher to students, a master to slaves, a god to humans, but admonishes his children "like a gentle father" (Hom. *Od.* 2,47). So Clement calls to his readers, "Come, come, my youngsters." We must all become as little children; then we shall share our father's kingdom with his legitimate son, the beloved. In putting ourselves under God's care, and in showing ourselves true friends of the first-born son, we ourselves become first-born sons. Clement is here combining a basic principle of several Greek philosophers, including Plato, that like is associated with like, with Paul's thought in *Galatians* (which he does not in fact quote) that the Christian becomes the child of God and heir to the promises, through a kind of legal fiction of adoption.

Some reject the call; for them judgment is in waiting. Clement quotes the familiar ninety-fifth psalm, already quoted in the New Testament in *Hebrews* 3,7–11, to reinforce the threat of punishment. But if there is threat, there is also grace. "Today if you will hear his voice. . . ." *Today* is renewed every day; Clement's wordplay is here brilliant and illuminating. The threat and promise alike come from the Divine Word. The Lord loves mankind—the great thought recurs again and again—and calls men to a knowledge of the truth by sending the Paraclete. Here is another wordplay. The Paraclete is the Comforter, or, better, the Advocate of *John* 15,26, that is, the Holy Spirit; the root is the same as the word for call. We might perhaps say that he advocates knowledge of the truth by sending the Advocate. The knowledge in question is godliness. Salvation cannot be bought with gold; in that sense it is priceless. But God accepts payment in the coinage of love and faith. And as Clement—sadly, for there is nothing of Tertullian's *Schadenfreude* about him—reflects on those who will not make the payment; he turns from the Pastoral Epistles to Plato (*Rep.* 10,611 D) and Homer (*Od.* 1,57–8). They grow round the world like seaweed round rocks; they yearn, like Odysseus, for an earthly home.

If we would learn godliness, what better teacher than God? Once again we remember that Clement planned to complete his trilogy with a work entitled *The Teacher*. God's instrument in teaching is the collection of the scriptures. Again we have an illuminating misquotation: "The Lord is at hand; take care not to be caught empty-handed." The first part comes from *Philippians* 4,5, but the remainder is not in our New Testament. Clement goes on to plead with earnest eloquence. The Word shines on all men; where the Word is concerned, there are no Cimmerians—a Homeric reference to dwellers in darkness (*Od.* 11,13–6). He calls for his many hearers to be gathered (if our manuscripts are right) "into one love"—a marvelous phrase. For there is one ultimate Being, and Clement here applies to him the Pythagorean and Platonic term "Monad." So the many separate voices blend in a single choir under one conductor, and their song is "Abba, Father," the first word of the child.

VIII   *The Claims of Tradition (10)*

Clement now turns to an objection. It is an objection still used today by avant-garde intellectuals in Africa. It is that there is no good reason (*logos* again) to overthrow a way of life inherited from previous generations. Clement's immediate answer is rhetorical. We might as well behave like children all our lives! No, when we are wrong, we need to be corrected or to correct ourselves. Then, whimsically, even on a voyage a new route is hazardous but attractive. Tradition is poison. It is tradition which has led the Greeks, like horses with the bit between their teeth, to run away from the Christian charioteers towards the precipices of destruction. Clement has in mind Plato's myth which compares the soul of man to a chariot drawn by two horses, one ruly, the other unruly, under the guidance of the charioteer Reason (Plat. *Phaedr.* 246 A ff.). This is, in other words, a hidden wordplay on *Logos*. He reinforces it by two more plays on words, one between *hagios* "holy" and *enages* "accursed," and one between *ethos* "tradition" and *theos* "god." The Greeks ought to live according to

God, not according to tradition; we might say that their lives should be godded not dogged.

Clement goes on to a curious description of pagan priests, with matted hair, dirty rags for clothes, nails like talons, and the appearance of never washing. He could hardly say this if it were demonstrably untrue; it certainly was not true of the priests of Isis, but we must not idealize all shrines because of the architectural glories of the Parthenon, and many were no doubt sleazy. This should be enough to send the worshippers to the true God, escaping from their earthly prisons—another Pythagorean-Platonic thought. And now Clement has one of his touchingly tender passages. God in his love of mankind does not let us go. God is a father; he goes in search of his creature. Dogs when lost find their master's scent; a horse may throw its rider but will still respond to his whistle. Man is God's ultimate creation; shall he serve another master? And at this point Clement does a moving thing. He does not stand on a pedestal and exhort his audience to repent. He identifies himself with them, and says, "Let us repent" or rather, for that is what the word really means, "Let us change our minds and turn from ignorance to knowledge, from folly to wisdom, from indiscipline to self-discipline, from unrighteousness to righteousness, from godlessness to God." Then, in a splendid phrase, he adds, "Glorious is the danger in deserting to God's side." The form of the phrase shows that Clement has in mind the climactic phrase of Plato's *Phaedo* with its promise of immortality (114 D), but there is an even more fascinating parallel with a phrase from Horace: "There is a delightful danger in following a god" (*Od.* 3,25, 18–9). Did Clement, one asks, know Horace's lines? God gives his grace freely; we have only to respond freely to inherit glory, a glory which Clement describes in words from the lost *Apocalypse of Elijah*.

And now Clement does speak as a Christian to non-Christians, and calls to them to have faith. They do not deliberate before they get drunk; why this deferring of the question of turning to God? "Have the same faith in us," says Clement, "that you have in intoxication, in order to become sober." He turns to the language of athletics, as so often, and issues an invitation to strip and compete on the track of truth, where the holy Logos is umpire and the Lord of the universe is president. Human craftsmen cannot give life to their creations, only the Father, the supreme artist (here Clement is quoting Pindar) can do that. The image of Olympian Zeus is an image of an image, illusory, unspeaking (Clement has in mind Plato's denigration of the artist: Plato claimed that the material object was a copy or image of the archetypal Form, and a work of art a copy or image of the material object). The image of God is the Logos, the Word, the Light which is the archetype of light. The image of the Logos is to be seen in the true man, that is the mind in man who is therefore said to be made in the image of God, and it is from his likeness to the divine Reason that he is endowed with reason. It is a closely argued passage, highly characteristic of Clement with its assimilated Platonism and its wordplay on the Logos.

Tradition has been fostered by opinion (which in Plato is contrasted with knowledge); it creates a taste for subservience and an unreasoning concentration on the insignificant. Ignorance is the cause of superstition and of its defilements. The remedy lies in the water of Reason washing off the dirt of tradition. What is the route to heaven? The Lord is the Way. And it is man's true nature to be in fellowship with God. We give each animal its natural task; we do not force the horse to plough (an interesting comment on changing practices in agriculture) or the bull to hunt. Man is born to see heaven (there is a pun on *thea*, sight, and *theos*, God) and should naturally turn to the knowledge of God. Then comes another marvelous passage: "Farm, if you are a farmer, but acknowledge God while you farm. Sail your ship, if you are in love with the life at sea, but call on the heavenly pilot as you do so. If you were on campaign when knowledge took hold of you, listen to the general whose command is righteousness."

The themes recur again and again as Clement repeats himself in his earnestness. The Greeks are drunk, idolatrous, ignorant, enslaved by tradition. They should say good-bye to fancies, opinion, tradition. They can see that the herms are mere stones, that the halo and rainbow (Iris) are natural phenomena not gods, that the sun and moon are no more gods than the day, month and year they mark, that Ares is no more a god than is a battle, that water is no more a god than is a shower of rain, that fortune is no more a god than action. The gods of the Greeks are insensible, dictators of stone and wood. Man is God's creation, his peculiar possession; he cannot serve another master. It is false to think that stocks and stones and animals are holy things but men are not; better to treat men as holy, and animals and inanimate objects for what they are. It is wretched to treat a raven as a messenger of God, and persecute the man of God, who does not croak or crow but speaks, and speaks with reason and love of mankind. God's love of mankind is ineffable, but it is inseparable from hatred of evil; his anger brings punishment, his love of mankind calls to repentance. Nothing blocks the path of man who is really eager for knowledge of God. As Menander says,

> The good man is at all points a savior.

But some are like deaf adders; they must spit out their poison, slough off their skin, check their snake-convolutions. And again a rhetorical climax, with the anaphora of the repeated word: "Have faith, man, in one who is man and God. Have faith, man, in one who suffered and is worshipped. Slaves, have faith in the dead man who is the living God. All men, have faith solely in the God of all men. Have faith, and receive salvation as your reward." The noblest hymn to God is a man who has found immortality, a man who is built up by righteousness, a man on whom are stamped the words of truth.

The themes continue. The very animals are more blessed than men in error. They are ignorant, but they do not pretend to truth; this is an allusion to the Socratic claim that his wisdom consisted in his knowledge of his ignorance. The Greeks have made themselves, by turning their backs on the divine Reason, more irrational than irrational animals. They have been boys, adolescents, cadets, grown men, but never good. (We remember that the Christians were early called "The good" with the implication of "The goody-goodies.") We enjoy sweets and do not like medicines; so we enjoy tradition and do not like truth. But truth is not hard to grasp, with hands, mouth, and heart (*Deut.* 30, 14), that is, will, action, and word. Then tradition is discarded, like the toys of childhood.

The power of God has shone upon the earth and filled the whole world with the seed of salvation. The Lord has accomplished this great achievement in a short while through God's providence. He it was who began to perform the drama of salvation. He was our champion and one with his creatures in a team of champions. He is the Word, he signs the cease-fire, he is mediator and savior, the spring of life and of peace.

IX *The Message of Salvation (11–2)*

Man was originally the child of God, playing in innocent freedom. He was led astray through the serpent pleasure. The Lord wanted to free him again, bound himself in flesh (and Clement, who has criticized the mystery-religions, calls this a divine mystery) to worst the serpent and enslave death the dictator. The Lord set and man rose.

There follows a passage which expresses well a dichotomy in Clement's mind. The Logos, which, we must always remember, means Reason, has come to us from heaven. We ought not to bother our heads with education from Athens, the rest of Greece, or Ionia. This at first sight might seem to be a dissuasive from Greek philosophy. But he goes on to say that the Logos is our teacher and has filled the whole world with the power of holiness so that the whole world has become an Athens, a Greece, by the power of the Logos (or, ambiguously, for reason). We might say, in a pun which Clement could not make but would approve, that the universe is our university. This suggests that we should not go exclusively to Athens, but it does not exclude Athens. In fact, Clement puts his position in the next sentence. The disciples of Christ have grasped firmly and broadcast what the leaders of philosophy could only offer clues to. What is more, Clement synthesizes four passages from Paul (1 *Cor.* 1, 13; *Gal.* 3, 28; *Eph.* 4, 24; *Col.* 3, 9–11) to express Christian universalism; it is to be noted that the new Christian man is neither Jew nor Greek, but in him the streams of Judaism and Hellenism flow together.

The ethical problems which worried the men of the Hellenistic age are trivial, says Clement. Philosophy is an extended process of deliberation wooing wisdom with a passion which has no end; the thought seems to come from Pantaenus. Piety is a shortcut; it is all that matters. "Receive Christ; receive sight; receive your light." Clement continues with an extended passage which makes play with the idea of light. In a vivid image he compares mankind with chickens being fattened (for death) in darkness in the ancient equivalent of those Animal-Machines which Mrs. Harrison has so eloquently attacked in our own day. The Logos brings us light. Night gives way to the day of the Lord. He is the sun of righteousness, and our song to him—and Clement is quoting one of the earliest of hymns—is "Hail, Light."

Knowledge of God is open to all. The price is a little faith. We need no magical protection. The Word is our savior, our amulet. Let light displace darkness. Let the child come to the father. Then he follows God, he obeys the Father, in his error he recognizes him; he loves God, he loves his neighbor, he fulfills the commandment, he pursues the prize, he claims the promise.

It is God's predeterminate purpose to save the flock of mankind; this is why the good God sent the good shepherd. The language is that of the gospels (*Jn.* 10), but it takes up ideas found also in Plato (*Polit.* 266C; 268C) and Philo (Clem. *Str.* 1,23,156). And now Clement has an extended military metaphor, but it is carefully couched to proclaim the pacifism which the Christians of his day espoused. Christ sends out the trumpet call of peace and assembles his soldiers of peace. He assembles his bloodless army by blood and the word. What a wealth of allusion there is in those last words! The normal soldier sheds the blood of others, and seeks to avoid losing his own blood. In Christ's victory, says Clement, the only blood shed is his own; for Clement is not here alluding to those martyrs who shed their blood with their Master's. And the word is the word of command, the divine Word, the divine Reason, and the use of reason and speech rather than violent action to change the world. The trumpet of Christ is the gospel; his armor, the armor of peace.

God becomes a fellow-citizen with men. We must become servants and imitators of God. Christ wishes us to be saved; in one word (again the richness of meaning) he gives us life as a free gift of grace. He is the Word of truth, the Word of incorruption, a goad towards salvation. We must purify ourselves, so that God may see us as his delight as well as his creation. Both are appropriate to one who knows Christ; he must be seen to be worthy of a kingdom and must be accounted worthy of a kingdom.

Tradition is a dangerous reef, a Charybdis, a Siren: Clement uses the language of his audience. It is a garotter, a false guide, a trap, a chasm, a pit. He piles on the metaphors and mixes them with the abandon of a Boyle Roche, so that tradition becomes a wave belching out fire. The nautical metaphor predominates. He calls on his hearers to bind themselves to the cross as Odysseus to the mast. The Word of God will be their pilot; the

Holy Spirit, as a word from heaven (another double entendre), will bring them into the port of heaven.

The image changes from Homer's *Odyssey* to Euripides's *The Bacchants* as he calls them from Cithaeron to the hill of the Lord, from drunken frenzy to sober salvation, from the Maenads to the innocent lambs of God (there is a characteristic wordplay on *mainades*, Maenads, and *annades*, lambs), from the staff of Teiresias to the cross of Christ as support, from the blindness of Teiresias to the light of Christ, from mysteries which involve eating raw flesh to mysteries of sanctity.

It is Jesus, the Word, who calls, and he calls all men, and Clement presents his call in half a line from Homer (*Il.* 17,220). He, being Reason, offers reason, that is himself; he offers immortality. They have been images as faulty as Plato's material objects; Clement is eager to straighten them till they fully resemble the archetype. He calls them to love Christ, man's brilliant charioteer, who has yoked together the team of mankind and is driving his chariot straight for immortality; it is of course the image from Plato's *Phaedrus* (246 A ff.) where Logos is the charioteer of the soul, again adapted to Clement's purposes, with the language linked to that of Christ's entry into Jerusalem.

Philosophers—Clement means the Stoics—call ignorance a form of madness. If we grasp the truth firmly then our minds will be healthy. And if, as the Greek proverb has it, friends hold all things in common, and if man is dear to God through the mediation of the Word, then all things become man's, and the man who honors God comes to resemble God and is adopted as a child of God. The whole life of men who have come to know Christ is good.

So to a brief peroration: enough of words. Clement pleads his own love of mankind and calls his hearers to choose between life and destruction.

X *An Evaluation of Clement's Appeal*

Clement's appeal is rooted in two concepts. The first is *philanthropia*. This means literally "love of mankind." Its first appearance in literature is in Aeschylus's *Prometheus Bound* (11; 28) where Prometheus, a god, is punished for his love of mankind. It is primarily applied to those gods who show a particular concern for human beings, Prometheus, Heracles, Asclepius, Love,

Peace, and not to the Olympians except for the popular Hermes. From this comes a natural extension to the attitude of rulers towards their subjects, and so as an ideal for other forms of government (Isoc. *Paneg.* 29). In the middle of the fourth century B.C., *philanthropia* became a political catchword at Athens, as the bond holding the state together; in its various forms it appears seventy times in Demosthenes. In the Hellenistic age it naturally retains its attractiveness as an attribute of monarchs. From this it passes to Hellenized Judaism. It is a favorite word of Philo, who frequently applies it to the Torah, and who wrote an influential treatise *On the Love of Mankind.* From Hellenized Judaism it passed to Christianity. It appears in the New Testament in Titus: "God our Savior's kindness and love of mankind appeared" (*Tit.* 3,4). Theophilus of Antioch is found using it (*Ad Autolyc.* 2,27) in the second century, but it was the Alexandrians, Clement and Origen (influenced by Philo), who really established its Christian usage. It becomes a particular attribute of the Christian God; Julian, trying to restore paganism in the fourth century, says bitterly, "I suppose his love of mankind will some day reach us too." Thomas Magister (896) centuries later looked back on its usage, and identified two meanings: an attitude of goodwill from superior to inferior such as God may show to man or a monarch to a subject, and the loving disposition of one individual towards another. For the Christian writers the two coalesce: the love of mankind shown to other human beings is a direct response to the love of mankind received from God, and that, as Clement makes clear, is shown primarily in the Incarnation.

Alongside this is the concept of the Logos. Here too pagan, Jewish, and Christian thought come together. We have seen how Heraclitus used the word Logos for the principle of balance and proportion which gives the universe stability; we have seen how the Stoics "lifted" this to represent the divine Reason. This in turn struck a chord among the Platonists, who preferred the word Intelligence, but thought in much the same terms. Meantime, the Jewish thinkers, in their exaltation of their one God, had tended to exalt him out of sight. So they looked for intermediaries. One of these was the Memra, the word of God, which was written about in such a way that it seemed to have an almost independent power. "The Word of the Lord which came to

Hosea. . . ." (*Hos.* 1,1). As the Greek for "word" is also *logos,* this formed for Philo and other Alexandrians a link between Greek and Hebrew thought. A cognate concept was the Wisdom of God, who is even described as "the word spoken by the Most High" (*Ecclus.* 24,3). This Jewish thought was taken up in *The Gospel according to John,* where the Logos is seen as the creative power of God. What John contributes fresh, as Augustine was to see (*Conf.* 7,9), is that "the Logos became flesh" (*Jn.* 1,14); in other words, the distinctive Christian contribution lay in the belief that in Jesus the self-expression, the creative power of God, the divine Reason, the pattern which lies behind the universe, is revealed in a human life.

Is his appeal persuasive? We have no evidence that it convinced anyone, none that it failed.

CHAPTER 3

The Tutor

I Introduction

*T*HE *Paedagogus*, here translated "tutor," was a tutor in the exact and literal sense of the word. He was not in the intellectual sense a teacher. He looked after the child's security and well-being. He was a slave, a family retainer, who accompanied the boy wherever he went. In one sense he was a menial. He would be responsible for carrying a torch in the dark, for carrying the boy's writing-things or other equipment, sometimes (as we see depicted on terracotta statuettes) for carrying the boy himself. But he was also responsible for the boy's behavior; he was in this sense a moral instructor; and this included functions complementary to those of the academic teacher in that he was responsible for keeping the boy up to scratch and ensuring that he applied himself to his academic work. There is an enlightening exchange between Socrates and young Lysis in Plato's dialogue of that name (Plat. *Lys.* 208C), in which it is made quite clear that the boy is under the tutor's authority, and Socrates even jestingly calls him a tyrant or despot; the passage is six centuries before Clement, but the system did not change. Nearer to the time of Clement Plutarch writes (Plut. *Mor.* 4 A): "When children reach the age to be placed in the charge of tutors, you must take great care over their appointment to avoid putting the children in the hands of prisoners of war, non-Greeks or slaves who are continually passing from one owner to another. It's ridiculous the way many people carry on nowadays. They take their best slaves and put some in charge of their farms, some of their ships, some of their business-affairs, some of the private houses, some of their finances. But come up with a slave who eats and drinks too much, and is useless for any other occupation, and they put their sons in his care. A good tutor ought to have the inherent qualities of Achilles's tutor Phoenix."

At first blush this is a surprising likeness for the Logos. But Clement has in fact worked out very carefully what he wants to say. The doctrine of the Trinity was taking shape in the church. There was God the Father, the Creator, endowing man by nature with his first impulses toward the truth. There was God the Son, revealed in Jesus. There was God the Spirit, the continuing living presence of God, leading men into all truth. All, for Clement, is of the Logos. But it was natural for him, without pressing the correlation too far, to think in terms of an exhortation to the truth, moral challenge (which was for Clement the major fact about the historical Jesus of Nazareth), and application in the search for truth, and the revelation of full knowledge. The tutor was a slave, and this is precisely what Paul said of Jesus, that he took upon himself the form of a slave (*Phil.* 2,7). So that the slave-tutor was a peculiarly apposite image for this second aspect of the work of the Logos.

II *The Work of the Tutor (1,1)*

Clement begins characteristically with an echo of Pindar (fr. 194 Sch.). "It is a foundation which has been laid"; the architectural metaphor is common in Paul. A foundation of truth, a foundation of knowledge (*gnosis*); so early is the keynote sounded. It is a yearning for eternal life operating through "reasonable" obedience. The whole phrase is striking and lovingly shaped, and introduces the idea of the *logos,* the eternal reason, the concept which formed a point of coincidence between Stoic philosophy, Alexandrian Judaism, and Christianity. This first brief paragraph is a conspectus of Clement's central thought.

Human life is divided into three aspects: character, actions, and passions. The exhortatory Logos has taken charge of the first, so Clement shows that he is writing in sequel. There is also a Logos to direct our actions, and a Logos to cure our passions. In writing of these Clement uses the technical language of Stoic philosophy. But these are all in the end the work of the same Logos who draws us out of our attachment to the world and, as a tutor, leads us to the salvation which comes from faith. This is the first appearance of the concept of the Tutor; it will be noticed that the image is generally applied, not specifically to the second of the three functions. The rest of the introduction is an elaboration of these images. We should note that the image asso-

ciated with the third function passes from that of the doctor to
that of the teacher. We should note an entirely typical allusion
to Homer (1,1,3: Hom. *Il.* 4,218). We should note the introduction of the great term *philanthropia* to represent God's love of
mankind. The final words of the introduction speak of the magnificent education offered by "the Logos with his universal love
of mankind, first exhorting, then as tutor, and as culmination, the
comprehensive teacher."

In this first brief section Clement has laid the ground plan of
his work. He has identified the three functions of the logos, and
set this work within the context of a serial exposition. He has
made clear his openness to Greek culture in Pindar and Homer,
and in particular the integration of his thought and expression
with Stoic ethical philosophy. He has introduced us to a number
of key-words and key-concepts. And by a combination of clarity,
judicious use of metaphors, and occasional rhetorical highlights
he grips our attention and heightens our appetite for more.

III   *Sin (1,2)*

Our Tutor resembles his Father God, sinless, spotless, passionless; so Clement gives the Stoic concept of passionlessness
(*apatheia*) a Christian place. We are not, and we should strive
to be, like him. This is the first appearance in this work of the
idea of the imitation of Christ, a potent way of life at all times
in the history of Christianity, most familiar to us from Thomas à
Kempis's classic, but of course scripturally based. But the thought
of the imitation of God belongs also to the Stoic-Cynic tradition,
and is found, for example, in Musonius.

Best to live without sin. This belongs to God. Clement does
not say that it is impossible for men; he implies that it is improbable. There is an ambiguity here in the Christian tradition.
Jesus commands his disciples to be as the Father in heaven (*Mt.*
5,48); yet the Christian witness also was that all have fallen
short; and every movement for renewal of Christianity has been
in tension between the claims of perfection and the fact of sin.
Clement offers a second-best; namely, to avoid deliberate wrongdoing. This belongs to the sage, the wise man. This last was a
Stoic concept, and when pressed the Stoics did not acknowledge
that many had qualified. It was, in the modern jargon, élitist,
and not useful to the ordinary man. So, as a third best, avoid an

excessive number of involuntary faults. This is the mark of those who have an efficient attendant tutor; they may sin, but they are recalled from sin, not left to wallow in it.

The thought of the passage is based on Philo (*Agr.* 175 ff.), but Clement Christianizes it, links it with thoughts and expressions from the New Testament, and then illustrates it with a series of quotations from the Old Testament (some but not all from the Philo passage), a series of allusions to pagan authors, and then a series of passages from the New Testament in which Jesus is shown as calling men from sin, sickness, and death; for Clement they symbolize the same state. Clement's favorite pun asserts itself. Sin is involuntary, therefore irrational (*a-logon*). Therefore, it requires the Logos, the Divine Reason, to heal it. The good tutor is Wisdom (a concept dear to Hellenistic Judaism, with a cross-reference to the Stoic sage), the Logos of the Father, the Creator of man (the language is Platonic). So Clement rounds off the section by bringing together the creative breath of *Genesis* with the Stoic world-order; he is viewing both in the light of Christ.

IV *The Love of Man (1,3–4)*[1]

The Lord then forgives us as God and tutors us away from sin as man. This leads Clement to a meditation on God's love for man. Behind this lie two of the great Christian words. *Philanthropia* or love of mankind we have already noticed. It was in love of mankind that the Word became flesh; Clement makes the point in this section. The other word is *agape* or love. This as a noun was virtually born within the framework of revealed religion. It is the ceaseless, patient seeking of the well-being of another, whether or not he responds. God is love (*agape*), and His love is shown in that while we were yet sinners Christ died for us and gave himself for us. It is this of which Clement is here speaking.

But his treatment is rather odd, and it expresses itself in contorted syntax. It is partly that Clement is trying to force Stoic concepts about the objects of choice into a Christian mold, partly that he has not analysed as clearly as usual what precisely he is seeking to say, partly that one suspects some fault in the text. Man, to receive God's love, must either be an object of choice in himself or an object of choice for the sake of all else. The second possibility involves contradiction. Man is chosen for himself and thus belongs to the chooser. Clement seems to deduce the worth or capacity of man to receive love from the love directed to him by God in the Incarnation. And it is for us to respond with our love to him who guides us in love towards the highest life. We live in the depths of darkness. If we guide one another it is the blind leading the blind, but the Logos is keen-eyed and sees the innermost heart; for it is the nature of good to do good.

And now Clement says firmly something which was not at all obvious. The Logos is tutor to women and men alike. Moral values are not different for men and women; there is one tutor for both. Clement rises to a peak of eloquence; "One church; one morality; one conscience; a common life, a bond of marriage; breathing, sight, hearing, knowledge, hope, obedience, love— they are all the same. Those who have a common life, common grace, common salvation, have also a common virtue and a common standard." Clement rams the point home with a couple of lines from Menander, and the scriptural idea of one flock, one shepherd.

It would be hard to overestimate the importance of this passage. This was an attitude not found in traditional Judaism: the Jew gave thanks that he was not born a woman. It was not found in Greece, least of all in the Athens where Pericles declared that the greatest glory of a woman was not to be spoken of by men for good or bad. It was not found in Rome, where despite the freedom of some aristocrats the woman was under the authority of first the father and then of husband. It is authentically the spirit of Jesus, whose freedom in speaking with the woman of Samaria startled his disciples, who denied a two-fold standard of morality over the woman taken in adultery, and whose attitude to Mary and Martha speaks of a new type of relationship. It is true to the early church, where Mary, mother of John Mark, played a prominent role, Nympha presided over a house church, Phoebe was deaconess of Cenchreae, and Priscilla was named before her husband Aquila. This partnership between men and women was part of the Christian revolution, the Christian transvaluation, and Clement is in the true tradition in offering it.

V   *The Dependence of Man (1,5)*

If human beings need a tutor, they must be children, and
in the next, longer section Clement establishes this. Scripture
speaks, as in a riddle, of "children." "Those children are—us."

What follows is eminently characteristic of Clement. In the
first place he displays his extraordinary assimilated knowledge
of the Bible and his capacity to turn it to his purpose. Thus he
brings together at one point all the first three gospels; at another
he brings together the parable of the sheep and the goats, and
the idea of the lambs and their shepherd; at another he starts
from the Pauline text "I betrothed you to Christ, thinking to
present you as a chaste virgin to her true and only husband"
(*2 Cor.* 11,2) and takes this to apply to the children of the
church (a reminder of the early age of marriage for girls); at
another he strains the language of newness as if it spoke of
youth; at another he prolongs a familiar passage of Isaiah as if
it read "Wonderful Counsellor, Mighty God, Everlasting Father,
Prince of Peace *in his extension of education* " (*Is.* 9,6); at
another he applies words which speak of Jesus's sonship to his
childhood (*Jn.* 10,38). To all this he adds allegorical interpretation: any passage which speaks of a young animal, a colt or a
lamb or a fledgling, speaks of our need of a tutor.

Allied with this is wordplay, though it is not necessarily play
to Clement. The Epicureans claimed that a seemingly organic
relationship between words must reflect an organic relationship
between the objects they signify, and Clement is not averse
to applying Epicurean theory at this point. So we have a
piece of fantasy about "Hosanna," linking it, as we might say,
to HOnor and SAtisfaction and NAme. We have an attempt to
establish an organic link between child and mild, and an even
more complex one between *atalos* (tender), *hapalos* (soft) and
haplous (simple). We have the stock association of *paidia* (play)
with *paideia* (education).

Alongside the scriptures stand the Greeks. Greek thought about
education, *paideia* (as Werner Jaeger termed his great book)
permeates the whole. There are details as well: a citation from
some unknown poet, and other passages which appear to be
allusions to Homer or the dramatists; an echo, a shade unex-
pectedly, of a famous rhetorical phrase of Pericles to the effect

that "the springtime had gone from the year"; a general linking of thought and language to Plato. Most surprising is the way in which Clement links his joyous sense of the Christian children pleasing God by their play with a passage from Heraclitus, philosopher of pessimism, suggesting that Zeus (really Time) plays in this sort of way.

One or two passages are of particular interest. We may notice Clement's sense that Christian education continues throughout life. It is a splendid thought in itself; it is also ammunition against the Gnostics, who claimed to have arrived. An important theme, in which, as we have noticed, there is a kind of wordplay between novelty and youth, is the newness of Christianity: the Christians are a new people, who have received and bring knowledge of new blessings. Another passage contains one of the very early references to Mother Church. We first encounter this symbolic usage in a Marcionite interpretation of *Galatians* 4,26 at about the middle of the second century. Later, in 177, it was used by the martyrs at Lyons. There is an extended account of Isaac, and he is taken as the "type" of the Lord; this is in accordance with regular Christian thinking. Finally the whole is summed up in the thought of Jesus as a child. The Logos, being God, and becoming man for us, wanted to become like us in every way (Clement brings together here the language of *Hebrews* about Jesus with the language of Plato about the Forms), and so received from Scripture the name "lamb of God," the son of God, the Father's little darling.

VI Scriptural Evidence and the Milk of God's Nourishment (1,6)

There follows the longest and most elaborate section of this book. It is a polemic against the Gnostics, who suggest that if Christians are children they are receiving only primary education, not real knowledge at all. On the contrary, says Clement, we have received adult (perfect) education; we are enlightened; we have received super-knowledge, revealed knowledge. "In baptism we were enlightened; in enlightenment we became sons; in sonship we grew to mature perfection; in mature perfection we received immortality." The language is that of the mystery-religions. Freedom from evils is the beginning of salvation, and salvation consists in following Christ. Faith and regeneration are all that is needed. We cannot think God's teaching incomplete; the lesson he teaches is eternal salvation from an eternal Savior. Man can be enlightened: that is why (to adapt the Greek pun) his child is called "sun." Of course, we are not yet at the goal; time is not eternity. Where faith is, there is the promise. And enlightenment, which dissipates ignorance and implants the faculty of sight, is knowledge (Clement has in mind Plato's comparison of the Form of the Good in producing spiritual insight and the sun in producing physical sight). Faith is the universal means of salvation for all men. God in his justice and love for mankind treats all the same; so does Clement against the élitist Gnostics assert the universal and impartial love of God. The Law was our tutor (*Gal.* 3,23–5). Paul said that in Christ we need no tutor, but Clement prefers to treat Christ as our tutor.

He goes on to examine a number of passages in the Pauline letters, and we need not follow him through the details of this. There is, in connection with a phrase in *Corinthians* (1 *Cor.* 3,1–2) an extended discussion of milk, and its relationship to the nourishing blood of the Savior, and to the purificatory power of water. There is a suggestion that blood becomes milk by a change of quality without any change of substance. The discussion is naturally based on theories from Greek philosophy and physiology, and indeed on passages from Homer, in one of which Clement has conflated two references. One particularly interesting passage brings together in a single thought Paul's vision of the mystical body of Christ and the Stoic concept of the universe as a single living being. Clement is interested in ideas; he is also interested in language, and though he scorns an excess of "word-chasing" he is genuinely concerned for precision. He applies to God the title "Nourisher"; here Christian and pagan mysticism come together, since the same idea is found in the Hermetic writings; he goes rather further when he says that the fatherly breasts of love of mankind furnish the children with spiritual milk.

The sections ends with a brief discussion of what Paul means by perfection: not final achievement, but separation from sin and birth to new life.

The whole of this difficult section is directed against Gnostic claims. We may not today find Clement's approach attractive

CLEMENT OF ALEXANDRIA

or fruitful, but he is concerned about a real problem and a real distinction.

VII   The Tutor and his Tutelage (1,7)

Clement has now established that our state is rightly compared to that of little children. Only the Father is a full-grown adult; the Father, he is swift to add, who is revealed in the Son. He now gives the Tutor his name—Jesus. Jesus calls himself "shepherd," and in the Old Testament the revealed God appears as educator (more strictly "chastiser": *Hos.* 5,2).

His tutelage is religion, learning how to honor God, education directed to knowledge of truth, an escort to heaven. The word "tutelage," says Clement with a bit of "word-chasing," covers the experience of the child who is guided and is learning, the work of the guide and mentor, the actual process of guidance, and the things learned, such as the commandments. Divine tutelage is to set a person straight on the road of truth which leads to the vision of God. Clement uses two images: the commander-in-chief on the field of battle, and the pilot of a ship, who in relation to other winds keeps the ship steady and allows it to be driven by the wind of truth, using as rudder his pupil's ears; this slightly fantastic image was a commonplace in Greek educational writing. Clement characteristically illustrates miseducation by a series of failures by human teachers in Greece and Persia.

"Our tutor," he goes on, "is the holy God Jesus, the Logos who guides all humanity—the very God who loves mankind is our tutor." He quotes a number of Old Testament passages in which, in common with other Fathers, he treats divine appearances as referring to the Logos. When Jacob says that he saw God face to face (*Gen.* 32,31), Clement comments, "The face of God is the Logos, in whom God is brought to the light and revealed." The word for "face" is the later "person" of Trinitarian theology; some may find Clement's usage more helpful. The moral instruction of the Old and New Testaments are the substance of the tutelage, he suggests reasonably, and more fantastically, interprets the rod from Jesse's root, and even the rod and staff of the shepherd of Psalm 23, as referring to the rod which was the teacher's insignia of office and instrument of chastisement. In the course of this discussion he uses of Jesus a very interesting

[76]

and remarkable phrase. He calls him "mystic messenger" or "mystic angel." He means that Jesus proclaims and reveals the hidden truths about God.[2]

VIII   *Love, Justice, and Goodness (1,8–13)*

The remainder of the book explores in a variety of ways, with some digression, the relationship between love, justice, and goodness, a theme still topical today. Clement discusses it primarily from his understanding of scripture rather than existentially, though we should remember that he would not have made such a distinction. And there is a sense in which he starts from his own religious experience; scriptural references to the severity of God are to be understood in the light of the love of mankind which is shown in his becoming man. It is this active readiness to share human suffering which makes the Lord an irreproachable tutor. "There is nothing that the Lord hates." Clement quotes from someone who wrote impeccable Greek; the sentiment comes from *The Wisdom of Solomon* (11,24), but the words are different. If he does not hate he loves; Clement uses a general word (*philein*), but when he turns to God's love for man he uses the great word of Christian love (*agapan*). Man receives this love supremely, being the noblest work of creation and God-loving. "So God is man-loving, the Logos is man-loving." To love is to seek to benefit. All that God does is for man's good. A familiar Greek phrase contrasts practice (*ergon*) with theory (*logos*). Clement shapes his sentence like this, but the meaning is other: "He demonstrates this in practice by tutoring him through the Logos, who is the true workmate of God's love for mankind." It is a passage of wonder and splendor.

The good which God offers man is beneficial, not necessarily enjoyable. Justice gives that which is appropriate to each— Clement's treatment of justice is Stoic rather than scriptural— and that is beneficial, but by no means enjoyable. Hence God's severity; it is medical treatment for a diseased life. The thought of moral evil as a disease of the soul is still Stoic, but behind it is Plato's view of punishment as remedial (*Gorg.* 478D).

This basic thought continues. Clement pursues it in thickening clouds of language through different images: military mutiny; disruption of political community; a vine which needs pruning; a musical instrument out of tune. His supporting illustrations may come from ancient rhetorical theory, or from *Ecclesiasticus* (misquoted), or from Plato (Clement cites his favorite passage from *Republic* 10,617E "Responsibility rests with the chooser; God bears no guilt.") God is not angry (a hit at the Gnostics); his severity is a technique of improvement. He is not vengeful; vengeance is answering evil with evil.

Clement cites a succession of scriptural passages relating to the goodness and justice of God. Running between them are threads of interpretation. We may isolate three of these. The first is his Platonism: it is very hard not to call it his Neo-Platonism. Clement is in the line of succession which leads from Plato through Numenius and Albinus to Plotinus. God is for him the One, the divine monad, scripturally "He who is" (*Ex.* 3,14), and Clement blurs in his language the Hebrew Creator who creates out of nothing and the Platonic Craftsman who works on pre-existent materials. Secondly, we may note that the Gnostics are never far from his mind, and he is careful to oppose Gnostic dualism explicitly; the Creator-Craftsman and the good Father are one and the same. Thirdly, there is an important piece of incidental theology when Clement says that the Logos is called just because of his revelation of mutual love with the Father, and the title reflects their equality of power (1,8,71).

Rebuke then is part of God's love for mankind, and Clement identifies twelve forms, which are not easy to distinguish in English; Clement indulges in his familiar wordplay in presenting them. They are, roughly, admonishment (a rebuke full of concern), censure (directed to shameful acts), blame (directed to carelessness or indifference), castigation (a strong form of censure), exposure (the public identification of faults), instruction (a rebuke which makes the offender think for himself), visitation (an expression of serious disfavor), invective (a very strong rebuke), accusation (directed at the guilty), animadversion (a disguised rebuke), ridicule (working through sarcasm), retribution (directed to legal offenders or disobedient children). He illustrates them by scriptural quotations, all of which are attributed to the tutorial work of the Logos. Fear then (as the Gnostics will not admit) can be used as a source of salvation. We are diseased and need a spiritual doctor; we are lost and need a guide; we are blind and need an enlightener; we are thirsty and need the spring of life; we are dead and need life;

we are sheep and need a shepherd; we are children and need a tutor; all humanity needs Jesus (1,9,83). Clement takes up the thought in a passage which may exemplify prayers of this period: "Feed us, your children, like sheep. Yes, Lord, fill us with your pasture, your righteousness. Yes, tutor, pasture us on your holy mountain, the church, which towers high above the clouds and reaches the heavens." It is not so different from evangelical prayer today.

Clement continues with a panegyric of the tutor, the good shepherd, the generous giver, benefactor, friend of mankind, who preferred to be brother rather than master. To him is due not the fear of a slave for a tyrannical overlord, which involves hatred, but the fear of a subject for a good emperor, accompanied by respect: we get a sudden glimpse of what it meant to be within the Roman Empire during the Indian summer of the Antonines. The threats which turn us from sin are the obverse of the exhortation which directs us to salvation. Clement backs his thesis with passages from the Bible, with the Stoic (but not the Epicurean) philosophers, with Bacchylides and the Pythagoreans. At one point (1,10,95) he unusually attributes the inspiration of the Old Testament not to the Logos, but to the Life (*Jn.* 14,6), a reminder of destiny as well as origin. The insistence that the two Testaments present the same theme is a further thrust at the Gnostics. Another unexpected but pregnant cross-reference comes in the application of words from the story of man's creation (*Gen.* 1,26) to the generation of the Logos. Christ in fact fully realizes the statement that man is made in God's image; the rest of mankind can only reflect it. We are to follow his steps, and we shall in the end put on his divinity; we shall be in true tune. Again Clement shows his extraordinary capacity to find relevance by expounding the consequences of this in Stoic terms. The book ends with an intellectualized account of virtue as following the Logos, which here, as in Stoic philosophy, is equated with Reason.

IX   *Christian Behavior: Food and Drink (2,1–2)*

With the second book we come to face practical problems of daily living (in Stoic language, external things), and indeed the task of the tutor in the Greek world was very much to inculcate what we should term good manners.

Food. We are to eat to live, not to live to eat: the *mot* comes from the Cynics who attribute it to Socrates. Our diet should be simple, directed to growth, health, and controlled energy. Avoid elaboration; avoid excess. Congestion and digestion (to adapt his pun) are not the same thing. The love-feast must be an expression of love; in the Greek it is simply called "the love" and Clement applies to it the language of Christian love: it is a banquet controlled by reason, i.e., the Logos. We should not forget how much the love-feast, the taking of a common meal together, meant to the early church at least till the third century. It was not the Eucharist, though it was at first associated with it; in itself it was a fellowship in the basic things of life, not a memorial of Christ's death. The general tenor of Clement's teaching is consistent. It is to avoid overindulgence. He backs it by wordplay, by snippets of Stoic, Pythagorean, Platonic, and even Epicurean philosophy (Epicurus was a great exponent of simplicity of diet), by the Old Testament, and by Plato's seventh letter. Avoid appetizers and aperitifs; they are not necessary. Don't eat and drink at the same time; they don't go together (in Greece the symposium followed the meal). Behave decently. Don't make a mess of your hands, your face, or your couch. Don't pull faces. And don't talk with your mouth full; it sounds awful (2,1,13). It is all very human. But there is more to it than that. It is because the Christian is following the example of Christ, and in all that he does is conveying Christ to his fellow-men. All is to be done to the glory of God.

Drink. "A little wine for your stomach's sake" (1 *Tim.* 5,23). All right, but it is a small dose for strictly medicinal purposes. Otherwise, water is best, and the young should certainly abstain from wine; they're hotheaded enough already! Besides wine swells the sex organs and encourages sexual curiosity. For the 18-30 age-group, he advocates moderation. The older are permitted freer refreshment, provided they keep mind clear, memory active, and body under control. Wine *is* dangerous, and Clement cites Aristotle and a doctor named Artorius as authorities for his statement. Half-drunk, people wear wreaths, like tombs. Wholly drunk, pouring a new day's intoxication in before yesterday's has worn off, they are to all intents and purposes dead, dead to reason (the Logos). They are drowned in drink, the helmsman of the mind being buffeted from side to side and landing them on the rocks. So drink to quench thirst, or to warm the body in winter, but beware of the slippery slope; no need to look for special vintages. There is only one wine for the disciplined drinker, and one viticulturist—God. Drink decently; don't pull faces, squint, dribble, splash it about as if you were washing your face, or gulp noisily. Militarist nations get drunk. Christians are the people of peace (the central traditions of the church were pacifist for three centuries). How did Jesus drink? As for those women who throw their heads back, displaying an indecent amount of neck, distending their throats, they're just letting all standards slide; Clement is polysyllabically sarcastic about them. Women should not reveal too much of their bodies: it's a risky business for the men who are attracted by the sight, and for the women who are aiming to attract them. And drunkenness, to return to the point, is out.

X. *Christian Behavior: Possessions (2,3) and Comportment (2,4–8)*

A short section follows on possessions. It is interesting that Clement's thinking here, though it is related to his Christianity, does not arise from it; it is closely based, even to identical words, on the first-century Stoic-Cynic Musonius Rufus. Gold and silver cups, which he starts from, are meant only to lead the eyes astray. They are quite impractical; they are too hot to hold for hot drinks, and they spoil cold drinks. All extravagances in furnishing, chairs and beds and fancy drapes, are of no real value. The evidence of scripture and Plato come together, as so often in Clement. The criterion is utility. No farmer in his senses would go for a silver pick or a golden shovel. The same applies to fitting out the home. Anything else is snobbery. Food, clothes, furniture should be appropriate to the individual, his age, his work, and the particular occasion. Then, as so often, just when Clement is seeming at his most unoriginal and, in philosophical circles, conventional, something theological, profound and original, slips out. The Christian religion, he suggests, is basically simple, with one God, and the Christian's way of life must conform with this monotheistic simplicity. Wealth is the citadel of vice. The best wealth is poverty of desires: this comes from Socrates. Extravagance is unreasonable, contrary to the Logos. Why be so concerned about things you can buy in the market?

Wisdom is not to be purchased with earthly coinage, but with the true currency, the imperishable Logos, the royal gold, or perhaps gold of the Kingdom.

Parties. When the Logos is, so to speak, in the chair, there is no place for irrationalities such as sex and drunkenness, or wild music and dancing. Clement would not approve of pop festivals; he describes people who indulge themselves in this way as undisciplined, unseemly, and uneducated. The values seem humanist, but we must see them in the light of his insistence that the Logos is our commander-in-chief, standard, and tutor. Flutes are out; they belong either to shepherd-life or to orgiastic superstition. In general Clement regards the effects of music as irrational (and therefore inappropriate to the Logos); this is derived from Greek thought and found, for example, in Plutarch (e.g., *Mor.* 704 F). But he doesn't rule it out altogether, only the sensual or debilitating modes, and singing played an important part in the life, fellowship, and witness of the church from the first. Some references to musical instruments in scripture might at first seem embarrassing (e.g., *Ps.* 150). Clement characteristically evades the embarrassment by allegorical interpretation. The trumpet is the power of resurrection; the lute is the tongue; the harp is the mouth; the tambourine is the church; the "instrument" is the body; the strings are its sinews. Music can be used to arouse military ardor or sexual passion or wild behavior, but man is meant to be an instrument of peace; the essential pacifism of the early Christians recurs. So in a party the demeanor of the Christian should be one of gaiety towards God, and a serious concern for our fellowmen. Our behavior will vary in inessentials with time and place, and there is a behavior appropriate to a party. Pick up a ten-stringed lyre by all means; it will speak to men of Jesus, since in Greek the first letter of Jesus's name was also the symbol for ten. In drinking, sing a song of gratitude for your share in this part of his creation. So with wordplay and with allusions to familiar anecdotes Clement makes his point that the Christian properly shows joy and that excess destroys joy.

Laughter. Clement's comments are surprisingly brief and negative; one would rejoice to see a real Christian philosophy of laughter, and he does not supply it. Buffoons are to be banished from our commonwealth: Clement sees the Christian community as the true fulfillment of Plato's *Republic,* and echoes his thought and language. If we banish buffoons, we can't be buffoons ourselves. Don't strike postures or pull faces just to raise a laugh, or use the spoken word (reason, the Logos) for that purpose. Because man, as Aristotle observed, is the only animal capable of laughter (*Part. An.* 673 A 8), he doesn't have to laugh at everything; horses don't whinny the whole time. Clement wants his laughter under control; he is afraid of degeneration into obscenity; he doesn't mind mild pleasantries, and prefers the smile to the belly-laugh. In this section he quotes Homer more than the Bible. The overall result is to make us wonder how much we, who inevitably rely on written sources, really know about ancient humor.

Obscenity. Avoid it, with ears, mouth, and eyes. It is common, pagan, uneducated, and shameless. The four adjectives are interesting; they imply four separate standpoints: aristocratic, Christian, middleclass (always with the reservation that Clement regards the Logos as our tutor), and ethical. It might seem that Clement was just another specimen of inhibited attitudes, but it is not so. He says explicitly, with a typical verbal play, that there is nothing obscene about the sexual organs, about the sexual act, or about sexual language. Only when abused, as, for example, in adultery or pederasty, do they become obscene. One could wish that all Christians had shown such balance and sanity.

Social intercourse. Avoid jeering at anyone; it's a small step to insulting behavior and violence. Develop communal feeling within the church. Protect young people from examples which might lead them astray. Married women and other men should be careful not to see too much of one another, and, if social obligation compels them, should be on the guard, remembering that drinking does not help thinking (2,7,54). Younger people at dinner should keep their eyes down; they should be seen and not heard; if they have to sit they should not cross their legs or rest their chin on their hand. For all, moderation, a largely vegetarian diet, and early to bed without waiting for the others. The older folk can rib the youngsters a bit for their own good. Speech should be under control; Clement is not afraid to applaud and accept the Epicurean aim of *ataraxia,* freedom from disturbance. Silence in women is a virtue, in the young a privilege without danger; speech (reasoned speech, speech which has learned from the tutelage of the Logos) is the blessing of age and experience. Two people should not speak at the same time, or they're soon shouting one another down. Use a level voice. Avoid logorrhoea. Don't click your fingers to call the servants; use words for the purpose of rational intercourse. Don't hawk and spit. Don't keep wiping your nose while you're drinking. If you have to sneeze or belch, do so quietly. Don't pick your teeth so that the gums bleed. The Christian's society is calm, tranquillity, serenity, peace.

Perfumes and garlands. This is a long and rambling section, which occupies rather more than an eighth of the whole book, and makes one realize that this was a living, existential issue among the Christians of Alexandria. Clement begins with a direct pellucid assertion: "There is no necessity for us to use garlands and perfumes" (2,8,61). The rest of the chapter works this out, starting, with a good deal of symbolism, allusion, and wordplay, from the sinner who poured the ointment over Jesus. Chrisms symbolize the Christ. Precious stones allude to the Logos, and gold, the symbol of royalty, to him in his changelessness. Next he expresses the views of the Greeks, represented oddly by Aristippus's philosophy of pleasure, and accompanied by a parade of learning, typically Alexandrian, about aromatics of various kinds. Then comes more symbolism. Christian men need only the odor of goodness, women the royal unction of Christ. In the literal sense, unguents have their uses. In moderation they can please without overwhelming the senses; they can keep off insects; they have their use in athletics. But aren't they really debilitating? Yes! The Lord offers the only incense that matters, the scent of love's gift. (This passage makes clear that incense was not used in Christian worship at this period.) Utility then is the answer. (Clement disowns Epicurean philosophy, but the Christians and Epicureans in some ways moved in parallel lines.) Health. Refreshment not excitement. In this area pleasure without utility is a sign of debauchery. Foolish women dye and perfume their gray hair, and the perfume makes it grayer still. So with garlands; they are associated with revelling and drunkenness. Crowns of flowers strip the countryside and are bad for the head. Clement gives us a bit of ancient physiology about the coldness of the head. Flowers are lovely and in enjoying them we honor the Creator. (2,8,70. This little passage is of some importance. There is less appreciation of natural beauty in pagan authors than is commonly supposed. We find it in Christian writers such as Clement and Tertullian who see natural beauty as the handwork of God. In Plato's *Symposium* in the ascent of the soul to the perfect Form of Beauty there is no mention of beauty in nature.) To use flowers for garlands is to exploit them; the flower and its beauty wither. It is a fine passage for any concerned with defense of the environment. Symbolism breaks through again. The husband is the wife's garland, marriage is the husband's garland, children are for both the flowers of marriage, God is the gardener of the fields of the flesh, Christ is the garland of the church. The earliest Greeks, says Clement following Eratosthenes, didn't use garlands; it was a degenerate practice which came in after the wars with Persia. The wreath symbolizes freedom from care; hence its use for the dead. Further, to make wreaths of flowers for our living is to mock the Savior's crown of thorns. The first revelation of God to Moses was in a burning thorn-bush. The revelation in Jesus is through a crown of thorns. The power is one and the same. It is the Logos who is one as the Father is one, and who is the beginning and end of time. There is here a sketch for a Christian philosophy of history. Then Clement realises that he has digressed; he has left the sphere of the Tutor for that of the Teacher. He returns to the right use of flowers and perfumes for medicinal purposes and controlled relaxation.

XI *Christian Behavior: Sleep (2,9) and Sex (2,10,83–102)*

There is some indication that Clement took special care over his style in the short section on sleep, and was careful to burnish it. He brings up Homer and Plato in his support, and an epigram of Ariston of Chios to the effect that "Sleep is like a tax-collector and exacts from us half of our life-time" (2,9,81).

His general theme is moderation. Feather-bedding, apart from being the product of pleasure-loving luxury, is bad for the body, hinders digestion, and does not help you to return to yourself. So sleep on a flat surface, not one which "gives." Silver feet and ivory inlay on the beds help no one at all. Of course, says Clement, with a dash of common sense and a sideglance at the upper-class church members, such things are not barred. If you have them, you have them. If you haven't, don't go out after them. Jacob at Luz had a stone for his pillow (*Gen.* 28,11). We should follow reason (the Logos, but the passage is very Stoic), and seek no more than warmth in winter and coolness in summer. Be a man; don't demand a soft bed. Sleep should be a physical relaxation not physical abandon. Go to bed sober, not weighed down with food. Clement is sarcastic about the grunts and snores and belchings and gurglings of those who do not observe this. There is no need to sleep from dusk till dawn. You can study, or get down to practical jobs, or (for women) work in wool. And it is the body which needs rest, not the soul.

Clement treats sex at much greater length. Here, as so often, what impresses is the balanced sanity of the man. In the first place he makes good his claim in the section on obscenity. There is nothing obscene about sex, and he talks about it naturally and without embarrassment. Further, he recognizes that total abstinence and total promiscuity are alike unnatural. He has in mind the Encratites who regarded marriage as fornication, and the Carpocratians who believed in free love ("Give to everyone that asks you"). There must be rules, and he aims to provide sensible guidance.

He starts by the asseveration that sex exists for the procreation of children; and it is only with the coming of efficient contraceptives that this view has been seriously challenged within the church. Characteristically, this leads him to use sowing and agriculture as a metaphor, and to interpret the parable of the sower symbolically. Man shows that he is made in the image of God in that he works with God in procreation. Clement's general thought, as so often, is a blend of Christianity and Stoicism. He turns to an allegorical interpretation of the ban on eating the hare and the hyena (*Lev.* 11,5), setting himself in passing against the more extravagant fantasies of the bestiaries, such as the hyena's hermaphroditism. Clement treats this prohibition as a warning against homosexuality, and especially pederasty, and indeed all uncontrolled lust of the sort which leads to illegitimate unions; he backs his views with a good deal of frank physiology (we are not here concerned with its accuracy), and with the authority of Moses and Plato.

We should consider all boys as our own sons, and all married women (they married very young and aged rapidly with constant childbirth, so that they would be most tempting while still in their teens) as our own daughters. More quotations follow from Moses and Plato. He cautions against homosexuality; sow in your own field only; no sex with your neighbor's wife; sex with concubines produces bastards; don't sow where you don't want to harvest; avoid menstruating women; avoid pregnant women. Sexual passion is a dictator; the idea comes from a well-known anecdote about Sophocles, which Clement later quotes (2,10,95).

What then of marriage? Clement treated this in a lost work *On Abstinence,* which enables him to be brief. Sex does undoubtedly reduce energy; at the same time the Lord wishes mankind to multiply. So marriage must be accepted, and put in its place. The object of marriage, Clement repeats, is procreation: it is not the casual secretion of the seed. It is inappropriate to the very young and the very old; it has its times and seasons. We need a tutor to guide us. The mystic rites of sex should not be performed in the daytime, on return from church or shopping, in the early morning, at the hours of prayer, Bible-reading or good works, but in the evening after dinner and thanksgiving, before going to sleep. And not all through the night under cover of darkness: let modesty be your torch. Keep the chastity of marriage: no prostitutes! Otherwise, you'll soon find that love takes wings and changes to hate.

So Clement turns to the evidence of scripture, which he backs with Sibylline Oracles directed to pagan readers ("your own poetry" 2,10,98), and Plato, whom he misquotes and describes somewhat oddly as "disciple of a non-Greek philosophy," perhaps referring to the Myth of Er which ends *The Republic,* or to his affinities with Biblical teaching (2,10,100). He is particularly strong against any thought that sins don't matter if they're not seen; the moral obliquity remains. Then, he uses an excellent phrase found also in Plutarch: don't take off your morals with your clothes. So don't let sex get the better of you. Like a farmer, sow your seed at the right moment. Clement ends where he began.

XII   *Christian Behavior: Clothes (2,10,102–2,12)*

The final sections of the second book treat clothing. The approach is Stoic-Cynic, but Clement links it with Christian fundamentals: secure external things for the body, govern the body by the soul, and "do not be anxious for your life (soul) what you will eat, or for your body what clothes you will wear; the life (soul) is more than food and the body more than clothing" (*Lk.* 11,22–4). Fulfill your needs: to go beyond that is to court extravagance, and that comes from the devil. It is luxury, dissipation, epicurism, gulosity, gluttony (the style is comic or satiric). Then comes a marvelous Christianizing of a phrase from philosophy: "If we are seekers, don't let us destroy in luxury the spirit of enquiry, but kindle it into a fire for the pursuit of truth." More sarcasm and satire follow at the expense of "gaudiness, the dyeing of wool, variegated colors, elaborate jewellery, gold ornamentation, artificial wigs and curled locks, eye-shadow, depilation, the use of rouge and white lead for make-up, hairdyes, and all artifices to make us appear what we are not," and a complex pun on *kosmos,* the order of the universe and the order of an elaborate appearance. Then the Christian message driven home by the parable of Dives and Lazarus, linked in complex symbolism with the hay which is useless and thrown on the fire, and the grass which though cut down springs up again. (There is also a warning against reading too much class-prejudice into Clement's Platonic language: he speaks of the "vulgar rabble" but they include the aristocratic Dives.) Then from scriptural evidence he turns to the pagan world and contrasts Spartan simplicity with the luxury of the Athenian upperclass. A Platonic touch follows: to care about ornament is to care about the image of Beauty, not Beauty itself, and this again is linked with a wordplay, image-idol, which gives it a religious connotation (2,10,106). The whole passage is as good an example of Clement's expository and rhetorical methods as could be found.

The aim of clothing is to protect the body; Clement makes a personal assertion of it. The principle is the same for men and women. The necessity is common; the provision should be similar, though women, being weaker, may have softer clothes but not silks which cling to the flesh and reveal more than they conceal! No dyes; they don't keep out the cold! White is the color of truth. Prodicus (the fifth-century sophist) was right to portray Virtue in plain white and Vice in showy colors not her own. John the Baptist and the prophets are taken as examples of simplicity in dress; Joseph's coat of many colors is interpreted allegorically to give it a favorable meaning. Clement disapproves of

Spartan mini-skirts, and tells a delightful story, known (though not so fully) elsewhere (Plut. *Mor.* 142 D). Theano was a Pythagorean. An admirer said to her, "What a lovely arm!" "Yes," she said, "and it's not public property." "What lovely legs!" "Yes, and they belong to my husband and to no one else." "What a handsome face!" "Yes, and that belongs to the man who married me, and to no one else." Women's beauty should not be a trap for men. Then Clement turns to have another fling at dyed clothes and other luxury, and makes a new point when he says that a covering should not appear finer than the thing it covers.

From clothes he moves to shoes; the treatment is based on Musonius, as is so much of this book, with no more than a side-glance at the Bible. Shoes are for covering and for protection for the sole of the foot against rough ground, and for the toe in case of stubbing. Women in particular must resist the temptation to elaborate footwear. They should wear plain white shoes, except in travelling, when they should wear greased leather with nailed soles. Women should not have bare feet; they are too delicate. Men can properly have bare feet except on military service. (The exception, surprising in a Christian context, arises partly from Clement's philosophical sources, partly from the fact that there were Christian converts in the forces, though they were not admitted to full church membership till they contracted out.) Bare feet are best for exercise, otherwise shoes should be simple.

From there Clement turns to jewellery and other ornaments. Children rush to touch the fire, admiring its brilliance, and not realizing its dangers. Silly women do the same with precious stones. Why pursue oysters and their products, when the real pearl, the sacred stone, is the Logos? Beauty is not to be imposed from outside. If a human being wants to attract by his beauty he should put on his natural excellences, justice, self-discipline, courage, and piety. These, except that piety appears in place of wisdom, are the four virtues picked out in *The Republic* and later called by Ambrose the "cardinal" virtues. Piety appears in similar catalogues elsewhere in Plato (e.g., *Gorg.* 507C). Clement contrasts this with catalogues, lengthy, tiresome, satirical, of female ornament from Aristophanes and elsewhere. A young painter, painting a Helen, tricked her out with gold ornaments.

The great Apelles commented: "Lad, you were incompetent to make her beautiful, so you made her rich." Clement looks on the painted Jezebels of his day as Helens of that sort. They should find their true gold in Christ. Artifice should not set up in competition with nature, falsehood with truth. Modesty and self-discipline are enough for charms and necklaces, eyes anointed with the Logos, ears pierced to hear divine truth. The Logos will exhibit true beauty.

XIII   *True Beauty (3,1)*

Clement begins the third book with the assertion that the greatest of all lessons is to know oneself, because to know oneself is to know God, and to know God is to become like God. Here he is drawing together the Greek and Christian wisdom, with the old Greek proverb and the doctrine that "like knows like"; the result is something extraordinarily like the assertion of the twentieth-century theologians that God is the depth of our being.

He doesn't in fact quite say that, although he comes close to it. He accepts Plato's teaching (*Rep.* 4,441 A) that the soul is tripartite, consisting of Intellect, Temper, and Desire, and calls Intellect "the inner man," man under the authority of God. Clearly, he deliberately uses Intellect rather than Reason (Logos) in order to distinguish between them, and goes on to say that the man who takes Reason (Logos) as his partner in life is consistent, has the form of the Logos, becomes like God, and is genuinely beautiful, not just embellished. Nothing destroys beauty more than a bath in the uneven flood of emotional pleasure. God is beauty.

Man is God because his will is fixed on the same things as God's will. He reinforces his assertion by a citation from Heraclitus: "Men are gods, gods men; this is Logos." This, for some reason, does not seem to have been garnered among the fragments of Heraclitus; it bears some relation to fragment 62, which makes a similar statement about mortals and immortals, but it is not the same. For Clement the Logos, the Word of God, the Reason in man, is the mediator, the minister of God, and our tutor.

There is another beauty to be found in love.

XIV *Against External Embellishments (3,2–3)*

It is the soul not the body we should seek to beautify; the body should be beautiful only with the adornment of self-control. Some women embellish themselves like Egyptian temples, which have magnificent exteriors, while a cat or crocodile or local snake lies in the inner sanctum. So it is with women who doll up their outward appearance, but within, where the true beauty, the true image of God should reside, all is loathsome; they have prostituted themselves. They spend their housekeeping money on ministering to their desires. A woman should not need to dye her hair blonde, put rouge on her cheeks, or pencil round her eyes; there is here an intimate glimpse of the ancient use of cosmetics. Women of this kind, says Clement, are sallow and subject to disease, not interested in housework; they are only concerned to make a spectacle of themselves; they damage the image of free women; they subvert family life. He calls in comic writers, surely rather doubtful evidence, in his support.

Reason—the Word, the Logos—wants to save us from this. Our tutor advises us to pass by another's river. Clement varies his interpretation of the saying (*Prov.* 9,18) from a warning against lusting for the wife of another, to a warning against the insatiable stream of indulgence. Love of luxury is worse than gluttony. There comes a point when you can eat no more, but lust for gold is never sated, even for a Midas. The desire for embellishment always grows. A flowered dress is the sure sign of the harlot (this may seem an extravagant judgment, but it could have been true in Clement's day). It is ridiculous for birds and animals to acquire beauty naturally and women to seek it artificially, turning their faces into masks (there is a pun in the Greek: we might say that their faces become fronts, or their guise a disguise). The Logos (he is quoting the New Testament : 2 *Cor.* 4,18) tells us to look below the surface. Moses did not permit an image as a substitute for God; how can an image be a substitute for man? No, it is spiritual beauty that we should seek. Esther found the true adornment in righteousness (a slight wordplay); her beauty ransomed her people from death; she used it as for a mystery.

Clement uses a picture of Helen from Euripides (*Iph. Aul.* 71-7) to reinforce his view that external adornment is a sign of sexual promiscuity. And what did it lead to? A war which shook the world!

Extravagance spreads like a disease and afflicts men as well as women. Look at their effeminate hairstyles! Clement, like some of our contemporary moralists, thinks that a man who elaborates his hair must be a queer. He does not see that he is falling into the very error he condemns—judging the inner man by his outward show. These men-women strip all their body of hair except their heads; they don't really honor hair. Clement can't resist a wordplay and tells the story of Diogenes up for sale, speaking "like a man," a genuine tutor, and telling an effeminate buyer that he needed to purchase a *man*.

Equally bad are the men who try to pretend they are not getting old. The Ancient of Days was not ashamed of hair as white as wool (*Dan.* 7,9), and no one else can turn a single hair white or black (*Mt.* 5,36). (One remembers the actress who hissed of a rival "I'd like to tear out her blonde hair by its black roots.") As a man grows older he ought to have more respect for the truth; a counterfeit head cannot display a true soul. Rejuvenation should be in the spirit; it is there that we must put on a new man.

It is not long before Clement returns to effeminacy; his pre-occupation with it seems obsessive, and we trace something morbid in a normally healthy outlook. He is strongly opposed to depilation. If the hairs of our head are numbered (*Mt.* 10,30), so are the hairs on our cheeks and the rest of our body. It is our lusts not our hairs which we should pull out by the roots.

There follows an eloquent indictment of urban life. It is no doubt overstated, as indictments penned by moralists generally are. It also no doubt reflects some of the corruptions of life at Alexandria. Luxury has turned the world inside out. Nature is in confusion. Men play the woman and women play the man. Sex is marketed like bread. Clement would welcome a return to ancient Roman law, practice, and attitudes. The man who listens to his Tutor has peace in his home and shows that peace even to his own hair.

The sections ends with a curious digression on the habits of the primitive tribes of Germany, Scythia, and Arabia, which includes an exhortation against bloodshed, since human blood has a share of the Logos, a reference to *Hebrews* 2,14–6.

Much of Clement's repetitive intensity suggests his own repressions. This apart, he does believe in a natural state of affairs because he believes in an ordered ordinance of a God who loves mankind. He believes in a natural distinction between men and women. He believes that nature under Providence prescribes the degree of bodily hairiness. But it doesn't really work for three reasons. First, the homosexual, against whom he inveighs so strongly, has his impulses "by nature"; he may be in a minority but it is a natural minority. Further, the impulse to lust is a natural one. Nature pulls more than one way. Nature is amoral. Morality has to be rooted elsewhere. Clement would accept this, but it invalidates his argument here. Second, man is always interfering with nature. We interfere with nature when we cut our hair at all; it is arbitrary to suppose that it is less natural to pull out a hair from the armpit than to trim a beard. Third, alternatively one might say that man is a part of nature so that everything men do is in some sense natural. Clement's argument is not soundly based.

But we should not blind ourselves to the fact that he is showing a genuinely constructive concern about social abuses.

XV *Warnings Against Luxury and Other Dangers (3,4–6)*

Some people in avoiding manual work themselves have recourse to large numbers of slaves. Clement lingers almost lovingly upon the list of luxuries they serve, in a mood which suggests that he is crushing his own desires. Then, as so often, epigrammatic truth flashes out: "The true eunuch is not the man who cannot but the man who will not pursue pleasure." (Origen took literally Jesus's approbation of those who become eunuchs for the kingdom of heaven's sake; Clement has the words in mind here, and takes them seriously but not literally.)

His concern turns to the company kept by women. Their attendants corrupt them with stories of love. There is a proverb (also quoted by Philo, so evidently familiar in Alexandria) which says, "Don't company with numbers if it does you harm." Clement seems to think that women are easily led astray to indolence, luxury, vanity, led astray by superstitious stories and old wives' tales. They turn to magic. They have one husband, set their heart on another, and are promised a change by charlatans. They are malleable, weak, and gullible. The moral is, "Choose your company carefully." There are women who become the prey of immoralists. Clement's indignation at this loses power when it is immediately followed by an attack on the practice of keeping pet birds, a preference for the irrational to the rational. These women would rather be uneducated than self-controlled; they spend all their money on gewgaws; they are like plumaged birds themselves!

And the baths! How dangerously tempting. The women parade themselves, trying by their accoutrements to knock back lovers, who will take them stripped of all accoutrements! They wouldn't strip for their own husbands, but anyone can see them at the baths, and they actually have men-slaves with them as they undress. It all starts with looking. "To look too curiously is to offend," says Clement, alluding to familiar words of Jesus (*Mt.* 5,28), and goes on to provide his own version of a piece of educational lore: "Respect parents *and servants* at home, all you meet in the streets, *women in the baths*, yourself when alone, *and the Logos everywhere*." The italicized words are Clement's additions to the stock phrases, and tell us something very attractive about the man.

There is nothing wrong with receiving a share of worldly goods, and sharing it with others out of love for mankind (*philanthropos:* a divine quality which man can share), provided we keep a sense of proportion. Love of beautiful things can easily become a selfish and tasteless acquisitiveness. It is ridiculous to value a possession above a person. The simple fact is that the good man has his treasure in heaven. He may seem to be poor, but he is really rich. The unjust man may have the riches of Cinyras or Midas, but he is wretched and life will not be granted him. Wealth is like a snake; it is not easy to avoid being bitten if you take it in your hands. Virtue is real wealth, and virtue is reason (*logos*) passed down through our tutor into practice. This is education, and it is better than silver. Even with material goods prosperity is shown not in possession, but in sharing with others. Possessions are not to be entrusted to any except Christians. True wealth is righteousness, the reason (*logos*) which is the gift of God; its only bank is the human soul; and he that has this has everything.

What is of particular interest in all this is that the church, which once had not many rich or noble, is plainly now attracting the wealthy with all the problems and temptations which inevitably followed.

XVI Simplicity of Living (3,7–8) and Practical Christianity (3,9–12)

Luxury devoted to pleasure shipwrecks a man. It makes him crawl on his belly instead of standing upright, to be as greedy as a sparrow and as lustful as a goat. Scripture provides us with examples of, and exhortations to, frugality. Away with our extravagant furnishings and massed servants. Our tutor gives us two attendants, Do-it-yourself and Be-satisfied-with-a-little.

Then comes one of those passages which warm us to Clement. He is a male in a society dominated by males. But not for him the way the Stoic Epictetus renounced the family. Clement says that if there are a wife and children the home is no load weighing us down; the home learns to march together along the road to heaven. A wife who loves her husband will join him in the journey on the same terms. Travel light; the essential piece of luggage is the staff of help given to others. True riches are like a well which fills up again as you draw from it. He who has the Logos, the Almighty God, (a notable phrase), lacks nothing.

Simplicity of living is an excellent training for hardship. To spend wisely is as good as having boundless resources; there is here a characteristic wordplay, since *euteleia* means literally "spending well" and idiomatically "being economical."

In all this the finest precept is by the use of examples. But examples may be of two kinds. There are good examples which encourage us to emulate them, as for instance, Penelope in the *Odyssey*, an example of chastity and married love; Abraham and the first disciples, examples of obedience (Clement typically quotes Hesiod in talking about them); the victorious athlete, a challenge to those who come after. Others are bad examples and warnings of what to avoid; the Spartan serfs who were encouraged to get drunk so that others might be disgusted; the "Gentiles," that is those who do not follow Christ (Clement has transformed a term of racial superiority into a term of moral criticism); the man walking in front of you who falls into a pit; the Sodomites; and Cain and Balaam and Core (*Jude* 11). So our tutor, in his love of mankind, finds many ways in which to help us, with rebuke or with encouragement.

There follows the most interesting section of the whole book, Clement's summary advice on Christian behavior. It can most conveniently be presented under its several heads:

The Public Baths. There are four reasons for going to the baths: cleanliness, warmth, health, and pleasure. The last is ruled out for Christians; so, though less emphatically, is warmth. This leaves cleanliness and health, and Clement very oddly says that women may visit the baths for both reasons, men for the second only. He probably means that men should for cleanliness wash in a river; he would regard this as indecorous for women. Constant use of the bath is debilitating, and wrinkles the skin prematurely. It is dangerous to bathe when tired or just after a meal. And we ought to be able to wash ourselves and not require an attendant to do it for us.

The Gymnasium. Physical fitness is desirable, and physical exercise a necessary means to that end. Clement thinks that the healthiest forms of physical exercise are associated with useful work; nothing demeaning in handling a hoe, working the mill, drawing water, chopping wood (Clement here has a sounder approach than his revered Plato, who saw manual work as degrading to a gentleman). And, of course, there is always walking from town to country or country to town. So too women have spinning, weaving, cooking, feeding the animals, making the beds. There are many educators today who think that the high schools have made a fetish of games, that boys and girls spend too much of their lives "striking different-sized balls with different-shaped pieces of wood," and that there are healthier ways of keeping fit physically.

Clement, however, does not rule out recreational exercise. He mentions in particular wrestling, and ball-games, which in the ancient world were mostly variants on a simple game of catch. He also allows fishing, and Izaak Walton reminds us that across the centuries fishing has been thought to prepare the clergy suitably for their task of fishing for men. But our athletic exercises should be controlled. He believes in moderation in all things. We should be seeking health, not competitiveness. Wrestling should be a straightforward test of strength, not of cunning and craft. We should avoid ungraceful attitudes. We should take exercise before meals, and be careful not to exhaust ourselves on an empty stomach. And we should be simple in our equipment and look after ourselves. Clement does not approve of athletics for women.

Clement is completely free from cant. The Greeks and Romans had little in the way of team-games, though they did compete for their city, and he uses no arguments about team-spirit. Highly organized competitive athletics has gone with a highly organized competitive economy; this lay in the future, but Clement has an intuitive awareness of its dangers.

Clothes. Tendency to luxury must be controlled. Luxury is like the unruly horse in Plato's *Phaedrus* (246Aff.) (there called Desire), trying to unseat the charioteer, the Logos (Reason, the Word, here identified as the Tutor).

We should wear plain, suitable, clean, white clothing. White is appropriate to the children of light. Thick clothing may be used to preserve the warmth of the body in winter: Clement does not favor the excesses of the Cynics who tried to discipline the body by exposing it to extremes of heat and cold.

As mentioned earlier, women may have softer clothes than men but should avoid luxury.

Ear-rings. Pierced ears? As well the sow's pierced nose, and her ring grovels in the mud. Reason—the Logos—says No.

Finger-rings. A gold finger-ring is permissible, not for display, but for practical use as a seal, essential as long as all servants are not honest. Other rings are to be discarded; "a wise man finds a golden ornament in education" (*Ecclesiasticus* 21,21). Further, men who wear a ring should wear it not at the knuckle as women do, but at the base of the little finger, leaving the hand free for work.

Women seem to be afraid that if they do not wear jewellery, they will be taken for servants. Their freedom of mind should be visible in their natural demeanor.

Clement allows one exception to the prohibition of over-adornment, and it delightfully reveals his understanding nature. If a woman has a husband with a roving eye, she can adorn herself to attract his eye back to her. But only to attract her husband.

An interesting section deals with suitable emblems for the seal. Clement recommends a dove (an early symbol of the Holy Spirit); a fish (an old religious emblem taken up by the Christians because I-CH-TH-U-S, the Greek word for "fish," is an acrostic of "Jesus Christ, God's son, Savior" in Greek); a ship sailing before the wind (the ship is sometimes an image of the church; the nave of the church-building derives its name from *navis* "a ship"); a lyre (Jesus became assimilated to Orpheus; Clement is not afraid of the fact that the dictator Polycrates used the device); an anchor (an obvious symbol of security, similarly used by Seleucus); a fisherman. Some of these symbols, such as the fish and the anchor, are found from much this period in the catacombs at Rome. He disapproves of idols, weapons (the Christians being committed to peace), goblets, and naked figures of lovers.

Hair. Unless men have curly hair (a curious exception) they should shave their scalps, and even curly hair should not grow too long. But men should wear beards and not go clean-shaven; this lends a tone of paternal dignity. The moustache should be trimmed away from the mouth with scissors, but not shaved.

Women may keep their hair soft, but should fasten it with a single pin, and should not practise elaborate hairdos which one scarcely dares to touch.

Wigs are out; fancy the hand of blessing being laid on a wig! Dyeing is also out. There is nothing to be ashamed of in the honorable estate of old age.

Make-up. Clement deprecates the use of make-up. Beauty is the free flower of health; it comes from moderation in food and drink, and from a good digestion.

The behavior of women. Inward beauty is called for, not external ornament. A woman is beautified by her own labor, by wearing clothes she has made herself, by chastity and self-control. Undisciplined behavior is the mark of the harlot. Eyes should be kept demurely down; to catch the eye of a man is the first step to fornication. Clement has other practices of which he disapproves: showing the teeth while chewing mastich; scratching the head with a prong of ivory or tortoiseshell (dead animals!) rather than with the fingers; rouging the cheeks; sitting in the doorway to catch the eyes of the passersby.

Walking. Our walking should not be a crazy onrush. It should be dignified but not laggard. It should not be designed to attract attention. And a man should stand on his own feet and not require servants to push him up a hill.

The true gentleman. The true gentleman should avoid effeminacy. He should not treat his servants as beasts of burden. He should be fairminded, loving, and forgiving. Clement quotes Peter (1 *Peter* 3,8) with a misquotation of "humble-minded."

The ideal girl. Clement's characterization of the ideal girl is taken from Zeno the Stoic. Her face should be clean; she should not lower her brows or raise her eyes; she should not throw her head back or allow her limbs to gangle; she should keep her mind sharp for conversation, and assimilate the good things said; her movements and attitudes should not encourage lustful thoughts; she should flower into a combination of modesty and firmness. And she should avoid extravagant harlotry of adornment.

Recreation. Men should avoid gossip, woman-chasing, and dice. How a man spends his time reveals his inner disposition.

Company. We should spend our time in the company of good men. It is curious but not uncharacteristic that Clement, who could have reinforced this with Paul's use of Menander's "Bad company corrupts good character" in the letter to Corinth (1 *Cor.* 15,33), chooses instead a fantastic allegorical interpretation of the Mosaic food laws.

The shows. Clement's section on the shows strikes us as odd, but we must remember that he is writing from Alexandria not Rome. He says, therefore, nothing about the gladiatorial displays, only the athletics meeting and the theater. His prime concern is not even about the content of these; it is that men and women gather promiscuously to look, not at the show, but at one another. He then turns to the theater, and argues as fervently as any Moral Rearmer that the shows put on are immoral and tend only to reinforce the unhealthy sexual excitement. The plays, he says with one of the puns in which he delights, are full of *spermologia*: the word usually means "idle chatter"—literally "seed-picking"—but it could be construed "talk of sex." From what we know of the theater under the empire we can well think that Clement's strictures at this point are reasonable. With Freud behind us, we can see that the same analysis could be applied to the wrestling-bouts, chariot-races, and, above all, the gladiatorial contests; they too pandered to an unhealthy sexual excitement. If we are tempted to think that Clement overstates his case we should remember that at Rome under Marcus Aurelius, the Stoic on the throne, more than a third of the days of the year were public holidays, and on most of these the "Games" were celebrated.

Religion and life. "We are not all philosophers." Oh yes we are! The man who loves his neighbor is a philosopher in practice. So in the daily practice of buying or selling we show our philosophy. Here Clement says two very interesting things to traders. "Name a fair price and stick to it." "Don't use an oath to reinforce your bargain." It was exactly these two principles which the early Quaker business-folk insisted on and found that they won the confidence of their customers so that their sacrificial principles became a source of material gain.

Behavior in church. Women and men alike should go decently clothed to church, quietly, walking naturally, with sincere Christian love, pure in body and in heart. And women should be veiled, unless the church happens to be meeting in her own home. We are reminded that a church at this period is a gathering not a building, and that nearly all churches were "house-churches."

Behavior out of church. Too many people take their color from their background: Clement's illustration is the polyp, where we might more readily think of the chameleon. They throw off their solemnity when they leave church, and engage in serenading, music, drinking.

The kiss of peace. Christians used to greet one another with a holy kiss. Clement seems to imply that some decidedly unholy kissing had crept into the churches. He distinguishes between the kiss of Christian love given with closed lips, and the noisy, poisonous practice of a smacking buss with lips open. Love, Christian love, is an inward disposition; it may express itself naturally in a kiss, but the kiss is of itself no guarantee of the inward disposition and it is the inward disposition which counts.

Discipline of the eyes. Men should not look at women. Clement is quite sane over this surprising advice: "Surely a man can use his eyes and keep his cool? Yes, but it's as well to be on guard against falling. It is possible to slip as a result of using the eyes; it is not possible to lust as a result of not using the eyes." But he must have missed a lot of innocent joy.

Behavior of married couples at home. Don't kiss your wife in front of your servants. Start at home and show that marriage combines joy with self-discipline.

XVII *What the Bible Says About the Christian Life (3,12)*

And now Clement draws to his conclusion in a massive flurry of scriptural quotations calling men to a life of righteousness and illustrating this by detailed practical precepts. We need not follow him in detail, but we may notice one or two points.

First, there is some confusion between the Tutor and the Teacher. The confusion is increased by an ambiguity over the Logos, the Word. It is an ambiguity which continues to the present. Strictly, the Logos is the Reason behind the universe, the Power by which God expresses himself, and for Clement as for John, that Power is revealed in Jesus Christ. But the Word implies something spoken or written, and it naturally leads the reader to think of the scriptures, which are also called "the Word of God." When Clement speaks, accurately in terms of ancient education, of the tutor as leading the child to the schoolmaster, he seems to identify the tutor with the scriptures and the schoolmaster with Christ. But at the end Christ is both tutor and schoolmaster. There is in fact some confusion in Clement's mind, though he might say that both are expressions of God's reasonable power.

Second, Clement here on the whole concentrates upon the Jewish and Christian writings. He does not intersperse these with more than a very few references to pagan writers, one from the Stoic Chrysippus, one from Pindar, and one, or possibly two, from Menander, and that, I think, is all. It is therefore the more interesting that he begins the chapter with two almost blatant references to Aristotle and Apollinides, and ends with two equally obtrusive references to Bacchylides and Homer. He sets his Christian injunctions in a pagan framework.

Third, among the Christian and Jewish quotations are a few that do not come from the Bible, as, for example, "Good works are an acceptable prayer to the Lord," "A heart that honors its Maker is an odor of sweet fragrance to God"; we do not know the source of these.

Almost the last words of the book are a prayer: "Be gracious to your children, Tutor, Father, Charioteer of Israel, Son and Father, both one, Lord. Grant us who follow your ordinances to fulfill the likeness of the image and to apprehend as far as we may the God who is a good not a harsh judge. In all things prepare us who have our citizenship in your peace, who have emigrated to your city, and have sailed untossed through the surges of sin, to be carried along in calm by your Holy Spirit, your ineffable Wisdom, by night and day to the perfect day praising with joy and thanks the only Father and Son, Son and Father, the Son who is Tutor and Schoolmaster, with the Holy Spirit, in all things praising the One, in whom are all things, through whom all things are one, through whom is eternity, whose members we all are, whose glory is the Aeons, the All-good, All-beautiful, All-wise, All-righteous, to whom be glory now and for ever. Amen."

XVIII   *Clement's Hymn*

At the end of *The Tutor* in all our manuscripts except the Palatine and New College manuscripts, there appears a hymn.

Clement's hymn is so important and fascinating that we must quote it in full. It is written in lilting, marching anapaests with a fine sense of onward movement.

> Bit for untamed colts,
> Wing for sure-coursed birds,
> Sure helm for ships,
> Shepherd of the royal flocks,
> gather your children
> all together
> to praise in holiness
> to hymn without guile
> with blameless lips
> Christ who guides his children.   10
>
> King of the saints,
> almighty Word
> of the supreme Father,
> source of wisdom,
> support of our labors
> with never ending joy,
> Jesus Savior
> of mankind,
> shepherd, ploughman,
> helm, bit,   20
> winging your holy
> flock through heaven,
> fisher of men

who find salvation,
charming by bliss
away from the sea's malice
the holy fish
of the bitter wave.

Holy shepherd
of men who find the Word,   30
King, be leader
of your stainless children.
Tracks of the Christ,
road to heaven,
Eternal Word,
infinite Aeon,
everlasting light,
fount of mercy.

Guardian of righteousness,
glorious life   40
for them that praise God,
Christ Jesus,
milk from heaven,
pressed out
from the lovely breasts
that adorn your bride,
your Wisdom.
We are babes,
breast-fed
with tender lips,   50
filled
with the dewy breath
of the breast of the Word.
Let us sing together
unison praises
to Christ our King,
in sacred payment
for life and teaching.
Let us sing simply
of the child of power,   60
a choir of peace,
those born of Christ,
an obedient people.
Let us hymn together
the God of Peace.

The imagery is noteworthy. One image piles on another. This is characteristic of John's Gospel, which is full of the names of Christ: the bread of life (6,35 and 68), the resurrection and the life (11,25), the light of the world (8,12), the door of the sheepfold (10,7 and 9), the good shepherd (10,11), the true vine (15,1), the way, the truth and the life (14,6), the lamb of God (1,29 and 36). It is interesting that Clement does not draw much on this list, nor exclusively on it.

Theophilus of Antioch, an older contemporary of Clement, has an important passage on the names of God—Light, Logos, Mind, Spirit, Wisdom, Strength, Potency, Providence, Sovereignty, Lord, Judge, Father, Fire (*Ad Autol.* 1, 3). He shows that there was interest in the church in the language which might appropriately be used in speaking of things ultimate, and in the limitation of such language. Some of the imagery is obviously applicable to Christ, Light, Logos, Lord and Judge, and all the rest, even Father (*Jn.* 14,9) is associated with him.[4]

Later, in the early seventh century, Isidore (7,2) has a long disquisition on the names of Christ. Notker and Sedulius also expand on this theme. Here is Notker's list:

Messiah, Savior, Emanuel, Sabaoth, Adonai,
Only-begotten, Way, Life, Hand, Like-substanced,
Beginning, First-born, Wisdom, Virtue,
Alpha, the Head, the last letter Omega,
Fount and Origin of God, Paraclete, Mediator,
Lamb, Sheep, Calf, Snake, Ram, Lion, Worm,
Mouth, Word, Splendor, Sun, Glory, Light, Likeness,
Bread, Flower, Vine, Mountain, Door, Rock, Stone,
Angel, Bridegroom, Shepherd, Prophet, Prince,
Deathless, Sure, God, All-Ruler, Equal.

A Greek manuscript of the thirteenth century now in Paris (39) actually brings the list to ninety-two without using all of Clement's. It is worth noting how widely Clement draws on the New Testament and how little on the Old, by comparison with Notker. Thus the idea of the "tracks" or "footsteps" comes from 1 *Peter* 2,21; the idea that we are babes at the breast from 1 *Corinthians* 3,2 and *Hebrews* 5,12–3; the milk of the Word from 1 *Peter* 2,2; the Peace from *Romans* 15,33 and *Hebrews* 13,20. The earliest images of Jesus in Christian art are symbolic representations of the Shepherd and, a little later, the Teacher.

That hymns were growing up in the church at this period Clement himself attests (*Str.* 7,7 etc.). We can trace them back to the New Testament. After the Last Supper Jesus and the disciples sang a hymn; we know that it was *Psalms* 115–8. A particularly fine hymn is found in Paul's letter to *Philippians* (2,5–8); other fragments are embedded in the Pastoral Epistles (1 *Tim.* 3,16; 6,15–6; 2 *Tim.* 11–3; *Tit.* 3,4–7) and in *Revelation*, such as the great "Worthy is the Lamb, the Lamb that was slain, to receive all power and wealth, wisdom and might, honor and glory and praise!" with the antiphon "Praise and honor, glory and might, to him who sits on the throne and to the Lamb for ever!" (*Rev.* 4,12–3). In A.D. 112 Pliny, "investigating" the Christians of Bithynia, found that they met before dawn on Sunday morning and sang a hymn antiphonally to Christ as God (Plin. *Ep.* 10,96).

This hymn thus falls into a familiar category. It looks very much as though it were designed for antiphonal singing; it falls into well-marked divisions (1–10, 11–28, 29–47, 48–66). It is carefully written. There is a controlled use of hiatus in the Greek, four times between lines (33, 48, 52, 53) and four times within lines (11, 31, 42, 43). Of the music we know nothing, and cannot even guess.

CHAPTER 4

Miscellanies: Books 1-3

I *Introduction*

At the beginning of *The Tutor* (*Paed.* 1,1) Clement identifies the three branches of human experience—character, action, emotion. It is right to begin with character, and this was the function of his *Exhortation*. Once character or disposition is right the rest will follow. Next comes *The Tutor*. The function of the tutor was to inculcate right habits of action, not to teach. The culminating treatise was to be *The Teacher*. The tutor is a guide, the teacher a methodical instructor; the tutor is spiritual, the teacher intellectual; the tutor deals with actions, the teacher with principles; the tutor inculcates self-discipline, the teacher knowledge. Or, to put it differently, Eudorus, an Alexandrian (Stob. 2,39) made an ethical division between impulse, action, and principle. *The Exhortation* gave us the first, *The Tutor* the second, and we are awaiting the third. All this was to Clement's mind the work of the Divine Word, forming our disposition, guiding our behavior, and, over and above everything else, systematically instructing us. But Clement at this point breaks off. He never wrote *The Teacher*. The suggestion, made by some, that *Miscellanies* was this culminating work, is merely ludicrous: it is neither systematic nor culminating. This is not the expected hymn to the glory of the Logos. Two things have happened. First, Clement got cold feet about his masterpiece. He started putting it off—and that is fatal! Second, he had a lot of miscellaneous material in his scrapbooks. As we often do, he put off the more exacting task by pleading the less exacting. He produced *Miscellanies*. From time to time he promised the other work. He will, he tells us, deal elsewhere with the First Cause (2,8,37). He will postpone the full Christian interpretation of the Greek mysteries (6,2,4). He will write more about the true

Gnostic later (6,18,168). For the moment, he's concerned with *Miscellanies.*[1]

Miscellanies is the least-known of Clement's works, except to specialists. The first problem is associated with the title. Clement himself said that he was not worried about the exact title (1,10,48). Its full title seems to have been *Miscellanies of Gnostic Notes in accordance with True Philosophy* (1,29,182; 3,18,110; 5,14,151; 6,1,1. See Eusebius *HE* 6,13; Photius *Bibl.* 111.) The word translated "miscellanies" is however itself not clear. It comes from a form of the verb for "strew" or "spread." The title is usually cited in the masculine *stromateis.* This ought to mean "bedmakers" or possibly "merchants of bedclothes"; it has been supposed that the slave who made the beds was also responsible for flower-arrangement, and that we should be thinking of the sort of extended meaning seen in "anthology" (literally "a posy of flowers"). In use, however, *stromateis* seems to have been equated with the neuter *stromata,* meaning "bedclothes," or with *stromatodesma,* "laundry-bags." The last meaning is tempting: you never know what is coming out of a laundry-bag, and the plural is explained by the fact that each book is a separate bag. But this is not how the church historian Eusebius understood the word: he says that Clement "spreads out" holy scripture and excerpts from the Greeks. Probably then we do best to think of the title as representing a patchwork-quilt. Clement himself tells us a little of what he is intending: a work in which divine truth is mixed up with philosophical teaching, as the grain with the husk (1,1,18); or again, a work full of casual variety, like a meadow in which flowers and trees grow wild, without planning, in intermingled profusion (6,2,10; 7,18, 111); or again, a variegated work, as *stromateus* implies, passing immediately from one point to another. This suits the patchwork-quilt. He justifies himself, with a change of metaphor, on the ground that different fish need different baits. The title was one of many appropriate to a miscellany (Aul. Gell. *NA* pref. 6–8).

We have not done with the title. Clement also describes his book as *Notes, hypomnemata, aide-memoires.* The term has an interesting history. It can be used of any memorandum, of a note in a banker's ledger, or the minutes of a committee, or a doctor's clinical notes. Lucian in his essay on *How to Write History* (16) uses it of a skeletonic outline of historical facts without elaboration or interpretation, a sourcebook rather than real history. There was, however, an extended use of the word, which is relevant here: it was applied to philosophical treatises. Thus, when Arrian calls his reminiscences of Epictetus "notes," he means us to understand first that these are a serious contribution to philosophy, second that they are factually accurate, third that they are the barest bones, and much more could be said. Finally, we should remember that in Plato's *Phaedrus* the word is used in connection with Plato's theory of knowledge and his view that knowledge is a recollection of things apprehended before birth (249 C). Clement, a devout Platonist, would not be sorry that his title should bear these overtones.

There are three more significant words in the title. The notes are "gnostic"; they have to do with knowledge, *gnosis*, with all the overtones of religious revelation which ring through that word. But Clement deliberately dissociates himself from the Gnostics, from "knowledge falsely so-called," as a New Testament writer puts it (1 *Tim.* 6,20). These notes are "in accordance with true philosophy." True philosophy plainly refers to Christianity, but the phrase suggests more, for it takes Clement's religious revelation away from the context of debased Hebraism and near-Eastern syncretism in which Gnosticism flourished, and places it squarely in the tradition of Greek philosophy.

We should note what Eusebius says about *Miscellanies* (*HE* 6,13,4–8): "In *Miscellanies* he has composed a patchwork, not only from holy scripture, but from the writings of the Greeks, recording anything which seems useful in their views, and expounding generally held opinions alike from Greek and non-Greek sources, and correcting the false doctrines of the leaders of heresy. He unfolds a wide area of research, and provides a project of considerable erudition. With all this he includes the theories of philosophers, so that he has made the title *Miscellanies* appropriate to the contents."

II The First Book: Introduction

The first book of *Miscellanies* treats of Greek philosophy. Clement's general position is clear and consistent. True philosophy is found in Jesus Christ. Greek philosophy, however, has a propaedeutic function. It holds for the Greeks essentially the same position that the Old Testament holds for the Jews, in making them ready to receive the gospel.

The opening words of the manuscript are lost: a whole page is missing. We lose the impact of his initial statement; we miss his own view of the nature and object of his work. When we join him he is stressing the importance of leaving a record for posterity, a plant to bear fruit. Wisdom is to be shared; it operates from love of mankind. So at the outset we have one of the great Christian words—*philanthropos*. But full knowledge (*gnosis*) is not for all. It calls for work, service, purity of intention, faith, constant search. Scattered through these worthy sentiments are quotations from the Bible and reminiscences of Plato. Clement shows his hand from the beginning (1,1,1–10).

He now turns to explain what he is about. He is not composing a piece of exhibition oratory. These are notes, a nest-egg for his old age, a medicine against failing memory, a kind of sketch of words and people, lacking the sharpness and vitality of the originals. Who are these people? Clement alludes to them cryptically—an Ionian encountered in Greece, a Coele-Syrian and an Egyptian in Magna Graecia, an Assyrian and a Palestinian Jew in the East, and, finally, in Egypt the genuine Sicilian bee. We have already discussed their identity (p. 14); we can be certain of nothing, save that the Sicilian bee is assuredly Pantaenus. These maintained the true tradition of blessedness in their teaching, handed down from father to son, from Peter, James, John, and Paul. It is a touching picture of the intimacy of the early church, which is sometimes forgotten. But the revelation is to the few. The sacred secrets, like God, are entrusted to word (*logos*) not to writing. This is a fascinating statement. In the first place, it is a clear assertion of the limitations of scripture, which we might not expect from other parts of Clement. Second, it indicates the importance of oral tradition in the church. But in addition there are overtones implicit in the ambiguity of *logos*. The written, and, for that matter, the spoken words, are useless without reason to interpret them, and that reason must be informed by the divine Word (1,1,11–3).

The notes are in any case a poor substitute for the original. Clement omits some matters for which his hearers are not ready ("Don't give a sharp knife to a child!"), and refers cryptically to others. He is guided by knowledge (*gnosis*) derived from revelation (the term is taken from the Eleusinian mysteries). He promises to proceed from the origin or genesis of the world to the point where the thorns and weeds are eliminated for the planting of the vineyard. He scarcely fulfills this somewhat poetic outline.

III   The Place of Philosophy

To warm up for a wrestling-match, you wrestle. Preparation for the mysteries is itself part of the mysteries. So Clement is going to use Greek philosophy. He means by this that Greek philosophy is not the full Christian revelation, but it is in essence the same thing; it belongs to the same family. It is like a pearl necklace with one outstanding gem; in one sense it is one pearl among many, in another it is *the* pearl. Clement changes his image. He is a farmer watering the soil of his readers with the stream of Greek philosophy, to prepare them to receive the seed of the Spirit. Some people see in philosophy a corrupting influence; Clement sees it as a work of divine Providence. This is unequivocal (1,1,14–8).

He suggests to the unconvinced that it is at least useful to see the limitations to the usefulness of philosophy—a typical use of verbal play to point a paradox. He also suggests that a display of erudition produces a confidence in a teacher; it is good to meet a student on his own ground. But he himself reasserts that philosophy is a clear image of truth, a gift of God to the Greeks. Truth itself is veiled, and *Miscellanies* so present it. Clement is ambiguous here; at one point he seems to suggest that truth is more appreciated if it is difficult to come by, at another that it is dangerous to reveal truth to spiteful opponents, at still another that truth is a seed which needs to be buried in order to grow. The opponents are formidable. Clement singles out two groups without precisely identifying them. One is clearly the Epicureans ("slaves to pleasure, professional disbelievers"). The other is the sophists of the movement we call the Second Sophistic. Clement is eloquently sarcastic about them ("like old shoes which let in the water and fall away till only the tongue is left"), and brings quotations from Democritus, Homer, Solon, *Matthew*, Paul, Cratinus, Iophon and *Isaiah* to bear upon them (1,2–3).

In Homer and Hesiod the word "wisdom" is applied to practical skills, to a craftsman, a musician, a navigator. Scripture applies it to all theoretical and practical skills and claims that they all came from God. But there is a special spiritual sense, which is linked with spiritual knowledge (*gnosis*). Those who are justified by philosophy have a treasure to draw on in emergency: it is their spiritual sensitivity directed towards the worship of God (1,4).

"Before the coming of the Lord, philosophy was necessary to lead the Greeks to righteousness, and it is still useful in drawing them nearer to the worship of God. It is a primary education for those who are going to harvest their faith by a process of demonstration. . . . God is the origin of all good things . . . including philosophy." That in a nutshell is Clement's position, and he states it without favor or fear. Philosophy holds the place for the Greeks which the Law holds for the Jews. It is a bastion against the sophists. There is only one river of truth, but a lot of streams disgorge their waters into it. The school syllabus is a preparation for philosophy, philosophy is subordinate to wisdom, the knowledge of all things, divine and human, and their causes; its object should be the knowledge (*gnosis*) and honor of God. Scriptural passages have been cited against philosophy, but only by forcing their meaning. It is interesting and important that Clement, who interprets the scripture so freely himself, is aware of the dangers of forced interpretation. He does himself now offer an allegorical interpretation of the story of Abraham, Sarah, and Hagar. Abraham is the type of Faith. At this period Wisdom (Sarah) was barren, and permitted Abraham to father offspring on Philosophy (Hagar). But Wisdom is the true bride of Faith (1,5).

We need some preliminary mental and spiritual exercise, diverting the soul from material things to truth. Clement quotes Plato (*Rep.* 4,424A) on the importance of education (with some interesting variants from the received text). He also quotes *Proverbs* (6,8) "Go to the bee": has he himself not been to the Sicilian bee? And then, in an exquisitely ambivalent phrase, "Men become good and noble by education not nature, like doctors and pilots." Good and noble, yes; it is the Greek ideal of the gentleman, the aristocrat, the man of culture, but, take the adjectives separately and they become Christian and classless. Of course we are naturally created (Clement uses the Platonic word) sociable and just, but this merely means that we respond to education and that we do not need it. One can have faith without education, but it will not be an understanding faith, and Clement drives his point home in a fine flurry of quotations in which Solomon, as the purported author of *Proverbs*, rubs shoulders with Anaxarchus and Hesiod (1,6).

Greek education and Greek philosophy come from God, but not as a fundamental principle; Clement uses a Stoic term, and is thinking of the Logos. It comes as rain, falling on field and dunghill alike. Life sprouts from it but not always fruitfully. Philosophy is useful to life, and Clement makes it clear that by philosophy he does not mean any single school or sect, not even Plato's, but an eclectic compilation of the truth in each. But we must pass from understanding to action: this is the true *gnosis* (1,7).

IV *False philosophy*

Clement has already touched on sophistic practice. He now comes back to it, in a stout scorn blending Paul and Plato. Sophistry uses words or arguments (*logoi*) to make false appear true. It aims not at truth, but at winning arguments, and unless rhetorical skill is joined to philosophy (love of wisdom), it is dangerous, diseased, and damaging, whereas the true Word, the Logos of salvation, is healthful. This section is rich in citations from Euripides, from no less than four plays; it has an otherwise unknown scriptural citation about "those who stretch the warp and weave nothing"; and it characterizes Plato as among the lovers of truth (1,8).

But Clement wants to insist that he is not opposed to philosophy, dialectic, or natural science. To stand on bare faith is like harvesting an untended vine—a good simile, since Jesus described himself as the vine. Athletes, pilots, doctors all train; Clement is closely following Plato here. The true Gnostic, like Odysseus, knows many things; he can distinguish sophistry from philosophy, the beauty-parlor from the athletics-track, cookery from medicine, rhetoric from dialectic, pagan sectarianism from truth. It is useful to handle words skillfully: Jesus did so on his encounter with the devil. We have to know how to answer questions; this is dialectic. To speak and to act are the work of the Word, the Logos; to act without the Logos (Reason) is to act irrationally. Here Clement indulges in his favorite wordplay:

it is important to realize, first, that where we have to render Logos by a variety of translations in English it is in Greek a single comprehensive term, and, second, that wordplay for Clement is not a trick of style but a use of language to reveal a substantial unity (1,9).

This leads to a fresh point. The right use of reason and words is good; so is right action. Jesus breaks the bread and tells us to eat—an action—in accordance with reason. There is a saving word and a saving deed, and both matter. This established, Clement returns to the warning against sophistry. We can be too concerned with words, and Plato and the Bible both warn us against this. Paul in particular warns us against false philosophy, enticing words, the wisdom of the world. This does not refer to all philosophers, but to Epicureans who eliminate providence and deify pleasure, and Stoics who believe in a material God, and the Ionian monists who make air or water or fire an object of worship. But the wisdom spoken in a mystery may have to be concealed from some; the pearls are not to be cast before swine, the seeds not to be sown in the path of jackdaws. It must be confessed that Clement's explaining away of his Lord's injunction to proclaim from the housetops is not free from sophistry (1,10–2).

V *The Story of Greek Philosophy*

Truth is one, falsehood has ten thousand byroads. The philosophical sects have fragmented the unity of truth, dismembering the Logos as the Bacchantes dismembered Pentheus. Yet all are illuminated by the dawn of light. This is Clement's great assertion (1,13).

And now he embarks on a potted history of Greek philosophy —and he is no doubt potting an already potted history—perhaps more than one as he is not entirely consistent. But even if he is drawing on handbooks he incorporates firsthand familiarity, and offers comments of his own. It would be inappropriate here to examine his summary in detail. We may, however, notice Clement's just insistence that Paul is familiar with Greek authors and thinks it right to attribute to them some authority. We may note his preliminary statements that all the Greek philosophers are later than Moses (which is true) and that their manner of philosophizing is Hebraic and allusive (which is surprising; we may recall that Numenius called Plato "Moses writing Attic Greek"). We may note his suggestion that the precept "Know yourself," attributed to various Greek sages, is an injunction to *gnosis,* Christian knowledge, the knowledge of God, since we cannot know the part without knowing the whole. Finally, we may note that Clement, for all his undoubted learning, makes mistakes; he confuses Aristotle and Aristarchus; he blurs Crates the Platonist with Crates the Cynic; he inverts the order of Cyrus and Darius. It remains a sensible enough summary and appreciation (1,14).

His next point is the debt of Greek philosophy to non-Greeks. He much overstates the position when he says that most of the philosophers and sages of the Greeks were foreigners by birth and education; this is sophistical rhetoric. His information is from handbooks; he takes what suits him and does not correlate. But there is a proper appreciation of the fact that Egypt, Mesopotamia, Persia, and India lie in the background of Greek thought. There is even a reference to the Buddha. It is interesting to see Democritus treated as he was at this time, as a master of the occult.[2] There is a good example of allegorical interpretation: Heracles's acceptance of the columns of the universe from the Phrygian Atlas signifies the learning of heavenly truths from non-Greek sources. That all is not from handbooks we see from a confusion, easy to make, between the myths in Plato's *Phaedo* and *The Republic.* One fascinating suggestion is that Pythagoras's "fellowship of the class-room" is an anticipation of the Christian church. This is important, for it shows the two points Clement thought essential in a church: that it is a fellowship, and that it meets to hear something.

Then Clement shows his faith and loses his sense of proportion. The Jews, he claims, are by far the oldest of all these peoples, and he forces some of the few references to the Jews in Greek literature to this effect (1,15).

Technical inventions and practical skills came to the Greeks from abroad. The list is formidable, fascinating, and miscellaneous. It includes astrology, divination, and forms of augury; the calendar; geometry; music of several kinds; the alphabet; medicine; navigation; metallurgy; military weapons; pottery; stone-masonry; hair-dye; boxing-gloves; linen-clothes; letter-writing. He gives his sources: naturally the school of Aristotle ranks high among them. But there is no attempt to order the list sensibly; one is conscious how far inferior Clement's treatment is in this regard to the accounts centuries before in Aeschylus's *Prometheus* (461 ff.) or Sophocles's *Antigone* (332 ff.).

He turns to the use of language and reminds his readers that Greek is only one language among others; there is a good anecdote of Anarcharsis, the Scythian, saying, "To me, all the Greeks speak Scythian"; he would have enjoyed the irony of our saying "It's all Greek to me." He quotes Paul: "If I don't understand the force of what is said, I shall be a foreigner to the speaker and he a foreigner to me." (1 *Cor.* 14,11). Then follows a decidedly odd catalogue of the Greek pioneers in some of the main branches of literature, all of whom Clement insists to be later than Moses. And then, after this unbalanced, tedious display of semi-learning, Clement returns to the main point. Is Greek philosophy, Greek culture, inspired by the devil? Or is it a partial but genuine apprehension of the truth? Clement takes the latter view; philosophy prepares the way for the royal teaching (1,16).

But what of Jesus's saying: "All that came before me were thieves and robbers" (*Jn.* 10,8)? Plainly it is not literally meant; the prophets were not thieves and robbers! And now Clement is at his most ingenious. He leaves it open that philosophy is inspired by the Logos, and being in the Logos cannot be before the Logos. But, granted the philosophers to be thieves, where did they steal philosophy from? They stole it from God, from the truth, and for the benefit of mankind, while being directed by Providence. Clement here has in mind Prometheus who stole fire from heaven out of his love for mankind. In one sense, he says with slight sophistry, he who does not prevent something from happening when he could is a contributory cause to its happening: so philosophy, stolen or not, came by will of God. In another sense he who does not prevent is not a cause; he is giving the individual freedom of choice and moral responsibility. So thieves though they be, the philosophers had a portion of truth, but they did not hold it in a spirit of true knowledge. Of course in the full revelation of truth this limited wisdom is seen to be folly. But all men are called; those who respond are chosen, elected. This is Clement's form of universalism; his successor, Origen, carried it further to involve the ultimate salvation of all, even the devil (1,17–8).

Clement now takes the primary text of those who favor the integration of Greek and Christian thought, Paul's speech at Athens (*Acts* 17,22–8). It is a dubious text. Paul's speech was not notably successful, and it looks as if, from what he writes later to Corinth, he came to regret his devious approach to the gospel. However, Clement is right in saying that Paul is familiar with Greek authors and takes them as a starting-point for his truth. Clement goes on to some Platonic quotations; again we find that he is quoting from memory, since he attributes to the pseudo-Platonic *Demodocus* some lines from the equally pseudo-Platonic *The Rivals*; Clement is aware of the doubtful authenticity. An apposite quotation from *The Republic* makes his main point that philosophy contains elements which are highly conjectural, but is centrally concerned with truth and with the good (*Rep.* 5,475D–E). He is thus able to use Paul's image of seeing the truth through reflections (1 *Cor.* 13,12), and this leads him to an interesting quotation which is not in the Bible as we have it: "You have seen your Brother, you have seen your God" (compare, for the general tradition, *Mt.* 25,40; *Jn.* 14,9; 1 *Jn.* 4,20–1). The pagans who have lived out the truth without full knowledge are better than the heretics who have diverged from the fullness of truth revealed to them—and we get a glimpse of a sect which celebrated the Eucharist through bread and water instead of bread and wine; one would have preferred Clement to have identified a more heinous heresy! (1,19).

So Clement can assert that there is only one authoritative truth (a wordplay here, for "authoritative" is *kyria*, and is the same root as *Kyrios* "the Lord"), but there are many partial truths, and one is the Greek. He appropriately uses an analogy of a multiplicity of contributory causes which is ultimately derived from Aristotle. But he further dares to assert that at one time philosophy "justified" the Greeks. There are grounds in the New Testament for claiming that the Gentiles did indeed receive justification. The obvious example is Paul's treatment of Abraham (*Rom.* 4,9–11), but there the point is Abraham's faith, as Martin Luther time and again insisted. Cornelius in *Acts* (10,34–5) is a better example; the word is "acceptable" rather than "justified." Luther would have started another Reformation at the thought that philosophy could justify anyone. Clement would have answered, first that the element of truth in Greek philosophy came directly from the divine Word, second that the response to truth is precisely faith and that philosophy as Clement uses the term includes faith, third that he does not claim more than that philosophy plays for revelation the rôle that elementary education plays for philosophy; it takes you up the first or second flight of stairs to the upper room; the word is the word used of the room in which the disciples were meeting at the beginning of *Acts* (*Acts* 1,13).

VI *Clement's Analysis of History*

The first book ends with an inordinately long account of the chronology of the ancient world. Its object is to establish the priority of Moses (who some Hebrew thinkers identified with Musaeus, the legendary teacher of Orpheus) and Hebrew "philosophy" to the major historical events, philosophical movements, and even mythological figures of the Greeks, and in the absence of our present knowledge of Minoan-Mycenean civilization, this can be done without difficulty. It would be exceedingly tedious to go through all the details of his account, though he preserves much of interest. There are mistakes: some of them are attributable to copyists, some to a certain innumeracy on the part of Clement himself. One of the oddest is the placing of Hoshea in the line of Judah's kings not Israel's; another is that Clement seemingly has made a proper name Hyperon out of two Greek words meaning "on behalf of whom." He covers a great deal of ground in Greek, Jewish, Persian, and Roman history, the last section including a precise designation, to the number of days, of the reigns of the Roman emperors. Julius Caesar's power is dated from November 11th, 48 B.C., and one wonders what tradition Clement had access to; perhaps Dio Cassius was right after all in assigning him extraordinary powers in 48. We note too that from Adam to the death of Commodus (A.D. 192) is said to be 5784 years 2 months 12 days; so much for Archbishop Ussher. The birth of Jesus is put in 4, 3, or 2 B.C. (the addition does not work out precisely), on the 25th day of the Egyptian month Pachon or the 24th or 25th of Pharmouthi (which would give a date in April or May) and his death in A.D. 28, 29 or 30. There was already a varied tradition. Clement has also a tradition that Jesus's ministry lasted for a single year.

In many ways the most interesting part of his historical section is a digression about primitive languages. There was an ancient controversy whether language was natural or conventional, or a combination of the two. Clement comes down firmly on the side of those who hold that language is natural, and uses this as a justification for the use of primitive terms in prayers (1,21).

Having established his general view of chronology Clement tells the story of the translation of the Hebrew scriptures into Greek under the Ptolemies by seventy scholars working independently and achieving a remarkable unanimity of expression. It was the will of God that the scriptures should reach Greek ears so that prophecy became Greek prophecy. This prepares us for the suggestion that Plato was indebted to the Hebrew scriptures, "Moses writing Attic," as Numenius put it (1,22).

We then revert to history for an account of Moses's life, which Clement draws from Philo's *Life of Moses,* with additions from other sources; not the least interesting part is an extended quotation from a Greek play in tragic form entitled *The Exodus,* written by an Alexandrian Jew named Ezekiel:

> But when the time of babyhood was passed,
> my mother took me to the princess's palace,
> first telling, recounting to me all the tale,
> my parentage, the gifts received from God.
> So while I was still enjoying boyhood,
> the princess guaranteed me all, a royal
> training and upbringing—I might have been her son.
> Then, when the fullness of the time was come,
> I left the royal home.

Moses's military leadership is taken as a model for Greek commanders, his legislation as a model for Plato's. We may note how Clement applies to Moses the language appropriate both to the class of soldiers and to the class of legislators, the two divisions of the Guardians in *The Republic.* We note that Clement, as often when he wants to make a point, turns to wordplay. The continual play on Logos returns, both in the calculations (*logismos*) which the military commander has to make, and in an allusion to the Right Reason of the Stoics. There is a play on the name of Apollo, interpreted as "not many" (*a-polloi*) in reference to the one true God, followed immediately by a pun in which the fire in the burning bush (*dia batou*) is conflated with the fire in the desert (*di'abatou*). Again, the law (*thesmos*) comes from God (*theos*). And we note that Moses and Plato alike are brought to the bar of true knowledge (*gnosis*). Moses then is a divine legislator, inferior to Christ, but far superior to the legislators of the Greeks, and his work is the archetype of theirs. The thought is Platonic that the Mosaic law is the Form, and the Greek instances are imperfect manifestations of that Form (1,23–6).

The function of law is in one sense negative, but in another positive and beneficent; it turns people from evil and directs them to good; and no one should run it down. There is a parallel with medicine taken from Plato's *Gorgias* (477 E 7 ff.). Mosaic philosophy in fact has four aspects: historical, legislative, ceremonial, and the ultimate vision; Clement takes this last term from the climax of the Eleusis mysteries, and identifies it with theology, the area treated by Aristotle in his *Metaphysics*. This is the area to be approached by true dialectic (Clement's thought and language are Platonic), sifting the true from the false, and ascending to the God of the universe. The faculty of discrimination is alluded to in another of these scriptural quotations which are not found in our scriptures: "Be reputable money-changers." The need for an analytical power of discrimination is also well expressed in a proverbial saying: "It's all one on Myconos." This is said in one explanation to refer to the fact that all the inhabitants of Myconos were bald; no such hairless identity is to be found in the books of scripture (1,27–8).

The Greeks are children, and their wisdom the progeny of the past; Clement uses the famous words of the Egyptian in Plato to reinforce his point: "Solon, Solon, you Greeks are perpetual children" (*Tim.* 22B). But all law comes from God, and Clement uses Jewish, Christian, and pagan writings alike to prove it. There is another wordplay, this time linking God (*theos*) with ordinance (*thesis*). The apocryphal *Preaching of Peter* testifies to Jesus's being called the Law and the Word. And on this note, with the reminder that he is seeking divine knowledge (*gnosis*) in accordance with true philosophy, Clement ends the first book (1,29).

VII *Faith*

The second book explores further what Camelot has called Clement's "theology of faith," and sets the true Christian Gnostic, who depends on faith, in foursquare contrast with the Gnostic heretics.³ Being a miscellany, it is not tidily shaped. It deviates and diverges. Yet it is not unplanned. It pivots on the great discussion of faith, knowledge, fear, and love in the twelfth chapter.

The opening creates some problems. It seems to lay down a programme. The Greeks have stolen from non-Greek (i.e., Hebrew) philosophy. In stealing they have—Clement uses two interesting words which at their best would mean "inspected the luggage thoroughly" and "put false coinage out of circulation" (as Diogenes the "Dog" claimed to do), but here mean "made fraudulent fabrications" and "debased the coinage." The themes are faith, wisdom, knowledge, and science; hope and love; repentance, continence, yes and the fear of God. Some have tried to make of this a simple division into two: the sphere of faith, and the sphere of hope and love, but Clement's mind is not so tidy. Faith is the main theme of this book, but there is an interlude on fear (2,7–8). The next book treats continence, but the programme is not systematically worked out. He goes on to elaborate. He will speak particularly of the use of symbolism and allusion; and of the limitations of the Greek educational system. He is not concerned to "hellenize." The word is ambiguous between "speak Greek" and "express Greek culture," and he means both: he is concerned with thought not languages, and he is concerned to find the roses among the thorns.

Faith is the way to truth. The non-Greek—"barbarian"—philosophy ("which we follow") is perfect and true; Clement's use of *barbaros* is interestingly paralleled by the way the Romans apply it to themselves, at once in genuine admiration of Hellenic culture and in a proud assertion that they themselves have something which matters more. Clement does not exclude science, the investigation of nature, but sees it as one of the lower steps in a process which, practised with right conduct, leads through wisdom to God. Truth is hidden and has to be discerned by faith. Faith, he says, using technical philosophical language taken from the Stoics, is a preconception directed by the will.

It is an assent in the field of religion, an assent (as some have put it) to an unseen object. It is an act of choice, an aspiration of the intellect, and as such the starting-point and first principle of action. The practice of faith becomes scientific knowledge; this state cannot exist except in religion directed by the Logos; faith does not depend on demonstration (2,2).

Basilides is wrong, Clement goes on, in claiming that faith is a product of nature (still more is Valentinus in separating knowledge from faith and claiming that the orthodox Christians, poor simpletons, have merely faith, while his own followers possess knowledge). This would leave no room for acts of choice, for moral responsibility, for penitence, and for the "blessed seal" (the term taken over by the Christians from other mystery-religions) of baptism (2,3). The Gnostic heretics are never far from his mind.

The Christian knows from scripture that we have freedom of choice. Clement quotes some passages and then reverts to technical philosophy. There are four containers of truth: perception, intellectual understanding, scientific knowledge, and assumption. By nature intellectual understanding has priority; in our actual experience perception comes first: this is a combination of Platonism and common sense. Faith moves through the objects of perception, leaving assumptions behind, and speeding on to rest in the infallible truth. First principles are incapable of demonstration, so that it is only by faith that we can apprehend the first principle of the universe; the Greek natural philosophers here failed. A new vision is needed, which the Logos can supply. Aristotle calls faith (but in Aristotle the word means "belief") the judgment which follows knowledge, and is therefore superior to it. Epicurus says that faith (belief) is a preconception of the intellect. This is equivalent to saying with Isaiah, "Unless you believe you cannot understand" (*Is.* 7,9), or with Heraclitus, "If you don't expect the unexpected, you won't find it" (fr. 18). A number of passages from Plato reinforce this. They lead to the conclusion that in wisdom, coming from faith, are (the thought is Stoic) "kingship, priesthood, prophecy, the power of legislation, wealth, true beauty, nobility, freedom." Wisdom is not easy to come by (2,4).

Clement now returns to his assertion that the Greeks simply borrowed from Moses, and supports it with a series of parallel quotations. Of particular interest is an adaptation of *Luke* (18,25): "A camel will more speedily pass through a needle's eye than a rich man become a philosopher." This shows the integrated quality of Clement's thought. At first sight it is replacing the kingdom of God by philosophy. But philosophy is love of wisdom, and in Hellenistic Judaism wisdom was a pure effluence from the glory of the Almighty (*Wisd.* 7,25), always at his side (*Prov.* 8,30), a mediator between God and man; there is a sense in which to love wisdom is to love the Logos. At the same time this is Hellenistic Judaism, a Judaism which has already come to terms with Greece. All these aspects are present in Clement's integration.

Faith then is needed. Wisdom is the scientific knowledge of first causes and of intelligible being. But the first cause of the universe is not accessible to demonstration, only to faith. God speaks, but we must listen with faith; a thrower requires a catcher, the man who lights a fire requires dry wood, the lodestone and the steel are both requisite. There is no repentance without faith; we must recognize that we are imprisoned by sin before we can seek to escape. Hope comes from faith. Faith is an assumption made by the free will, the preconception of a sound judgment before there is or can be apprehension, an expectation about the future. Right behavior springs from faith; faith is the foundation of Christian love (which is of course in Christian terms, as Clement does not need to say, the very being of God: 1 *Jn.* 4,9). Faith comes before our eyes as the first movement towards salvation, after which fear, hope, and repentance advancing with continence and persistence lead us on to love and knowledge. Faith is the very foundation of truth. Much of this is directed against the Gnostics in their division of the gods of the Old and New Testament (we have an otherwise unknown quotation "You have received as inheritance the covenant of Israel": 2,6,29), in their fatalism, and in their criticism of the inadequacy of faith alone.

VIII *Fear*

"Those who denounce fear run down the Law, and so the god who gave it." In these simple words Clement separates his Christianity both from the Stoics who saw fear as a passion unworthy of the true sage, and the Gnostics to whom the God of the Old Testament was a devil-god. Fear, he says, is not illogical; it is instilled by the Logos. The fear of the Lord is the beginning of wisdom (*Prov.* 7,1); if the Law instills fear, then knowledge of the Law is the beginning of wisdom. The laws deal (in Stoic language) with "intermediate" things, not matters of moral judgment. But the Law, the Mosaic Law, the Torah, directs us away from immorality. It is a tutor to bring us to Christ.

Clement now attacks the Gnostic views of Valentinus and Basilides explicitly. He is particularly hard on a mythical interpretation of the story of Christ's baptism, whereby the evil angels and their leader were struck with astonishment and fear by the voice of the Spirit, and jealous of Humanity for receiving the seed from above; in Basilides's version it was this Fear (personified) which gave birth to the aeon Wisdom. Clement is continually insistent that the God of the Old Testament and the God of the New are one and the same, and that both Testaments are inspired by the Logos. He will not allow the Gnostics to put justice in opposition to goodness; it is a problem in Christian ethics which is still with us today: do the demands of love run counter to those of justice, is love to be interpreted in terms of justice, or justice in terms of love?[4] He also has a hit at the Stoics. All fear is not a passion or perturbation. Such a fear applied to God is superstition. No one is afraid of God, only of falling away from God. Fear is good if it takes away evil (2,7–8).

IX *Faith, Knowledge, and Behavior*

Fear leads to repentance and hope, hope to love. Love is concord in all that has to do with reason, life, or behavior, in relationship with our fellows. A fellow is a second self. Parallel with this is hospitality or practical help for strangers. Love of mankind (*philanthropia*: the great word recurs) is the treatment of human beings as if they were personal friends. If the real man within us is the spiritual man (*pneumatikos*), then love of mankind is brotherly love towards those who share the same spirit. Natural affection is the preservation of goodwill. A long series of scriptural passages, and from *The Shepherd* of Hermas, follows and takes Clement a little way from his theme. He returns to assert the unity of the virtues and their basis in faith (2,9).

The Christian philosopher then is dedicated to contemplation, to the fulfillment of the commandments, and to the molding of good men. The combination makes the Christian Gnostic; if any one of them is lacking, his knowledge (*gnosis*) is left lame. In a brief but exalted passage, Clement brings together the language of the Old Testament ("knowing God"), the language of Plato ("contemplation"), and the language of the mystery-religions ("vision" or "spectacle"). The effect produced is that Christianity is the true fulfillment of all three. And it is the true *gnosis*, the true knowledge, the knowledge of wisdom, which cannot be separated from right behavior. Other alleged forms of knowledge, whether among Greek philosophers or Jewish-Christian sects, "puff up" (1 *Cor.* 8,1). True knowledge comes from faith, one that is scientific not conjectural. So the Christian Gnostic will take care to avoid errors of sense-perception, speech, and reason—there is allegorical interpretation involved in Clement's explanation—and action. Clement also plays with number symbolism. The universe has nine regions, and God is found in the tenth. Man has ten faculties: body, soul (or life), five senses, speech, reproduction, and the intellectual or spiritual. The last alternative brings together Paul and Plato, and the parallelism means that this is the faculty by which we know God. The Christian Gnostic is rooted in faith, and reason, his governing principle (*hegemonikon*, a Stoic term), is his soul's pilot. Clement has a side blow at another Gnostic sect, that of Simon, as he reaffirms the stability of the Christian Gnostic against the shiftiness of the heretics (2,10–1).

So we reach the great central chapter. Time is twofold, past and future. So is faith; faith in relation to the past, hope to the future, with love, for the Christian Gnostic who knows but one God, the unifying principle in the present, and fear its obverse, since we fear (not abjectly) and love the same God, and to fear to do wrong is a form of enlightened self-love. Blessed is the man who has faith, mixed with fear and love. Faith is strength leading to salvation, power leading to eternal life (but Clement has also Aristotelian language in mind; a potentiality actualized in eternal life). The Christian Gnostic shows his knowledge in relation to the past (faith) and also the future (hope, prophecy), and in his present action; Clement is a little uncertain whether he is operating a twofold or a threefold scheme. Platonists and Stoics alike agree that assent is within our power. Every opinion, judgment, assumption, act of learning, everything by which we live, is a form of assent, and this is faith. So knowledge and action, past, present, and future, Christianity and Greek philosophy, come together in Clement's mighty scheme (2,12).

X *Moral Responsibility*

Clement's treatment of responsibility is naturally based upon the current church practice of his day. The Christian on admission to church membership put aside his past. In baptism those sins were washed away from him. He knew himself to be forgiven. What then of sins committed after baptism? Clement, in common with the best thought of the church, recognized the weakness of human nature, and allowed one lapse, though any who so backslide should live fearfully. But one lapse might be forgiven. Frequent repentance simply means sinful practice; it is to substitute opportunism for a genuine self-discipline; it is a mock-repentance.

Impulse is a movement of the mind to or from something; a passion is an impulse which has got out of hand so that the soul no longer obeys reason (Clement has in mind Plato's image of Reason as the charioteer guiding the unruly horses of temper and passion). Disobedience and obedience to reason are alike in our power; and actions of our free will come under judgment (2,13).

There are such things as involuntary action, and Clement takes his account of them from Aristotle. They are of two kinds: those performed through ignorance, and those done under duress. The examples come straight from Aristotle (*NE* 1,1111 A 6 ff.): the man who doesn't know who he is, or who doesn't realize what he is doing (like Aeschylus divulging the Mysteries), or who doesn't recognize the other person and kills a friend instead of an enemy, or doesn't know the instrument and uses an unbuttoned foil, or the method like the wrestler who accidentally kills his opponent, or the consequence like the doctor who kills his patient with a medicine intended for healing. Clement's treatment is not quite clear. He seems to accept that such people are in some sense morally culpable, but not as culpable as those who are set on vice. It is acts of deliberate choice which are subject to judgment (2,14).

He goes on to analyse voluntary action. They may arise from desire, choice, or intention; corresponding to these are culpable error, misfortune, and crime. It is a culpable error to live in extravagant luxury, a misfortune to strike a friend thinking him an enemy, a crime to rob a tomb or temple. Culpable error arises from not knowing what we ought to do, or not being able to do it; Clement takes examples from tragedy. The discussion is complicated by the fact that this root in Christian language normally conveys "sin," but here it is determined by philosophical, not religious, usage. A misfortune is a culpable error contrary to calculation; a culpable error is an involuntary crime and crime is voluntary wickedness. But the Lord offers cures for our passions, thus showing our moral responsibility. There is repentance. There is forgiveness (2,15).

XI   *God and Man*

Clement now turns to a profound insight. We cannot speak of God as he is; we can speak only out of our own experience, and recognize that the truth is far greater than we can speak or think. This is an attack both on the Stoics, who criticized the Christians for attributing human emotions to God, and the Gnostic heretics who in treating man as an emanation of the divine nature in fact brought God down to man's level. What Clement is saying in other words is that God is not less than personal, and that we can speak of him only analogically (2,16).

Next comes an interesting analysis of the relationship of will to knowledge. Clement begins by coining a word to state a near-tautology: scientific understanding is a scientistical state: but there is a pun, highly Platonic, on the idea of stability. It is associated with experience, cognition (the knowledge of universals by species), intellection, comprehension (the capacity to make comparisons and distinctions), and full knowledge (*gnosis*, the scientific understanding of true reality). Scientific understanding is due to reason (the Logos). When we fail to do something it is because we do not want to, are not able to, or both, so that our faculties of reason are dependent upon our will.

In the true Gnostic the will, the judgment and the practice are inseparable (2,17).

The Greeks got their concept of ethical virtue from Moses, Clement asserts: courage, self-control, wisdom, justice (the four "cardinal" virtues), and toughness, endurance, dignity, continence, and above all piety. The analysis of the virtues is made in terms of knowledge; it has Platonic roots, with Aristotelian and Stoic blossoms. The virtues, if not all one (in Socratic terms), are inextricably intertwined: the man who has one virtue in the spirit of true knowledge has them all. We are to be assimilated to the Lord as far as it is possible for us with our mortal nature (2,18,80). The phrase is noteworthy; it is taken from Plato (*Theaet.* 176A–B) but christianized. What follows is treated similarly. It is an ethical analysis, using *Proverbs* and especially the Torah, and following closely Philo's exposition. But from time to time Christian language and Christian ideas push through, martyrdom (2,18,81), *philanthropia*, humanity or love of mankind, *agape* or Christian love, and an old pun between *chrestos*, good, and *christos*, anointed or Christ. The whole tenor is that the Torah is governed by humanity and by Christian love (2,18).

The true Gnostic imitates God as far as is humanly possible. Like the Stoic sage, he is king of his passions, and practises continence, endurance, and right living; his practice of sharing is more directly Christian; for a bad man the greatest blessing is not to be his own master. Adam's innate nobility lay in his freedom of choice (a commonplace with the Greek Fathers), and he abused it. Noah did not have the same innate nobility; he was preserved by divine providence. Abraham's son and grandson owed their blessings to their father. Clement's exposition, as so often, follows Philo, even to the typological interpretation. He passes to Plato's view of happiness as likeness to God (*Theaet.* 176 B), and the Stoic doctrine of conformity to nature, i.e., to God. This takes him to a Stoic analysis of human relations. Friendship (*philia*) is of three kinds. The best is founded in virtue: Clement christianizes and says, "The love (*agape*) based on reason (or the Logos) stands firm." The second is based on common helpfulness; the last derives from regular acquaintance. Clement links this with a Pythagorean view: the first is based on knowledge of God, the second on service of men, the third on animal pleasure. The Christian conclusion is that the true

Gnostic starts from knowledge of God and shows his likeness to God in the service of men (2,19).

To this end asceticism and self-discipline are essential, their fruits being the Stoic freedom from passion (*apatheia*). Clement takes as types of endurance Daniel, Job, and Jonah. The true Gnostic will have such endurance as a direct consequence of his knowledge of God. Clement pursues his theme through the Torah, the plays of Euripides, the ascetic philosophers, and the New Testament. Stoic thought returns with a pun: "to be different we must treat with indifference things that are indifferent." We are not stones, plants, or irrational animals and ought to have the self-control to prevent ourselves from being led irrationally astray. Clement attacks Basilides and Valentinus for treating the passions as actual spiritual entities, appendages of the soul. This would mean that sin was inescapable, and self-discipline impossible; further that the soul, being in essence spiritual and of the same nature with God, though fallen into the material world, is saved by its very nature. Clement insists on the need for repentance; salvation comes from a change associated with obedience, not from nature (2,20,115). "The flesh must be abused"; the *mot* was attributed to Nicolaus, one of the seven deacons of *Acts*. The "Nicolaitans" took it as an invitation to licence; Clement takes it as an invitation to asceticism. He quotes the Greek hedonists to reject them, and the Greek ascetics to approve them. The Torah uses fear to impose, like a tutor, discipline on us and lead us to Christ. Example is better still than precept. The true Gnostic is mightier than pleasure, prevails over passions, knows what he is doing, is greater than the world. Self-control is the greatest of all God's gifts (2,20).

How many works of the philosophers Clement had read at first hand is a matter of controversy. Like most of us, he had recourse to handbooks and encyclopaedias from time to time, and he undoubtedly did so in his account of the end or aim of life as seen by the several philosophers. He rejects hedonism. The view of Aristotle and the Stoics that the end is a life in conformity with virtue, he treats sympathetically as a partial truth. After working through these and other views he comes to Plato. Man's ultimate good is found in likeness to God (Plat. *Theaet.* 176B). This is in accordance with scripture. Clement in a masterly manner brings together all the diverse threads which make up this book when he writes, "The opportunity is laid before us of arriving at the endless end, if we obey the commandments (that is, God), and live in conformity with them without reproach and in genuine understanding through the knowledge (*gnosis*) of God's will. Our end is likeness, as far as possible, to right reason (or the upright Logos), and restoration to perfect sonship by the Son" (2,22,134). And this springs from faith (2,21–2).

XII *Marriage*

This is the real end of the second book, but Clement, like a good serial-writer, leads in to the third with a brief section on marriage. Ought we to marry? The theme was a philosophical commonplace, and the philosophers have given different answers. Clement, slightly whimsically, says that it is not for every man to marry every woman he meets on every occasion in all circumstances! He argues the case for marriage, following Musonius, on common sense grounds in a male society: the complementary physical equipment of the male and female bodies, children (as a patriotic and personal necessity) and, principally, the need for a wife's care in time of illness. Those who love wisdom find in marriage something more than mere pleasure, a partnership of like minds in accordance with reason (or, as always, the Logos), dependent not on outward looks but on inward character. Such a marriage must be kept pure, like a holy statue. And such a marriage may not be broken. Fornication and adultery are condemned; the Torah and the Gospel are at one, of course, coming from one Lord, says Clement, with a hit at the Gnostics. But repentance is always open (2,23).

When he plunges into the third book it is explicitly to assail the heretics. For the great Valentinus and Basilides he has some respect. Valentinus believed in monogamy. Basilides permitted marriage but exalted abstinence; some of his followers fell away, and Clement attacked those. He is strongly opposed to the Carpocratian sect. Clement traces this sect back to one Carpocrates and his son Epiphanes. Both look like divine names; Celsus calls the sect "Harpocratians" after Harpocrates, the Greek name for Horus; and Epiphanes means "God manifest." Equally it is possible that the founders of the sect took divine names on themselves. Clement quotes from a book *On Righteousness* purporting to be by Epiphanes. Chadwick and Oulton wrote: "This work merely consists of the scribblings of an intelligent but nasty-minded adolescent of somewhat pornographic tendencies. The work attempts to justify extreme sexual license by a communistic theory: the existence of private property is of human invention and has no divine sanction; communism is therefore to be practised in sexual relationships."[5] Clement accuses the Carpocratians of promiscuity; he levels at them a charge fired by Celsus at the orthodox Christians (Orig. C. Cels. 6.40), that they turned their love-feasts into a sex-orgy, their *agape*, so to speak, into an *eros* (3,1–2). Other heretics are also accused of sexual immorality. These include the Nicolaitans, who made of physical sex a mystic communion; the adherents of Prodicus, who claimed that as sons of the first God they enjoyed absolute freedom, and as kings (the Stoic sages) they were above law (Clement says they are not kings but abject slaves); and the otherwise unknown Opponents, who declared that the God of the Old Testament was a false god, and that therefore we should commit adultery so as to break his false commandment (3,4).

Clement is equally opposed to the ascetic sects, principally the followers of Marcion, who similarly believed that the Creator-God of *Genesis* was a kind of anti-God, and had no desire to people his world. Clement reasonably comments that they don't refuse to breathe his air and eat his food. Clement thinks that Marcion took his asceticism from a half-reading of Plato (3,3). Tatian, the Syrian author of a harmony of the gospels, is another ascetic to come under the lash. To Tatian physical intercourse was destructive to prayer, and marriage was an invention of the devil. Clement counters him with a careful exposition of scripture: marriage is not the same thing as fornication (3,5; 3,12). A third ascetic is Julius Cassianus, a former follower of Valentinus, who moved away into an extreme ascetic and docetic position (3,13 ff.).

Clement's own position is not wholly consistent. He sets out the Christian view as he sees it, at the beginning of the book: "We bless sexlessness, and those to whom God has granted that state. On the other hand we admire monogamy and the honorable estate of single marriage. We say that we ought to share suffering and bear one another's burdens; so that nobody should think that he's standing fine and firm, and then fall. It was of second marriage that the Apostle said, if you are on fire, marry" (3,1,4).

Promiscuity is immorality. Inhibitions about sex are a blasphemy against creation (3,5–6). Clement stands between the two. But he is closer to the ascetics. License is slavery to the passions, and this prevents knowledge of God; abstinence is self-control. Clement's ideal is not to feel sexual desire, and let sexual union be determined wholly by will. This is an interesting and unusual position, and Chadwick and Oulton are wrong in saying that he would like to get rid of sexual relations altogether.[6] He is opposed to those who abstain from sex out of hatred for the flesh, but in his own way he wants to get away from the actuality of his body. But he is not obsessed with sex. Dorothy Sayers once wrote a booklet entitled *The Other Six Deadly Sins,* and Clement argues that continence should not be thought of in merely sexual terms (we may think of the way "temperance" has changed its meaning), and should apply equally to money, luxury, possessions, outward appearance, language, thought (3,7,59). And he insists that marriage in accordance with reason (as prescribed by the Logos) is not a sin (3,5–9).

In a typical chapter Clement explores the possible meanings of the three gathered together where Christ is to be found (*Mt.* 18,20). Clement interprets this as husband, wife, child. In its own way this is a beautiful exegesis, a hallowing of family life. He alludes to other explanations: passion, desire, thought; flesh, soul, spirit; the called, the chosen, and those picked out for the highest honor; the one church, the one man, the one race; Jew, Gentile, and the "new man" in Christ; Torah, prophets, Gospel. It is of course a digression; it is also fantasy. It is typical of the range of allegorical interpretation.

Most of the rest of the book is concerned with scriptural refutation of the heretics. There are some texts which Clement finds embarrassing. It is to his credit that he does not ignore them or pretend that they do not exist, even though he explains them away by allegorical interpretation. Thus he is puzzled by the contradiction between the ban on the eunuch entering God's assembly (*Deut.* 23,1), and Jesus's approbation of those who make themselves eunuchs for the kingdom of Heaven's sake (*Mt.* 19,12), a verse which Clement's successor Origen was to take with tragic literalness. Clement will not go to extremes. He takes the first, of those whose lives bear no good fruits of conduct, and the second, of those who have freed themselves from sin (3,15).

So he reaffirms his positive teaching. Birth is not evil, or else the Lord would have been born in evil; even here there is an ambiguity, for he seems at one and the same time to speak of the Virgin Birth, and to use the thought to uphold the essential holiness of sex (3,17). Celibacy may—not must—be chosen. Christian marriage is a partnership, in the home and in the Christian faith, one man with one wife (3,18).

CHAPTER 5

Miscellanies: Books 4-End

I *Martyrdom*

At this point Clement seems to become aware that the structure of his work is incoherent and discursive. He feels the need to offer a preview of the rest and to justify himself. He is going next to deal with martyrdom; the perfect or full-grown man; faith and questioning; symbolism; a brief addition on ethics; the contribution of non-Greek philosophy to the Greeks; a conspectus of views on natural philosophy; prophecy; the true Gnostic natural philosophy. He *is* offering a miscellany. It sounds as if some readers had complained that they were getting nothing from the first books. Clement rejoins that you have to be golden yourself before you can discern the gold in the rock; you have to winnow the chaff to find the wheat (4,1–2).

Most people have a disposition like a storm, insecure and unpredictable (not controlled by the Logos). Man is compounded of rational (belonging to the Logos) and irrational, soul and body: Plato said the same, but allowed an irrational element within the soul. The body's natural destination is the earth, the soul's is God. To reach its destination it needs education by means of true philosophy. It needs to be free from the lusts of the flesh, from trouble and fear. Paradoxically, freedom from trouble is achieved through self-discipline, freedom from fear, escape from sin, which may itself be achieved through fear of sin. The true Gnostic is practising all his life the separation of the soul from the body; the thought is Platonic (Plat. *Phaed.* 81A). He therefore is not afraid of death (4,3).

This leads to the topic of martyrdom. The theme was existential, not abstract. For three centuries a Christian might expect to face death for his faith. Polycarp was burnt in 155, refusing to abjure the King and Savior he had served for eighty-six years. Justin won his sobriquet of Martyr at Rome in about 165. There was a major persecution at Lyon in 178. Seven men and five women were executed at Scilli in North Africa in 180. Perpetua and Felicitas suffered at Carthage in 203. These are only a few of the more notable contemporary examples. The martyr was the witness; he witnessed by his willingness to die and by his courage in dying. "The blood of Christians is seed," cried Tertullian. It was true. The death of Stephen seared the heart of Saul till he saw for himself the vision of Christ which Stephen had claimed. Tacitus tells that the crowds were moved to sympathy with the Christians who suffered under Nero. Tertullian himself seems to have been converted by the bearing of Christians before death. Clement develops the thought differently. The martyr is a witness to himself of the sincerity of his faith, to the Tempter that his jealousy of such love and faith is useless, to the Lord of the inspiration by which he has learned his lesson. Then and only then "you would be astonished at his love . . .; he puts unbelievers to shame." This is just. The martyr is being loyal to his Lord and true to himself: the effect on others is the consequence, not the purpose of his act. Further, love is alongside faith. Faith without love can be very unattractive; this was all Marcus Aurelius saw in the bearing of the Christian martyrs (MA *Med.* 11,3). Clement is right in giving his account a warmer, more sociable color. Christians, he says, call martyrdom "fulfillment" or "perfection" because it demonstrates the perfect act of love. And, he goes on, it is the faith and love and upright life and knowledge of God which make the martyr, the witness, not the particular mode of death (4,4).

The martyr then has a contempt for external things. Clement links this first to Stoic philosophy, of which this was a significant tenet, and then (without naming it) to Epicurean philosophy, seeing that the martyr makes a hedonistic calculus of pleasures and pains, and accepts present pain for future pleasure. Then he returns to the New Testament and offers a long exposition of the Beatitudes, with occasional help from Plato, the Stoics, and other parts of the New Testament. The interpretation is for the most part straightforward. Clement is saying what the New Testament is saying, that the follower of Christ is called to give up all and to seek first the kingdom of God, that the poor (whether in possessions or spirit; Clement is aware of the difference of text and not afraid of it) are blessed, that to lay up treasures on earth may divert from the lasting treasures, that the thorns of external cares may choke the seed. Only occasionally is he led into fantasy, as when the peacemakers who are blessed are taken to be those who have tamed the passions which war against reason. There is an interesting, and just, analysis of two kinds of penitence, one negative arising from fear, one positive arising from shame. He links his exposition to the concept of the true Gnostic. We are called to follow the Gnostic life and to seek the truth in thought and in action. There are two paths to the fulfillment of salvation: action and knowledge. Knowledge (*gnosis*) is a purification of the ruling principle of the soul (4,5–6).

If a man deny the Lord from fear of death, he does not destroy the Lord's authority; he denies himself and the very principle of life. To love the Lord is both to love your neighbor and to love yourself. (This again is closely parallel to that modern theology which sees God as the depth of our being.) Clement goes on to a profound statement about the nature and purpose of suffering when he writes of Jesus: "He himself being life, in that he suffered, was willing to suffer so that through his suffering we might live."[1] The blessedness of the martyr who shows his love in his willingness to die is expounded with reference to a number of scriptural passages, especially from Paul's letters to Rome and Corinth, and to passages from Greek tragedy, where Antigone, for instance, defies Creon to the death in the name of Zeus, and to a well-known passage from *The Republic* about the fate of the just man (Plat. *Rep.* 2,361E), and to a number of historical examples from the Graeco-Roman world. The exposition is particularly interesting for its reference to honors after death for those who live holily and punishments for those who live unrighteously. The true Gnostic, says Clement, will never see his ultimate goal in life, but in eternal happiness and in being a kingly friend to God (the Stoic phrase is noteworthy). For those who are eager for perfection the foundation of knowledge in accordance with the Logos is the holy triad "Faith, hope, love, and the greatest of these is love" (1 *Cor.* 13,13) (4,7–8).

The church is full of those who have had the courage and dedication to suffer. They include women as well as men. Clement is on the whole sensible and enlightened in his attitude to the differences between the sexes. He lived, we must remember, in a man's world. But (as we have seen: p. 72) Jesus had introduced a new spirit into the relationship between men and women, and the first generation of Christians had followed their Master's lead by the freedom of association between men and women (which led to scandal-mongering from those outside), and by their willingness to accept the leadership of women who were ready to take on leadership, as were Phoebe, Nympha, and Priscilla, in a mixed society. Clement accepts this higher role for women; it is for him reinforced by the fact that he had found a similar attitude in *The Republic*. There are physiological differences between men and women; Clement says that women are equipped for childbearing, which is true, and for domesticity, which isn't. He perhaps has a slight suggestion that women are intellectually somewhat less able than men, though he does not press the point. He does, however, say explicitly that unless men have become effeminate they will always do a better job than women at anything. This is prejudice, but it is prejudice derived from Plato (Plat. *Rep.* 5,455D). But this said, he also holds that true philosophy, true love of wisdom, belongs to our common humanity, and women have it as much as men and are as capable as men of dying for virtue and liberty (4,8).

Clement now characteristically gathers together some of the Lord's main sayings on martyrdom. One might have expected a comprehensive collection; he is content to be representative, and we are reminded again that he was working without advantage of concordances and the like. A long passage from a Valentinian named Heracleon is cited with general approval: its tenor is that deeds speak louder than words. Clement says that the Lord "drank the cup"; the apostles, in imitation of him, suffered for the churches they had founded (the plural is interesting: the Lord founded the church, the apostles the churches) so as to become true Gnostics and perfect (or fully grown); those who follow the steps of the apostles as true Gnostics ought to be sinless, and out of love for the Lord to love their neighbor, and in a crisis to be ready to drink the cup for the church (singular). But Clement's good sense and the general good sense of the church discourage the deliberate seeking of martyrdom by provocative action (4,9–10).

He is also very sensible in answering those who say, "If God really cares for you, why does he let you be persecuted?" It is really impossible to improve on what Clement replies. First, the judge who condemns the Christians is not a marionette or automaton but a free being who makes his own judgment. Second, injustice in this world can be reconciled with the existence of a loving God only if it is temporary, that is if life continues beyond the grave. Third, God uses suffering in this world to change it, so that the faith which proves itself in suffering becomes light to others. This is masterly; this short section is one of the finest things Clement ever wrote (4,11).

So he goes on to criticize Basilides, who suggested that the martyr was expiating previous sin, perhaps committed in a previous existence (even Clement's Platonism will not take this), though not the actual offense for which he was condemned, and Valentinus, who looked to the coming of a peculiar people who would do away with death, and who thus in Clement's view denigrated the work of Christ. The section on Valentinus is really a digression, but it serves as yet another reminder of the importance of these sects in Clement's mind, and of the seriousness of their challenge to the church (4,12–3).

He moves from the negative critique to the positive. The immense power of goodness; love; faith; and freedom—there in a nutshell is the Gnostic martyr, the man who has knowledge and the courage to die for it. But though we all have knowledge of a sort, all have not real *gnosis*. Some people say that this might be a stumbling-block to the weak, in whom the liberty of knowledge might become licence, and Clement is off on another digression about being scrupulous not to injure others by our freedom. (A worker among alcoholics need not be teetotal in principle, but he must be teetotal in practice.) Clement returns to the love, faith, and purity of the martyrs, which he illustrates from scripture, using particularly the glorification of love in John's first letter, and the passages relating to martyrdom in *Hebrews* and *The Wisdom of Solomon,* which he reinforces from Clement of Rome's letter to the church in Corinth (4,14–7).

II *Christian Perfection*

We have already been led insensibly into the subject of Christian perfection. Christians practise love of mankind; this means seeking the common good, whether by martyrdom, or education through word and act; it means love to God and the neighbor.

The same act is not the same whether committed in fear or in love; it is a very different matter to refrain from adultery out of fear and out of love. Desire needs control as well as action. Clement produces a reminiscence of a teacher of whom he disapproved, and an Egyptian anecdote which actually evaded Herodotus, in illustration. There is a difference between rational and irrational desire, between falling in love and falling in lust. The true Gnostic is seeking this spiritual maturity or perfection, and it is something men and women alike can share in. He recurs to this and illustrates it from pagan and Christian examples Then with a characteristic digression he gives a man-based view of the good wife, given as a helper to her husband, and in the same breath laughs at himself with delightful honesty, and explains that this means tactfully correcting all the mistakes her husband makes over the domestic economy (4,18–20).

Now perfection may be attained or approached in different fields, in piety, or endurance, or continence, or good works, or martyrdom, or knowledge. But there has never been any perfect in all ways except Jesus. Abstinence from wrongdoing is a step on the right road; the perfection of the true Gnostic means acceptance of the Gospel; it means co-operating with God's will for the restoration of our true birth and sharing in the fullness of Christ. It means understanding and perspicacity. It means doing good out of love, just because the act is lovely. It means pursuing the knowledge of God for its own sake, so that if (impossible!) he had to choose between knowledge of God and eternal salvation he would choose knowledge of God. It means a state in which he no longer has to be continent, but is free from the passions altogether (the Stoic concept). Clement deviates slightly to some etymological play on words for "right" and "knowledge," and symbolic interpretations, and quotations from Heraclitus and Empedocles and Democritus and Plato and Paul and even Epicurus. He reasserts that the true Gnostic chooses what is good in accordance with knowledge. There is a sense in which the true Gnostic has already become God. Man in general is molded in the form of the spirit born with him; the individual man is characterized in accordance with the stamp of the choices he has made impressed on his soul. God is impassible; the man who has self-control is assimilated as far as possible to God; he is deified into a passionless condition.

Clement has a fine simile. If you are at anchor, and pull on the anchor, you pull the boat towards the anchor, not the anchor towards the boat. If you are anchored to God in knowledge, and pull, you draw yourself to God (4,21–3).

God's forgiveness cannot undo what has been done. But God does forgive, and Clement has a noble rebuke for Basilides. Basilides said that God forgives involuntary offenses only; Clement rejoins that this makes him man not God. Divine punishment has three ends, all educative: to reform the offender; to discourage others by example; to show care for the victim (4,24).

The true Gnostic is richly blessed in his contemplation of the unseen God; he is as a God among men; he is one with Christ.

God cannot be scientifically proved; he is not an object of scientific understanding. But the Son, who is wisdom and knowledge and truth, can be the object of demonstration and description; and all the powers of the Spirit coincide in the Son. This is not a Nicene formulation; how could it be? It is a fascinating insight into the way the doctrine of the Trinity looked to an intelligent Alexandrian Christian a century and more before Nicaea. God has no beginning. He is the perfect first principle of the universe. He is the producer of the beginning. He is pure being, and as such the first principle of the area of action. He is the ultimate good, and as such the first principle of ethics. He is intelligence, and as such the first principle of the area of thought and judgment. So the only teacher is the Son of the holy supreme Father, the educator of men (4,25).

There is no reason to run down the material world; we can know God here. The true Gnostic is concerned with God in ethics, in natural philosophy, in ratiocination; wisdom is the scientific understanding of things divine and human, righteousness is a harmony of the parts of the soul (very Platonic!), holiness is the worship of God; the correspondence is not quite exact. The soul of the wise man and true Gnostic treats the body seriously. He is a temporary dweller in this world, but not an alien to it. So Clement is led to a peroration which ends the fourth book: "I would pray the Spirit of Christ to wing me to my Jerusalem. For the Stoics too say that heaven is really a city whereas the things here on earth are no cities at all and have the title without the substance. For a city is a thing that matters, a populace is an ordered commonalty, a gathering of men under a system of law, as the church is under the Logos, an impregnable city on earth, free from autocracy, the will of God done on earth as it is heaven. The poets create images of this city in their writings. The Hyperborean and Arimaspian cities and the Elysian plains are communities of the just. Yes, and we know Plato's city, a pattern laid up in the heavens." (4,26).

III   Faith and Hope

There is no knowledge without faith or faith without knowledge. We must know the Father to have faith in the Son; we must have faith in the Son to know the Father. (If this were purely a rational argument it would be circular, but personal relations are not like that.) We are, says Clement, believers in what is not believed and Gnostics in what is not known; then he adds, in a marvelous phrase, "faith is the ear of the soul." He goes on to establish on a scriptural basis the need for faith, against Basilides, Valentinus, and Marcion. The field of faith is not the field where normal enquiry can give a clear answer ("Is it daylight?"), or is never destined to give a clear answer ("Is the total number of stars odd or even?"), or can legitimately take different views ("Is the child in the womb an independent living creature?"), or can establish incontestable arguments. Remove these, and you have the area of faith. Clement now becomes very modern when he points out that questions concerning God are not answerable in the same terms as questions about sense-perception, or open to proof by argument. The Logos is not an analysable statement but a revelation. So we pass through a symbolic interpretation of the name of Abraham, based on Philo, and quotations from the Greek poets and philosophers, who stole their beliefs from Moses (says Clement), to the foundation of God's temple in faith, hope, and love (5,1).

Clement's treatment of hope is curiously brief. He is content to adduce a few passages from pagan authors, principally Plato, and some of these are of doubtful relevance. The truth is that if it were not for the familiar passage in Paul (1 *Cor.* 13,13) hope would not hold such an exalted position as it does, and there it is subordinate to love; further the English "hope" somewhat misrepresents the Greek *elpis,* which was a technical term of the mystery-religions, and almost equivalent to faith, though with a future reference. Clement sees this and identifies the objects of faith and hope as things to be known with the mind, and lying in the future. He has an interesting interpretation of the verse about the "violent" storming of the Kingdom (*Mt.* 11,12); the violent are not the contentious but those who are energetic in right living. This may well be the true interpretation. For Clement it is reinforced by a wordplay between *bia*, violence, and *bios*, life. A wave of quotations drives it home (5,2–3).

IV *Symbolical Interpretation*

Symbolical or allegorical interpretation is an essential instrument in Clement's toolkit. He proceeds to expound his philosophy at this point. He begins by showing that the Egyptians and Greeks as well as Jewish and Christian writers have used picture-language, symbols, allegories, riddling allusions, metaphors, maxims susceptible of more than one interpretation, and the like, in speaking of divine things. He illustrates this, entirely appropriately, first by Pythagorean maxims (e.g., "Don't keep a swallow in the house" means "Avoid chatterboxes"); then by an elaborate explanation of the tabernacle and its contents, which are interpreted as Christian symbols; then by a rather cursory account of some Egyptian symbols (the hawk of the sun, the ibis of the moon); then by an astonishingly miscellaneous collection of materials from Greek sources. Finally, he turns to some allegorical interpretation of the Old Testament. The injunction not to eat birds of prey (*Lev.* 11,13) is taken to mean "Have nothing to do with robbers," or again Joseph's coat of many colors is taken to indicate the extent and variety of his knowledge (5,4–8).

There are good reasons for veiling the truth in symbols. It means that they reveal their secret only to those who approach them in the right way. It means that we require an interpreter. It means that truth appears more brilliant, like a reflection in water. Clement reinforces the principle by appeal to the inner disciples of the Pythagoreans, to Plato's use of myth, to Aristotle's esoteric treatises, and to examples from the New Testament (5,9–10).

Clement now shows a profound understanding and philosophical analysis of the mystical approach to the knowledge of God.

He starts from "the road of negation." God is "not this, not that." It is in itself a safeguard against trivializing God, against trying to catch him within the pincers of human syllogisms, against reducing him to a malleable, pliable, tractable object of our finite attentions, and so against idolatry. So Clement approves the silence of the Pythagoreans that by withdrawing attention from the world of sense they might concentrate their minds upon God. We too easily, he rightly says, make God in our own image; Xenophanes had said it centuries before. He does not share birth, food, growth, extended life, physical attributes. Not this, not that. He is above space, time, name, and conception. Strip off from physical being, depth, breadth, length; you are left with a point, which has position and unity. Strip off position; you are left with unity. The problem is that the knowledge gained by strict adherence to the negative view is inevitably negative; we reach some sort of conception of the Almighty, knowing not what he is, but what he is not. Clement, however, gives this positive content through Christ: we cast ourselves into Christ's greatness and advance from that point by holiness to infinity (5,11).[2]

God cannot be expressed in words. Clement has an admirably modern sense of the limitations of language, and indeed of analytical thought. Even when we use words such as the One, or the Good, or Intelligence, or Absolute Being, or Father, or God, or Creator, or Lord, we are not really naming him. We are giving the mind some support to prevent it from going off in all directions. The knowledge of God is given by God himself; the Greek philosophers and the Christian scriptures attest the same. Salvation comes from learning the truth through Christ (5,12–3).

V   The Indebtedness of the Greeks

We have seen already Clement's claim that the Greeks learned from the "barbarian" philosophy such truths as they had discerned. He now elaborates on this in such a way as to spill across the borderline between two books. First come several pages of parallel passages. As the eye moves over them we note a preoccupation with Plato, who constantly recurs; of particular interest is the identification of Er in the myth in *The Republic* with Zoroaster.[3] Epicurus is said to have derived his philosophy from *Ecclesiastes;* some of us think that the connection is genuine but in the other direction. A number of passages from different poets exalt the seventh day. A fine passage from Epicharmus in praise of Reason (*logos*) is applied to the Logos. Menander is said to paraphrase scripture. The general message is that no people can live without faith in a superior being, and that the revelation was to the Jews, for others to learn from it (5,14).

Before proceeding Clement inaugurates a new book with a brief introduction. In the next two books he is going to expound the true philosophy shown by the true Gnostic. It has been supposed that he was directing them against the philosophical persecutors of the church. He offers a reminder that he is compiling *Miscellanies*; they are like a meadow or park where the flowers are scattered. Our knowledge (*gnosis*), our spiritual parkland, he goes on, is the Savior, into whom we are transplanted. With this introduction he returns to the theme of literary theft, and lists a long succession of passages in which one Greek author might be thought to have borrowed from another. Plato cribbed from Pythagoras, Aristotle from Plato, Epicurus from Democritus. . . . One is tempted to comment "*C'est imiter que de planter des choux*" (6,1–2).

So back to the Greek debt to the Jews: this time they are said to have plagiarized their miracles. The evidence is curiously thin; it would not have been difficult to produce more persuasive parallels. There is an interesting, though slightly irrelevant, note about a cave in Britain under a mountain with a cleft at the top, so that the wind gusting into the cave made a noise like the clashing of cymbals. The Greeks also, Clement claims, borrowed the doctrine of transmigration of souls from Egypt. This leads to a cursory and somewhat misleading summary of Egyptian religion (strangely inadequate in one living in Egypt; there is here a commentary on social divisions in Alexandria), and an anecdote of Alexander and some Indian gurus, which does little more than show that the Greeks had contact with India. But the Greeks did have some knowledge of the true God, only they worshipped him wrongly. It was he who gave the Old Covenant to the Jews, philosophy to the Greeks, and now the New Covenant to all. (Clement in this section draws upon the apocryphal *Preaching of Peter* for his commentary, treating it as authentic.) God is no respecter of persons. He wills that all who believe shall be saved. His punishments even are directed to conversion and salvation. So it is natural that he should have spoken to Greek as to Jew. And the Lord—and his apostles—preached to those in Hades, and on all grounds we must think that he spoke to all those who were ready to hear (6,3–6).

VI *True Philosophy*

True philosophy is not the view of any particular sect. It is systematized wisdom which offers experience in things concerned with living. It is solid knowledge (*gnosis*), an unshakably firm grasp of things human and divine, present, past, and future, revealed by the *Logos*, eternal in one sense, but temporally useful; it aims at right thinking and right living. The Greek philosophers were concerned with ethical virtue. So that in one sense philosophy consists in those views of each sect which are unquestionably true. These were borrowed from the Jews, but beautifully expressed in Greek (Clement claims truth for the Jewish tradition but allows the literary excellence of the Greeks). They all had a partial view of truth, like a perspective drawing. They were misled by their humanism. For true knowledge purification is needed, right action and revelation through Christ and his apostles. Philosophy then may be a stepping-stone on the way to knowledge, but the true Gnostic has no need to go back to philosophy as understood by the Greeks. Even if their philosophy was devised by human understanding, still that understanding came from God (6,7–8).

The true Gnostic must however be something of a polymath. The pruning-hook is designed for pruning but can be used for other purposes; man is made for the knowledge of God, but he is also an applied mathematician, farmer, and philosopher. Philosophy is not false; all useful things come from God; but there are tares of hedonistic philosophy and heretical religion among the wheat. But philosophy is elementary and limited in its scope. Full knowledge takes us beyond the material world. Faith and prophecy belong to knowledge. Knowledge and impulse are both powers of the soul. The true Gnostic takes his knowledge into realms which others find intractable. Further, the true Gnostic is free from passions. The Savior was free from passions. It would be ludicrous to suppose that his body needed food; it was held together by a secret power; he ate so as not to appear different (Clement, as we have seen, is here very close to docetism). So the true Gnostic, having love in its perfection, is free from desire, and being assimilated to God is free from passions, and having no fears or desires has no room for courage or self-discipline; Clement says, in a fine phrase, that through love the future is already present with him. If a man has true knowledge his ruling principle cannot be unstable. Knowledge is not inborn but acquired; it needs application, tending, and nurturing, then from constant practice it becomes a state or habit, and through love becomes permanent. The true Gnostic has few needs. Knowledge is his business, and he pursues anything which will help him: music and arithmetic, with their concern for structure and proportion; geometry, in which abstraction from the material world leads the mind to pure being; astronomy, raising the mind from earth to heaven; dialectic, drawing distinctions among existing things, as species from genus, and isolating primary substance. No hobgoblins to be scared of here (Clement's language echoes Plato, deliberately cf. *Phaed.* 77 E). The faith that can be shaken by plausible half-truths is not very deeprooted. These, properly used, are limbering-up exercises, and show their true colors in the light of the real truth (6,9–10).

This leads to a section on number mysticism. Abraham has 318 servants, in Greek characters TIH (*Gen.* 14,14). T is the Cross, IH the first letters of Jesus's name. Clement offers a wide selection of alternative interpretations. Such number mysticism tends to leave us impatient; to the early Fathers it was meaningful. Clement illustrates geometry by the tabernacle, music by the practice of David; we learn in passing that the early Christians had music at their common meals. Clement does not scorn practical uses of geometry in architecture and astronomy in navigation. He returns to the general principle. Greek philosophy is the ornamental fringe on the garment of truth (*Ps.* 45,14) not the truth itself (6,11).

We are not born virtuous, but naturally equipped for virtuous behavior. This is the answer to a logical quibble. How could a perfect God create an imperfect man? Adam was made neither perfect nor imperfect, but capable of perfection. Only the true Gnostic attains perfection or fulfillment. Knowledge is the highest good, and so all good consequences flow from it, but it must be pursued for its own sake. Righteousness in life, a foursquare quality (Plato: *Prot.* 349B again) follows. So the true Gnostic, even here, bears the aura of righteousness, the assimilation to the Savior, the sort of glory reflected in Moses's face from the presence of God (*Ex.* 34,29). This leads to a discussion of different degrees of glory (6,12–4).

Clement now enters upon an interesting exploration of different approaches to knowledge. He uses an image from grafting. There are four types of grafting. In one the graft is fitted between the bark and the wood; this symbolizes ordinary Gentiles who receive the Logos superficially. In the second the wood itself is split and the graft inserted. This symbolizes Greek students of philosophy and also Jews; cut through their philosophical tenets, open up the Old Testament, and the new growth can be inserted. The third method uses a sharp knife to scrape off both suckers and lay bare the pith without damaging it, so as to bind them together. This represents heretics and coarse minds, who need driving to the truth. The fourth is budding, and this is the true Gnostic method: there is a pun on the word for "bud" which also means "eye."

Knowledge and love go together. Clement is guilty of a little sleight-of-tongue here as he uses the Greek word for Christian love, directed to persons (*agape*), for love of knowledge, and blurs both with the commandments. Everything—love, knowledge, and the keeping of the comandments—leads to immortality. True knowledge about God is found in the teaching that comes through the Son (here we have an adumbration of the unwritten *The Teacher*). Greek philosophy and Christian heresy have a contribution to make to the discovery of the truth, but are partial only. True knowledge leads to practical wisdom; the righteousness of the perfect or fully-grown man springs from love of God and "doing his own thing."

Clement returns to the reasons for hidden meanings in the scriptures: first, to awaken curiosity; besides, for those who were not ready to understand to be kept from wrong ideas. He defines a parable in two ways: a discourse which is not on the main theme but on a related one and which leads to discerning the truth, or a form of speech which offers a vivid presentation of the main point through something different. There is a sense, he says, in which the whole prophetic view of the Messiah's world-order is a parable (6,15).

As an example of interpretation in the light of true knowledge Clement expounds the Decalogue. Ten is a sacred number; there are ten types of organisms in the sky, ten sorts of living creatures on earth, ten faculties in man. Clement then proceeds to each of the commandments in turn, or rather not quite all of them, since there are omissions in our present text, whether because something has been accidentally lost, or because Clement has conflated and summarized, or for some subtle reason we fail to discern. He calls them by the title "word" or *logos;* this is in accord with Hebrew usage, but it also creates for Clement a relationship with the Logos. The exposition varies considerably. Sometimes Clement is content with the literal meaning. The fourth commandment leads him into a lengthy exposition of the mysticism attached to the number seven. The last few commandments are given symbolic meaning. It is adultery to hold a false opinion about God; it is murder to try to do away with the true teaching (*logos!*) about God; it is theft to parody the true philosophy, or to attribute to the stars what really belongs to God (6,16).

So Clement reverts yet again to the place of philosophy. The Greeks have grasped the truth of names, but the Christians ("barbarians" or "non-Greeks") have objective truth; there is a difference between speaking about God and speaking God, treating of accidents and treating of essence. Essential discourse is to say "God is the Lord of all"; it would be possible to base a treatise on religious language on this statement. But philosophy is the gift of Providence; all good gifts, medicine and physical exercise and commerce and understanding—and philosophy that makes for virtue—come from God. The Jews then had the Torah, the Greeks philosophy, up to the time of Christ's coming when there was a universal ("catholic") calling of both to be a peculiar people devoted to righteousness. Philosophy then has its place. It is a proper recreation for the true Gnostic. Further, even if we reject philosophy we must philosophize in order to reject it: this is a famous argument of Aristotle's (fr. 51 R³). But the Greeks must learn to abandon idolatry and to seek God as their teacher. For philosophy disappears at the touch of persecution, but "the word (*logos*) of our teacher" has flooded all through the world (6,18).

VII *The Defense of the Christian Gnostic*

The seventh and culminating book of *Miscellanies* in its present form is a defense and glorification of what Clement calls the gnostic Christian, the Christian whose Christianity is grounded in true knowledge. Clement speaks of Christianity or "Christianism," a word previously used by Ignatius. He displays a characteristically sane attitude to scripture: he is not going to weigh his work down with texts, but what he writes is full of assimilated scripture. Other influences on his thought also make themselves clear, Plato especially, as when he describes God in a phrase from *The Republic* (6,509B) as the cause "beyond" (7,1,2), and when he writes in the language of the familiar quotation from *Theaetetus* (176B) of assimilation to God (7,1,3). He goes beyond this: Clement is a fascinating mixture of the practical and the mystical. The true Gnostic serves his fellowmen, and his ministry is directed partly to their improvement and partly to serving their needs. The culmination is that he is not merely assimilated to God, he will *be* God. Saints, said Aquinas (*Summa* 1,108), are called gods by participation. The knowledge of the true Gnostic is shown in three ways: in basic knowledge about Christianity, in the fulfillment of things commanded by the Divine Word, and in passing on the hidden truths. The Gnostic is an initiate of the divine mysteries; no one can call him an atheist, a charge levelled at the Christians because they denied the familiar gods (7,1,4).

More allusions follow, mainly from Plato, and from a wide variety of works, but the description of the Logos as "all intellect" (7,2,5) comes from the early religious thinker Xenophanes, and the thought that the power or potentiality of the Father is revealed in the activity or actuality of the Son, who is called the actuality of the Father (7,2,7) comes from Aristotle. The language, however, has its basis already in the New Testament (e.g., *Mt.* 14,2; *Rom.* 7,5; *Gal.* 2,8; *Col.* 2,12) and the writings of the Apologists (e.g., Just. 1 *Ap.* 60,3; Athenag. *Leg.* 10,2). The Word is the Teacher, whose activity Clement has promised to explore, and he is characterized by his *philanthropia,* his love of mankind (7,2,8). As the magnet draws a whole series of iron rings, so through the magnetic power of the Holy Spirit the Son draws to salvation all beings, from angels to the humblest; the implication is to be noted that it is by contact with one another that the power of the Holy Spirit spreads (7,2,9). And so Clement repeats his great assertion: the two sets of ordinances, the Mosaic Torah and Greek philosophy, were alike given by the Logos (7,2,11).

At this point Clement fires off, a little surprisingly, a quotation from Aeschylus: "For the rest I say nothing" (*Agam.* 38). He now turns from Platonic concepts to Stoic language. The pure of heart enjoy the *apprehensive* vision. God is described in Stoic language as Law and Ordinance and Eternal Reason (or Word: Logos). The true Gnostic is simultaneously a member of this and of a higher world; he is set in his place in the ranks. However poor he is, he is paradoxically rich. The language is that used of the Stoic sage; the implication is that the Christian Gnostic is the true sage (7,3,18). He is also the true athlete— an image found in Paul as well as among the Stoics—in a contest with passions, in which the angels and "gods" are spectators, the Son is Umpire, and Almighty God is President. Man finds his true function (the thought and language go back to Socrates) in obedience to God, and the Divine Word watches us as the sun watches over the world. In the mosaic under St. Peter's at Rome Christ appears in the sun-god's chariot; already Malachi's vision of the sun of righteousness was applied to him (*Mal.* 4,2).

Clement now turns to attack the anthropomorphic gods of the Greeks and in so doing shows the breadth of his reading. Xenophanes and Pythagoras are there, and the little-known Pythagorean Androcydes. Plato of course recurs time and again; so do his successors Xenocrates and Polemo; Theophrastus is quoted at second hand, and a witticism is attributed to Cleanthes which belongs more appropriately to Chrysippus. There are *bon mots* from Cynics such as Bion and Diogenes, and from the sophist Antiphon. More surprising are the allusions to the Cyrenaics and Epicureans (the last in a difficult passage where the sense is corrupt: 7,7,37). Clement is not content with the philosophers; they offered him insufficient ammunition. He goes to the poets, to Homer and Hesiod, to the tragedians, Euripides especially, and above all to the writers of comedies. And interspersed with them all are relevantly contrasting passages from the Christian writings; the scorn of these all-too-human gods is intensified by the scorn for temples built by mechanic labor (the contempt for manual work is derived from the aristocratic Plato not from the carpenter Jesus) (7,5,28), and by a distaste for sacrifice. The true God is not circumscribed by place or hungry for food. Clement has a great section on prayer, which he describes as fellowship with God. In an interesting passage he speaks of prayers whispered without opening the lips; he is aware of silent prayer, but the ancients, who always read aloud, must have vocalized even when silent (7,7,39). He describes too the attitude of prayer, standing, with head thrown back and palms extended up to heaven, and with the body raised on tiptoe for the last words of the prayer (7,7,40). "Every place and every time at which we hold the thought of God is genuinely holy" (7,7,43). Rightmindedness speeds the answer to prayer; wickedness makes a prayer damaging to the one who offers it, for he is seeking the semblance not the reality (a Platonic distinction). The seeker asks for faith, the true Gnostic asks for love. God demands of us the things which are in our power— choice, aspiration, possession, use and disposition of the things which concern us. Pelagius said no more! For the true Gnostic the whole life is a holy festival (7,7,49).

Clement concludes this section of the book, the defense of the true Gnostic against the charge of atheism and impiety, with a brief homily on letting our yea be yea and our nay nay (though he allows deception "medicinally," as a doctor may deceive a patient for that patient's own good; this is honest, practical, and very dangerous doctrine). A brilliant passage combines a rationalist attack on Greek religion, by allusion to the suggestion that the gods were personifications of useful objects, with a profound characterization of the true Christian. The Greeks (by a process of reference back) call iron Ares and wine Dionysus. In exactly the same way the Gnostic, finding the means to his own salvation in the service of his neighbors, might well be called the living image of the Lord, not in terms of outward appearance, but in representing his power and emulating his preaching (7,9,52).

VIII   *The Nature of the True Gnostic*

Clement passes from the defensive to more positive assertions. The name *gnostic* means "one who knows," and Clement is somewhat torn between the claims of knowledge and love. Paul

had no doubt: knowledge would vanish away, love would remain
(1 *Cor.* 13,8). At the last Clement would not demur. He sees an
ascending scale, from faith to knowledge, from knowledge to love,
from love to bliss. Faith is a kind of shortcut to knowledge,
knowledge is the firm grasp of the things handed down by faith.
The Gnostic, the man of knowledge, treats all created things in
a spirit of thankfulness. He does not show hostility to others,
even if they merit contempt; his reverence for the Creator leads
him to love his partner in life. This marvelous phrase is slightly
marred by an association, more Platonic than Christian, with the
thought that the body is a prison (7,11,62). But even that reminds us that martyrdom was never far off in the first three
centuries of Christianity, and Clement indeed tells a story, otherwise unattested, of Peter encouraging his wife as she went to
martyrdom (7,11,63). The combination of Greek and Christian
thought, integrated by Clement's receptive mind, continues. The
doctrine that vice is ignorance (7,11,66) is sheerly Socratic.
Paul would not have said so: "the good that I would I do not: but
the evil which I would not, that I do" (*Rom.* 7,19). Then follows
one of Clement's profoundest passages: "Those who endure from
love of glory, from fear of sharper punishment, or hoping for
pleasures and delights after death, are children in faith. They
are blessed, but they are not yet grown men in love towards
God as is the Gnostic. The church is like an athletics festival;
it has different prizes for men and boys. Love is to be chosen
for its own sake, not for the sake of something else" (11,7,67).
We are reminded of the prayer of Rabia, the great woman
mystic of Islam: "O my Lord, if I worship thee from fear of
Hell, burn me in Hell, and if I worship thee from hope of
Paradise, exclude me thence, but if I worship thee for thine own
sake, then withhold not from me thine Eternal Beauty." The
Gnostic is the perfect, or full-grown, or all-embracing man of
Jesus and Paul (*teleios*: the word is ambiguous: *Mt.* 5,48; *Eph.*
4,13); he is the friend of God (*Jn.* 15,15).

And now we see the sturdy practical sense which goes with
the high abstractions of Clement's philosophy. The ideal Christian gives help to all in need, and gives in accordance with
need, not desert. Others may be hostile to him, he is hostile to
none. He is committed to a way of life, and nothing can happen

CLEMENT OF ALEXANDRIA

to make him compromise it. He has the faculty which the
Stoics claimed for their sage—the full knowledge of everything,
divine and human. Food and sex are conditions of life, not its
objects. And sex has its proper fulfillment in marriage. True
manhood is not to be found in celibacy; it is exercised when the
love of God is indissoluble from the life of a husband and
father. Here Clement is profoundly Christian. For Christ the
world is not to be escaped from, but redeemed (7,12,70).
Clement goes further. The sectarian Gnostics had set goodness
against justice and attributed the first to the supreme God and
the second to the corrupt and lower creator. Clement asserts
that this is a false dichotomy: God's goodness is always just.
This is excellent, provided that we measure true justice by the
goodness of God, and we do not limit our vision of God's goodness to the scale of human justice (7,12,73).

The Christian Gnostic is a laborer in God's vineyard. Clement
quotes *The Traditions of Matthias,* perhaps a lost gospel, for
another profound sentiment: "If a neighbor of one of the elect
sins, the elect has sinned. If he had comported himself as the
Logos suggests, his neighbor would have honored his life and
refrained from sin" (7,13,82). Right behavior depends on knowledge of God. "Works," says Clement in a flashing epigram,
"follow knowledge as the shadow follows the body." He goes on,
not less characteristically, to justify his view of the perfection of
the Gnostic through a detailed scrutiny of 1 *Corinthians* 6.

The book is drawing to a close. It was not intended to be the
last book of *Miscellanies;* he specifically defers some points
(7,15,89) and does not end on a note of triumph. A little while
back we were reminded of the shadow of martyrdom lying across
the church. Now we are led to recall the shadow of division. It
was with the Christians in the year 200 as it looks like being
in the year 2000. It was a major charge levelled by the pagans
and Jews against Christians, and Clement's answer, that Jewish
religion and Greek philosophy had plenty of sects of their own,
is good debating but unconvincing (7,15,89). Equally unconvincing is the magnificent rhetoric of his imagery. Wax fruit
may deceive us by its appearance: this is taken from a story
by a Stoic sage, who ought to have experienced "apprehensive
presentations," being so deceived. We do not refrain from travel-

[152]

ling along the main road because there are dangerous byroads. Weeds grow in the best of vegetable gardens (7,15,91). The heretics, says Clement, force the meaning of the scriptures. The right way is to interpret the scriptures by the light of the scriptures, and by the light of what is fitting to the Lord and to God Almighty (the argument could be circular but is not necessarily so). Ignorance is the state of the pagans, conceit of the heretics, knowledge of the true church; the pagans seek pleasure, the heretics division, the church joy. If we want instruction in farming we go to Ischomachus, in seamanship to Lampis, in military command to Charidemus, in riding to Simon, in business methods to Perdix, in cookery to Crobytis, in dancing to Archelaus, in poetry to Homer, in debating to Pyrrho, in oratory to Demosthenes, in dialectic to Chrysippus, in science to Aristotle, in philosophy to Plato (the references range from the obvious to the obscure); if we follow the Lord we are perfected in the likeness of our Teacher (7,16,101).

All sin (Clement uses the Greek word *hamartia*, which means literally "missing the target") springs from two sources—ignorance and weakness; here Plato's insights and Paul's are set side by side. The true Christian needs education of two kinds: knowledge, which is in effect the witness of the scriptures, and training through reason escorted by faith and fear. It is hard to overestimate the importance of this passage. The Christian education counters the deficiency identified by Plato; the philosophical training (admittedly under the escort of faith: the metaphor is from the slave, the tutor, who escorted the child to school and kept an eye on his behavior) counters the deficiency identified by Paul. The Gnostic is thus concerned both with contemplation and with action, with the two areas of wisdom identified by Aristotle. All of Clement's wisdom is here (7,16,101–2).

Most of the rest is an attack on heretics, whom Clement compares with burglars armed with skeleton-keys, or tunneling into a bank. His analysis of heresies is not without interest: some named after their founders, Valentinians, Marcionites, Basilidians; some, like the Encratites (or self-disciplined) from their practice; some, like the Docetes and Haematites, from their doctrines; some, like the Entychites (the take-it-as-you-comers, implying their sexual promiscuity) from their lawless behavior. But the true Church is single and pre-eminent, like the Monad, the Ultimate One (7,17,107–8).

Right at the end comes a short characterization of these *Miscellanies*. They are not ornamental gardens (of the type familiar to us from eighteenth-century châteaux, with their geometrical regularity), but like wooded hills, with fruit-trees planted among the natural growth, offering a nursery from which trees may be transplanted for an ordered pleasance. Different fish call for different bait (7,18,111).

IX   *The Eighth Book*

In the single surviving primary manuscript of *Miscellanies* there are eight books, and the last is followed by two works entitled *Excerpts from Theodotus* and *Selections from the Prophets*. But Photius, the Byzantine patriarch and lexicographer, testifies to having seen manuscripts of *Miscellanies* which lacked the eighth book, and went straight on from the seventh book to the treatise *Who is the Rich Man that is being Saved?* This suggests that there is doubt about the authenticity of the eighth book. In fact, there is not so much doubt about its authorship as doubt about where it fits into the scheme of Clement's writings. Hans von Arnim in a lucid Latin discourse showed that the eighth book, which deals with logical questions, was an unsatisfactory way for Clement to end *Miscellanies*, and was very different from the other books. At the same time, as he also argued, it contains much that is characteristic of Clement. It seems most likely that the eighth book and the two *Selections* are raw material which Clement had collected for future use. They are not closely related to one another. The first shows Clement as a philosopher, the second as a theologian, the third as a biblical commentator. The alternative view of Zahn, that the three together form the ruinous relics of a lost eighth book, is altogether less plausible.

The first of these fragmentary collections goes under the name of *Miscellanies* book VIII. It starts abruptly. Only the latterday Greeks are given to backbiting; the earlier philosophers did not dispute or doubt (*aporein*), an extraordinary assertion seeing how many of Plato's "Socratic" dialogues end in doubt (*aporia*). It has been left to a non-Greek philosophy to expel strife with the words, "Seek and you shall find." Clement draws two conclusions, first, that truth is attained by seeking; second, that the search should be peaceable.

Clement's basic principles of investigation are admirable. First, define your terms; see that the definition is clear and simple; examine your proposition in the light of your definitions. Demonstration in the strict sense produces in students a belief which is based on knowledge. Clement makes a subtle distinction between syllogism and demonstration; syllogism operates from *agreed* premises, demonstration from true premises.

Everything is not demonstrable; we are driven into an infinite regress. Demonstration depends on indemonstrable first principles which are accepted on faith. Clement is here doing something very interesting. The Greek geometricians deduced their whole system from a small number of axioms ("self-evident truths") and postulates ("let it be granted that . . ."). Modern geometry effectively took its rise from the challenging of the concept of axioms and the substitution of different postulates. Clement does not appear to acknowledge the distinction between axioms and postulates. What he offers is neither self-evident truths nor arbitrary assumptions, but first principles accepted on faith. ("Religion," said Donald Hankey, "consists in betting your life that there is a God.") This is right. There are, however, other grounds for demonstration which Clement acknowledges, in the clear evidence of the senses and the intellect. Theoretically, he is on more dubious ground here, but in practice we go along with him. Knowledge then advances by asking questions on the basis of previous knowledge. Clement exemplifies this by some biological examples which show the importance of precise definition.

Clement now digresses to attack the followers of Pyrrho. Pyrrho was a contemporary of Alexander the Great (though much outliving him), who concluded from the conflicting evidence of the senses and of reason that knowledge is impossible, and we ought therefore to suspend judgment. He founded the school of Scepticism, and the Platonists of Clement's day had only recently emerged from his influence. Clement directs against the Sceptics the implications of their own philosophy. You cannot suspend judgment and advocate suspense of judgment, because to advocate is not to suspend. The Sceptics are dogmatic about their Scepticism. And rightly, since for Clement philosophy is the establishment of dogma, he accepts a wide area over which suspense of judgment is right, but not over fundamentals.

There follows a long discussion of the methodology of investigation. Induction proceeds from the particular to the general. Alongside it Clement sets not the Aristotelian method of syllogistic deduction but the Platonic method of division. This is depicted in *The Sophist*, where the method is to agree a class in which the term to be defined is found, and then subdivide that class continually until we are left with a definition which applies to our required term and to nothing else. Thus, if the term is "angling," we may agree that it is a skill, and proceed (Plat. *Soph.* 218 D ff.). It is acquisitive not creative, uses capture not consent, is stealthy not open; it is directed towards living not lifeless things, creatures of water not land, fishes not birds; it employs a stroke not a net, by day not by night, from below not from above. At each point we reject the irrelevant classification and concentrate upon the true classification. It will be noticed that division may be a division of a genus into its natural species; it may be a division of a whole into its parts; it may be a division into accidental attributes; and Clement is sure that only the first will yield real knowledge. Clement's thought is thus basically Platonic, but he has been influenced by Aristotle also, and presents the familiar "categories"—"What?" "What size?" "What sort?" "What relations?" "Where?" "When?" "Acting" "Being acted upon"; our text lacks "Position" and "State," but we should doubtless supply them.

But Clement is still worried by the Sceptics and reverts to them. What causes suspense of judgment? Two things principally: the mutability of the human mind, and the inconsistency in things themselves.

He then, still following Aristotle (*De Interpretatione* 16 a 3), turns to the subject-matter of speech. This can be presented as names, or concepts, or the subjects of those concepts. Knowledge relates to the general not the particular; this surprises us, but it was a common view to Plato and to Aristotle, who saw the general as defined, the particular as infinitely various. (Man has two arms; a particular man may have had one cut off.) Clement uses Aristotle's categories for his analysis of terms. He notes the

[156]

existence of homonyms (which he calls equivocal terms, as when two people are both called Ajax), heteronyms (e.g., black and horse of the same object), synonyms (which he calls polyonyms) and the like.

The last section analyses causality. Causes are primary, immediate, or cooperative. Thus when a boy learns, the father is the primary cause, the teacher the immediate cause, the boy himself the cooperative cause. Another analysis (due to Aristotle) divides cause into four: the efficient (e.g., the sculptor), the material (e.g., the bronze), the formal (e.g., the mold), the final (e.g., the honor accorded to the finished product). These two principles are worked out in some detail, which it is not necessary here to follow.

We have in fact jottings of a system of logical analysis which brings together Platonic and Aristotelian thought. There is nothing specifically Christian; these are jottings which have not been worked up.

X *Theodotus*

The full title of the second of these collections is *Excerpts from the works of Theodotus and the so-called oriental teachings, contemporary with Valentinus*. It is not clear whether the oriental teaching is a description of Theodotus's work or an additional source. It is not an actual title, as we know from Hippolytus (*Ref.* 6,35,4–9). The matter is complicated by two further facts. First, we know nothing of Theodotus; he is presumably the Gnostic of that name mentioned in Ignatius (*Trall.* 11), but we cannot be sure even of that. Second, only some of the extracts are explicitly attributed to Theodotus; others are clearly linked with these; but there are some (6–7 and 42–65) which differ from the rest and therefore cannot come from Theodotus, though we cannot be certain whether they involve one or two additional sources. In addition to the excerpts there are passages of critical interpretation. It may be taken as certain that the majority of these come from Clement himself; they accord well with what he writes elsewhere. There remains a problem about one section (10–7). Here in place of Clement's usual spiritual Platonism we encounter a materialistic Stoicism. This led Bousset to suggest that the comments over a large section of the work (6–20; 27;

Ecl. 43–64) were taken from lecture-notes of Pantaenus. This will not do, since Pantaenus is quoted (*Ecl.* 56,2) and presumably is not quoting himself. There remains a problem. Unless additional evidence appears it is best to assume that Clement, with Stoic sources open before him, is not consistent with what he writes elsewhere. Elsewhere in *Miscellanies* he stresses that he is not just a Platonist, but takes the best from all the schools (*Str.* 1,7,37). In another place he ends by rejecting Stoic materialism, but uses Stoic language while explaining it away (*Str.* 7,7,36–7).

The quotations start from Jesus's words on the Cross: "Father, into thy hands I commend my spirit" (1,1). But these words do not receive their obvious meaning. Theodotus had stated that Wisdom armed the Logos or spiritual seed with flesh, so that the Savior came down wearing flesh; there is a significant difference from John's "The Logos *became* flesh." At the Passion it is Wisdom that Jesus commends to the Father; indeed it is the whole spiritual seed, the elect. Clement pertinently comments that the language is scriptural but the interpretation is at fault.

Behind this opening lies a complex system, some of which is expounded later. There was an original pair of Eternal Powers or Aeons: Depth (Bathos) and Silence (Sige); from them emerged the Fullness or Pleroma. The twelfth of the Powers, Wisdom (Sophia), offended and was banished from the Fullness. There she produced Christ, who left her to become absorbed in the Fullness. She tried again and produced the Artificer or Demiurge, who created the world and began to rule it tyrannically with a horde of associates. Meantime, Christ, now drawn into the Fullness, pleaded with the other Powers to save Wisdom, and the elect. The elect were formed by the Divine Word (Logos) early in the business of creation, who privily inserted a "male seed" in the psychic make-up of some human beings. The Aeons produced Jesus to be her Advocate or Paraclete. Jesus now appeared on earth as in one aspect corporeal and exposed to suffering, but also as a spiritual being (23,3). He required a material body to enter space and subdue its lord, a spiritual body to rescue the elect. The elect had forgotten the very nature of their being; it was Jesus's calling to remind them of it. This part of the system owes something to Plato's doctrine that knowledge is recollection.

Jesus was seeking to restore harmony to the Fullness. Here we come on an important aspect of Theodotus's teaching. Salvation is the restoration of Form; this again is Platonic. But the Form is closely associated with—we might almost say identified with—the Name. This goes back to Philo's identification of the Logos with the Name of God. To Theodotus the Name provides the very pattern of the existence of the Aeons; by contrast the Demiurge is characterized as "an emptiness of the Name." It is easy to see why Theodotus laid such stress on baptism; baptism is baptism into the Name (22,4). It is an occasion for joy. It is an escape from the evil principalities, death to the old life; it is a new life in Christ. The water, like the bread in the Eucharist and the oil in Unction, is sanctified and transformed by the power of the Name. But Theodotus adds a curious warning. Unclean spirits sometimes go down into the water with the man being baptized, receive the seal, and are impossible to heal.

The act of restoration is the crucifixion. Unfortunately, Theodotus does not seem completely consistent in his interpretation. The crucified body is said at one point to be the spiritual seed. There must be something wrong here, as the words show which follow. It is the spirit, which Jesus on the cross commends to the Father, which is the spiritual seed, the elect (1,2). By taking on flesh Jesus, said Theodotus, identified himself with Wisdom and with the Church of the elect. Clement adds that his invisible part was the Name (26,1). Through crucifixion and baptism Jesus gathered the spiritual seed, reunited them with their counterparts among the angels and restored them and Wisdom to the Fullness.

The picture of man in *The Excerpts* is characteristic of the Gnostics. He combines in himself an earthly and a psychic nature. The earthly nature is seen in the material body; it is evil, demonic. The psychic nature was formed in the fourth heaven and united with the material body in the act of creation. The seed of the elect leave the body behind. But not all men are saved. Adam's progeny fall into three races, fathered by Cain, Abel, and Seth, the first irrational, the second rational and just, the third spiritual. These psychic natures were created in heaven and transmitted through Adam but not by him; he was responsible only for their earthly integument.

For the most part Clement merely transmits what he has read, though even here his selection of extracts may be revealing. R. P. Casey, in a careful study, has shown how boldly Clement adapts his borrowings, controlling them in all instances by a more basic Christian commitment than the Gnostics showed. Thus "We"—i.e., we Christians—"state that the elect seed is a spark given life by the Logos, a pupil of the eye, a grain of mustard-seed, a leaven which unites in faith the races which seem divided. But the Valentinians . . ." (1,3). He accepts the Valentinian phraseology within the limits of Scripture, no further (cf. 1 *Pet.* 2,9; *Is.* 43,20; 42,3; *Deut.* 32,1; *Mt.* 13,31). "To Clement," writes Casey (p. 26), "the elect seed represented the influence of the Logos in the souls of all those who had freely elected to believe. They were chosen by God because they had chosen to believe in him. . . . Between the Valentinian view of the work of the Logos and Clement lies the whole expanse of his broad but subtle conception of faith." Here, as in other passages, he is going as far as he can in sympathy with the Valentinians. Elsewhere he is more critical. He thinks that the Valentinians are wrong in identifying the Paraclete with Jesus. Clement stresses that the Paraclete is the Spirit, sharing the very substance and power of God (23-4). Again Clement insists, against Theodotus, on the impassibility of God (30,1). It seems a curiously unchristian view, for one who believed Jesus's words, "Whoever has seen me has seen the Father." However, it became Christian orthodoxy, and it is fascinating to be admitted to the formative stages of that tradition. Especially important, as Casey rightly says, is Clement's doctrine of the Logos. Clement affirms first that there is a divine Logos who is, in essence, God in God (8,1); second, that the Logos became flesh in the prophets and in the Savior (19,1); third, that the Logos in God and the Logos in Jesus are the same; fourth, that nonetheless they acquire a distinction in their activity; and fifth, that this distinction can be expressed by describing the Logos made flesh as a son (though not in substance) and as first-created. This is to some extent a compromise solution, but we are again impressed by Clement's firm grasp of Christian principle and refusal to be led on wild-goose chases.

XI *Selections from the Prophetic Scriptures*

Selections from the Prophetic Scriptures falls into four well-marked sections. 1–26 deals with baptism; 27–37 is concerned with the Gnostic; 38–50 and 51–63 are scriptural commentaries. The title is at first sight misleading, but Clement is not referring to the prophets, but to the prophetic trend which he sees running through all scripture.

It is however not quite as tidy as this might suggest. It comprises a succession of brief, discontinuous paragraphs, arranged with some succession of thought, snippets, notes. The first few deal with scriptural passages with a cosmological turn. Clement is all ready for allegorical interpretation. Then he comes to the theme of baptism. The crossings of the Red Sea by Moses and of the Jordan by Joshua are given mystical meaning; the names Joshua and Jesus are the same. The water above the heavens, invisible and accessible only to the mind, is an allegory of the Holy Spirit. The old theme recurs that God mixes fear in with his goodness. To be in the body is like sailing an old ship: no use lying on your back; be constant in prayer (Clement has the storm on the Sea of Galilee in mind). A paragraph anticipates what he will later say about knowledge: we enjoy it here in measure, and on the basis of what we possess look firmly forward to the rest. The three witnesses of *Deuteronomy* (17,6) are Father, Son, and Holy Spirit: the doctrine of the Trinity is there, though without theological formulation. Fasting is a symbol of dying to the world. Prayer is said, a little oddly for Clement, to be stronger than faith. Teaching which leads to knowledge is a God-given miracle. God created us. We did not pre-exist. Clement dismisses this part of Platonism; he adds an argument: if we did pre-exist we ought to know where we were and how and why we came here. God brought us into being out of non-being, and, once born, saves us by his grace, if we appear worthy and suitable. In Clement's theology God calls but man must respond; we are not puppets, not slaves of determinism or predestination. The Lord buys us by his precious blood—but from whom? From the tyranny of our sins, says Clement. There follows a finely conceived account of God. "If anyone has a thought of God, it does not match God's worth—what could that be? So far as in him lies, let him think of a tremendous light of supreme beauty, unthinkable and unapproachable, possessing every good power and every attractive virtue, concerned for all, full of compassion, passionless, good, omniscient, completely prescient, true, sweet, brilliant, unquenchable" (21). He returns to baptism, and this leads him from water to fire and its consuming power.

In the next section Clement develops the theme of the true Gnostic. He begins with an attack on false Gnostics. The sea may be used for swimming, commerce, or fishing. The land may be used for travelling, agriculture, hunting, mining, building. Reading of the scriptures may be put to the encouragement of faith, moral encouragement, or the eradication of superstition. But knowledge, true knowledge, is essential. And the law of the true Gnostic directs him away from wicked acts, wicked thoughts and wicked words, from enmity for anyone, from envy, hatred, slander, and calumny. Long life is blessed only in those worthy of eternal life, who have caused no one pain except the bittersweet pain of turning him from evil, who are rid of their passions and free. "Virtue which comes from knowledge—Gnostic virtue—is always a lovely thing, gentle, innocent, harmless, blessed, ready for anything; it consists in the best possible relationship with all that has to do with God, and with men; it establishes a man in the image of God and makes him through Christian love a love of all that is noble" (37). This involves wisdom, self-control, righteousness, faith.

The remaining paragraphs are so miscellaneous as to be impossible to summarize. The majority of the passages quoted or discussed come from *The Psalms*; two are from the first chapter of *Genesis*. *Judges* and *Isaiah* are also represented, as is one of Clement's favorite works, *The Wisdom of Solomon*. The New Testament passages are all from the gospels, two from *Matthew*, three from *Luke* and one from *John*; there are also several citations from the apocryphal *Apocalypse of Peter*. We note an attack on Tatian (38); a curious description of the passions as "spirits" (46); a firm recognition that the Logos does not require us to depart from the world of creation, but to live in it without being dominated by passion (47); another curious description of the stars as spiritual bodies charged to share the organization of the world with the angels, not causes of generation, but signs of past, present, and future, and affecting the seasons, weather, crops, and health (55); an allegorical allusion to the second coming (56); a reference to the angels of the first creation, with some symbolical interpretation and some discussion of the hierarchy of angels (57). There is not much here to excite us or to add to our understanding of Clement; it is reinforcement of what we already know.

CHAPTER 6

Salvation for the Rich?

I *Introduction*

"YOU see your calling, brethren," wrote Paul to the church at Corinth, "how that not many wise men after the flesh, not many mighty, not many noble, are called" (1 *Cor.* 1,26). A century and more later the situation was not so very different. Celsus, the Platonist whose informed and reasoned attack on the Christians we know through the pages of Origen's answer, testifies to it: "We see them in our own houses, wool-workers, cobblers, laundrymen, vulgar, uneducated people. They do not dare to open their mouths in the presence of the grave wisdom of their employers; but when they get hold of the children in private, and with them silly women, they wax wonderfully eloquent" (Origen *C. Cels.* 3,55). Yet Celsus's very words show that this was not the whole story, since it tells of conversions in upper-class homes. The followers of Jesus were by no means the rag-tag-and-bobtail of Jewish society. The fishermen he called were independent operators, Matthew had presumably accumulated tainted money in the manner of his profession. Nicodemus and Joseph of Arimathea were men of some wealth. When the movement fanned out beyond the borders of Judaea, and Paul in particular went among the Greeks, and when the church reached Rome and the Latin-speaking West, it is a priori likely that its immediate appeal would be to the underprivileged (in another passage Celsus suggests that Christianity appealed only to the slaves, women, and children) and there can be little doubt that the ultimate ground of Roman persecutions was the fear of revolution. But even in the first century there were others. Pomponia Graecina, wife of Aulus Plautius, who commanded the invasion of Britain, was suspected of "foreign superstition" (Tacitus *Ann.* 13,32); it has been supposed that this was Christianity, especially as a member of the family, Pomponius Graecinus, is named in one of the Christian catacombs. By the end of the century, Christianity had reached the royal family. Flavia Domitilla, wife of the emperor Domitian's cousin T. Flavius Clemens, was certainly a Christian, and there is good reason to suppose that her husband may have been. Rich men were not unknown within the churches.

This created problems. Jesus had held a common purse with his disciples, and the early Christians had seen a simple communism as the natural expression of their common fellowship under the power and presence of the Holy Spirit. "They were all filled with the Holy Spirit, and spoke the word of God with boldness. And the multitude of them that believed were of one heart and of one soul; none of them said that any of the things which he possessed was his own, but they held all things in common." (*Acts* 4,31–2) Unfortunately we do not know how far this practice of common wealth spread outside the Jerusalem church, how long it lasted, or what were the stages by which it changed.

The gospel records preserved the story of a man of great possessions, described by Luke as a "ruler"—perhaps a member of the ruling-class, perhaps the president of a synagogue—who came to Jesus, and was told to sell all his possessions and give them to the poor and to follow Jesus (*Mk.* 10,17 ff.; *Mt.* 19,16 ff.; *Lk.* 18,18 ff.). The story is spelled out in a fragment of the lost *Gospel according to the Hebrews*. Here the rich man is puzzled by Jesus's injunction and scratches his head. Jesus replies, "How dare you say, 'I have kept the Law and the Prophets'? It is written in the Law 'You shall love your neighbor as yourself.' Look here, many of your brothers, children of Abraham, are clothed in rags and dying of starvation. Your house is filled with good things, and not a single one of them goes out of it to them." There is no reason to doubt that this is an authentic story of Jesus. But perhaps the principal gain from New Testament scholarship in the twentieth century has been the reminder that what we read in the gospels is what was in use in the churches at the time when the gospels were written. In other words this was an attitude to riches which the churches wished to instill in the second half of the first century.

Clement had to face some of these challenges in the church at Alexandria. It is evident that there were wealthy people associated with the church. It may be that they were exercised in conscience about their wealth, unable to give it up, unwilling to enter fully into the life of the church as long as they felt that they were living a lie. It may be that they were fully within the church, but that their way of life was being challenged by some of the more radical members. It was to the condition of these men of money that Clement addressed his monograph whose title, far clumsier in English than in Greek, is literally *Who is the rich man who is being saved?* We should probably entitle it something like *Salvation for the Rich?* We may imagine that it is based on a sermon, though in its present form it is too long for a sermon even in those days of heroic endurance, or perhaps an exposition and discussion in one of Clement's classes. As it stands, it is a pleasant example of the general treatment of a serious ethical issue.

Clement starts with an uncompromising attack on servility towards the rich. It is an illuminating opening, since it shows another attitude which must have been found within the church. Such servility gives to the wealthy honor which is the prerogative of God and corrupts them by reinforcing their pride. Clement has sometimes been accused of playing down the direct demands of the gospel in the interests of wealth, and it is possible that the very fervor of this attack arises out of his awareness of such a temptation. But he is clear about the corrupting effects of too much money. He describes the rich men as wallowing in a debauched and . . . life; our text is faulty, and we cannot be sure what other epithet he used—perhaps "filthy," perhaps "ephemeral." Wealth naturally engenders arrogance. The right attitude to the rich is not servile flattery. It is more humane, more *philanthropic,* more "loving-to-men" not to add to their burdens, but to help them to bear their burdens, through prayer, and through reasoned and enlightening discussion of their problems with them; this last Clement describes by a word which literally means "citizenship"; he sees it as the Christian's social responsibility (1).

Clement now turns straight to the problem. The Lord said that it was easier for a camel to "slip out through" a needle's eye than for a rich man to do so in the kingdom of heaven (*Mk.* 10,25, but "slip out through" is Clement's vivid language). Clement is not concerned with rich men who are deaf to the calling of his Lord. But sincere seekers stumble here in his view, because either they despair of eternal life and so exploit this life to the full, or, understanding that Jesus is talking paradoxically, they nonetheless seek the wrong means to eternal life (2). Those who love truth and love the brethren, who do not show coarse aggressiveness or profiteering servility towards rich men, have the duty to help them by expounding the Lord's "sayings" (*logia*: we may remember that a collection of such "sayings" was partially preserved in the sands of Egypt, and that the hypothetical Q, which has been postulated as a source used by the first three gospel-writers was—if it existed—another such collection). Clement now, using a favorite image of Paul, asks the rich man to consider himself an athlete. The image itself is an indication that he is writing for Greek readers, since Jews objected to the nudity involved in athletics, though the Jews of Alexandria were more liberal or lax. To enter for a race an athlete must have a hope of winning, and he must be willing to train. In the spiritual race, the Logos (the meaning is blurred between "natural" reason, and the Divine Word) is the trainer, Christ the Director of Games, the New Covenant the appropriate diet, the Commandments the suitable exercises; the things which make the difference to the outstanding athlete are love, faith, hope, knowledge of truth, goodness, gentleness, compassion, seriousness. Clement has Paul's letter to Corinth in mind, and he brilliantly equates the last trumpet which raises the dead with the trumpet announcing the end of the race and victory (3). So, with a prayer, Clement sets to his task.

Clement begins by quoting the passage from *Mark* in its entirety. His text differs slightly from the one we know, though the sense is not seriously affected. Clement immediately lays down his principle of interpretation. The Savior—not just an indifferent title, but Jesus in his work of saving men—does not teach like a human teacher, but a divine and mystical wisdom (the language has Gnostic overtones); his words are not to be taken literally, but we must look for their hidden meaning; the things which affect our salvation are concealed by a "supercelestial" depth of thought (Clement here uses a rare word from Plato *Phaedrus* 247 C, which indicates that he is linking Christianity with Platonic metaphysics) (5).

There follows a passage of some eloquence. "Our Lord and

Savior is glad to be asked a question wholly appropriate to him. The Life is questioned about life, the Savior about salvation, the Teacher about the principle of the doctrines he teaches, the Truth about true immortality, the Word about the Father's word, the Perfect Man about the perfect rest, the Incorruptible about lasting incorruption." Being God, he knows the question before-hand, and takes up the first word to turn his pupil to God, the steward (another Platonic word) of eternal life (6). So that our first instruction is to know God, to live close to him, to love him and to grow like him. Here again Clement brings Christianity and Platonism together; the love of God is a Christian concept, but the thought of "becoming like God" is Platonic (7). Next we are to know the Son, who offers so much more than Moses offers in the Law; this is why the young man speaks con-fidently of the Law, but makes supplication to the Son. And Clement adds a vivid metaphor, especially apposite to Alexan-dria: "He is tossing dangerously as he heaves to in the waters of the Law but comes to a safe anchorage in the port of the Savior" (8).

The young man had obeyed the Commandments, no question of that. But he was not yet perfect, though he was free to choose perfection. Clement stresses this freedom of decision as vigorously as any modern existentialist and goes on to say some-thing which Christians have too often forgotten: "God does not use compulsion; he hates violence" (10). Yet the young man made the wrong choice. Why?

"Sell all that you have." Here is the crunch. Clement will not have it that this is literally meant. It is not an injunction to throw away his possessions, but to banish his present attitude of mind towards them, his identification with them, his passionate embrace of them, his diseased excitement over them, his op-pressive preoccupation about them. Clement's common sense cannot see any good in being without means of livelihood; if that were true, every beggar would be blessed. In any event there is nothing new in the renunciation of riches; witness Anaxagoras, Democritus, and Crates. Of these the last is the best example, since he, one of the most attractive of the Cynics, really did renounce possessions. Clement cannot accept that the literal interpretation of Jesus's words can possibly be right. But it is strange that he uses the fact of the philosophers' acceptance of poverty as an argument against it being a Christian injunction; elsewhere he is willing enough to treat them as "forerunners." It is significant that he does not cite the obvious example of Socrates (11).

Clement now uses a very interesting phrase. He takes from Paul the words "the new creation" (*Gal.* 6,15; 2 *Cor.* 5,17), which he has eloquently expounded in *The Exhortation* (*Protrept.* 11), and applies them to Jesus himself. In its strict sense, the idea that Jesus was himself created would cause theological difficulties. But Clement does not mean this; he means rather that Jesus sums up in himself the new order, that with his coming the world changed. He *is* the new creation. Clement might have quoted, but does not, *Revelation*: "Behold, I make all things new" (*Rev.* 21,5). And, if new, then this commandment must be a new commandment, spiritual not literal (12).

Common sense pushes forward again. If a man is destitute, he is inevitably absorbed by immediate necessities and has no time for the higher things. Further, there are other commands of the Lord which cannot be fulfilled except through possessions. If we have nothing, we cannot practise sharing, we cannot feed the hungry (13). Material goods, he says punningly, are good and to be used for the good of others. Wealth is like a tool; it can be misused, but, used properly, it is of service. So that when Jesus speaks of getting rid of all that we have, he is referring to emotions in the soul (14). If we dispose of our outward possessions but retain our inward passions, we are no better off. If we free ourselves from inward passions, we begin to put our property to its proper use. Clement is here playing with Stoic ideas. According to the Stoics there is nothing good but virtue, and happiness lies in the assent of our will to what is good. Things outside our control, such as wealth, are, in the technical term, "indifferent." They are not to be pursued; they are not to be rejected either. It is a too comfortable doctrine, enabling, as it does, the rich to rest in their riches, and to advise the poor to endure their poverty as something "indifferent." Much that has subsequently passed for Christianity has been really Stoicism.

> The rich man in his castle,
>   The poor man at his gate,

God made them high and lowly,
And ordered their estate.

It is to be feared that Clement played his part in this non-revo-
lution (15).

Clement now enriches his interpretation with a fuller exposition. When a man has external riches and is not a slave to
them, but uses them for others, he receives blessing. But if he
keeps an estate where his heart ought to be, he will be judged
as he is; there is an allusion to a saying of Jesus not preserved
in the New Testament: "I shall judge you on the basis of the
condition in which I find you." There are two kinds of treasure,
and two kinds of poverty. Clement has noticed that where Luke
has "Blessed are you poor" (*Lk.* 6,20) Matthew has "Blessed
are the poor *in spirit*" (*Mt.* 5,3), and thinks that he is right to
make the addition. This accords with his readiness to avoid the
literal and obvious meaning. But at this point Clement's desire
to make a point leads him astray. For plainly the good treasure
of which Jesus speaks (*Lk.* 6,45) is not external; it is "good
treasure of the heart." Equally he should not suggest that
poverty of spirit is blessed, but poverty of external possessions is
identical with a refusal to hunger and thirst after God's righteousness (17). He returns to the need not to interpret Jesus's words
clumsily, crudely, or literally. Salvation does not depend on external things, but on faith, hope, love, brotherliness, knowledge,
gentleness, unpretentiousness, truth. The list, which starts from
the famous chapter in 1 *Corinthians*, is different from the earlier
catalogue of virtues, and the inclusion of knowledge is especially noteworthy. Clement takes a fresh example. Good looks
do not of themselves guarantee or imperil a man's salvation. So
"When you are being hit, offer your face freely"—evidently a
version of the command to turn the other cheek, which has survived in a different form. Clement is somewhat disconcerting
hereabouts. We half want him to emphasize that external possessions do not minister to salvation; he is insisting primarily
that they need not hinder salvation. It is all very Stoic. (18).

The thought becomes more contorted, and editors have had
difficulty in establishing the true text. Clement, now reversing
his earlier thought, says that the true rich man has riches in his
soul, and the word is wrongly applied to the man with external

possessions; the true poor man is poor in spirit, and the word is wrongly applied to external poverty. He imagines the man who is poor in spirit and rich towards God speaking to the man who is not poor externally and rich in passions (something has gone wrong with the antithesis on any count), and telling him to renounce the alien possessions in his soul by selling them for the true riches of a moral character ordered in line with God's commandment. The "alien possessions" are to be given to the poor (in the literal sense) who have need of them. What are these alien possessions? Clement does not express himself clearly, and probably he is not clear himself. He cannot mean money, since this would run counter to the whole tenor of his argument. Despite what he says elsewhere (*Str.* 4,29,1), he probably does mean a certain acquisitiveness, which he might regard as dangerous in the haves but desirable in the have-nots (19).

The rich man misunderstood Jesus. The disciples were disturbed precisely because they understood; they *had* given up their external possessions, but they had *not* given up their passions. "Salvation belongs to souls that are passionless and pure." We are back with the Stoics who claimed that their perfect sage was passionless (20). But Clement returns to the New Testament, as he always does, in maintaining that it is the power of God that makes salvation possible. But it needs activity from the seeker. Clement comments, "This is the only acceptable violence, to do violence to God, and take life from God by forcefulness." Tertullian has a similar phrase of the power of corporate prayer, but his words are directed to Romans who suspect the Christians of a violent conspiracy (*Apol.* 39). Clement has the story of Jacob's wrestling in mind (*Gen.* 32,24–32). God, he says, is glad to be beaten in that contest. Peter understood; he claimed that they had left all, referring not to trifling possessions but to diseased passions. Clement slightly contradicts what he has earlier said, but he is making a different point. This, he suggests, is what it really means to follow the Savior, to pursue his sinless perfection. Clement has a delightful and characteristic image. We are to use Jesus as a mirror, and dress up our soul by what we see there (21).

But there is another stumbling-block. Jesus commends those who leave their families; elsewhere he seems to call his followers to hate their families (*Lk.* 14,26). This cannot, said Clement, be literally meant—if we are to love our enemies we cannot hate our friends—and Clement is sane in reconciling the two commandments. We are indeed to avoid hatred and evil-doing, and we are equally not to put family-ties before right living (22). Our worldly father may have given us birth: the Savior has given us new birth (23). Salvation must come first (24).

Clement goes on to examine other phrases from the account in *Mark*. It will be remembered that Clement's text does not contain a promise of worldly possessions, but a question and response suggesting that possessions must be used with an eye to eternal life. But added to possessions, in both versions, is persecution. This is a difficult saying to interpret in any case; it was preserved in the church without its context, and different writers have provided it with different contexts. Clement sees the question "To what end is the present possession, here and now, of land, money, property, brothers—with persecutions—directed?" as the indication that Jesus disapproves of possessions *when accompanied by persecutions*. This is wrong-headed; it shows Clement at his worst and most obscurantist. He emerges ingeniously. Persecutions, like the rest, may be external or internal, and the latter are the worst, and Jesus is warning against inward temptations. Clement characteristically uses a phrase from Plato to describe these assailing powers. Then, in another of his vivid metaphors, he calls Jesus the soul's "defense attorney." The word ("Paraclete") is used in *John* of the Holy Spirit (*Jn.* 14,16). It is not unjust to say that by the time of Clement effective belief in the Holy Spirit had waned, but belief in the present power of Jesus had ousted it; it is just also to remember that in the New Testament the Spirit is at times called the Spirit of Christ (*Rom.* 8,9; 1 *Pet.* 1,11) (25). He goes on to another saying, which was in fact detached, "The first shall be last, and the last first" (*Mt.* 19,30 etc.), but instead of examining it he reaffirms his central position. The rich are not locked out, if they get their values right, and are alert to the Lord's every signal, as sailors to a good captain. There is nothing wrong in thrift and no guilt in being born into a rich family! If wealth were only the ambassador of Death it would have no place. But the rich man must keep along the right lines (Clement's phrase comes from chariot-racing), and must live as a fellow-citizen of God (a Stoic phrase with some New Testament justification, e.g.,

Eph. 2,19; *Phil.* 3,20). He must not be controlled by, but must control the power of, riches; the last phrase recalls the words of the Greek historian Thucydides, a man grimly aware of the corruptions of power, about "the insolent power of wealth" (Thuc. 1,38) (26).

What then must the rich man do to be saved? It is here that we see Clement at his best and realize that for all his middle-class morality and occasionally fantastic perversion of the clear meaning of the text, he has a close understanding of the heart of the Gospel. He brings together the story of the rich young ruler, and the lawyer's question about the greatest commandment. The first commandment is to love God, and Clement, like John (1 *Jn.* 4,19), knows that our love for God is a response to his love for us. More, to love God is to "put on" God, to become at one with him (27). Second to this, but no less important, is love of the neighbor. Clement tells, freely and well, the story of the Good Samaritan (cf. *Lk.* 10,30–7). He makes a point of the fact that the Samaritan has equipped himself to help those in need before setting out, and he does not fail to notice that the story does not end "That is your neighbor" or even "That is love" but "Go and act"; love flowers in good acts (29).

And now Clement extends his interpretation. He suggests that our nearest neighbor is Jesus himself, whose saving work we meet at every turn. Clement's thought is centered on Christ, not on man. He does not say that we are to love our fellow-humans for their own sake, and in so doing shall find that we have been ministering to Christ, but that we should love Christ and love our fellow-humans out of obedience to him. In his eloquent account of Christ's saving work he allows himself a word-play between oil (*elaion*) and pity (*eleon*) (30). To love Christ means to love those who believe in Christ, those whom Christ speaks of as his children and his friends. Clement quotes another saying of Jesus not found in the gospels: "For I will give not only to my friends but to my friends' friends as well" (31).

He invites the rich to a profitable business, bartering perishable possessions for imperishability, and keeps this obviously appropriate metaphor working. "Set sail, man of riches, for this fair; if you've any sense, circumnavigate the whole earth, do not shrink from danger or exertion to buy a heavenly kingdom here and now." The possession of jewellery is nothing. Clement puts in a phrase from some poem on precious stones; they are food for flames, the sport of time, the accident of an earthquake, a monarch's insolence. Better to live and reign with God in heaven (32). Better to serve the needs of Christians, who can requite this service with one another. They form an army without weapons, without war, without bloodshed, without anger, without offense, a bodyguard and soulguard, whose general is God. Their prayers can save a ship from sinking and steer it to safety (it is not clear whether this is intended literally or metaphorically), can conquer illness, can rescue from bandits, can defy evil spirits (34). They can offer frank rebuke, friendly advice, genuine love (35). And among them are those whom Clement, perhaps referring to a lost saying of Jesus, calls "more elect than the elect," the light of the world and salt of the earth, (to use a Gnostic term) the seed (36).

Clement reverts to what we may call his hymn of love. God is love, he says, echoing John (1 *Jn*. 4,8) and it was through love that he revealed himself to us in visible form. And now Clement adds a fascinating thought. "God in his ineffable aspect is Father, in his readiness to suffer with us he became Mother. In his love the Father became female; the primary evidence for this is the Son he bore himself. The product of love is love." There were some Gnostics who introduced a Mother as the cause of creation, and it is hard not to think that Clement is trying to express the fruitful part of this thought in a Christian context. Clement, like the Gnostics, is not afraid to project sexuality onto the ultimate. We can, after all, only argue from the familiar to the unfamiliar, and the Father-Son image comes from the New Testament. Clement cannot rid himself from the primacy of masculinity. But he is attempting a richer and profounder account of the creative power behind the universe, a power which for the Christians has its highest fruit in the Incarnation. To put it differently, once we have called God Father we have said too much—or not enough. In *Genesis* it is written: "God created man in his own image, in the image of God he created him; male and female he created them" (*Gen.* 1,27). As bishop Synesius puts it in one of his hymns:

> Thou art Father, thou art Mother,
> thou art female, thou art male.
>
> (*Hymn* 2,63–4)

And though Christian love (*agape*) is not the same as sexual love (*eros*), an account of Christian love which ignores sexual love will be found wanting. For it ignores the fact that Christian love can be a sublimation of sexual love, that social service is often a redeployment of the instinct and energy of sex; witness Florence Nightingale. It also ignores the fact that Christian love between man and woman may lead to sexual love; witness Martin Luther.

The Son in his love for us fits himself to the measure of our weakness so that he may fit us to the measure of his power. He sacrifices himself for us, and calls on us to do the same for one another (37). Love then it is which Paul calls "a more excellent way" (1 *Cor.* 12,31), and in expounding Paul's panegyric of love Clement has a magnificent phrase: love "is poured out for our brother; for him it is all aflutter, for him it is sanely mad." It is one of the finest of all oxymorons, a paradox of which G. K. Chesterton might have been proud. But with love must go repentance. The word for "repent," a New Testament word, means literally, as we have seen, "change one's mind." But it has a deeper meaning than that implies. It involves a change of one's whole attitude, a reorientation of personality. It is close to the Old Testament use of "turn back"—the word and thought of Clifford Bax's poem:

> Turn back, O man, forswear thy foolish ways.

It is to turn one's life around and face a new direction. Clement does not play this down at all. Penitence is condemnation of past actions, and earnest prayer that the Father will not hold them against us. Clement is under no illusions about human wickedness. He knows the economic and sexual exploitation of others, the lies and easy speeches which comfort cruel men, the inward passions that shake the soul, though here he lapses again into Stoicism, for Jesus was not unwilling to display anger or grief. As he writes of these things, the images heap up. A man may run on the rocks of vice; he may withdraw from the competition at the climax of the play; he needs nursing as through a long illness; he needs a trainer, a pilot. Clement knows that a rich man, almost more than any, needs someone to stand up to him and speak out to him; it is notable that at this point he addresses himself directly to the rich. But he knows also the grace and mercy of God, and piles on the scriptural quotations to demonstrate that forgiveness may be found (38–41).

And now, skilled and sensitive preacher that he is, Clement draws to a conclusion with a story, which he claims to be true. After the death of Domitian the apostle John moved from Patmos to Ephesus, and used to travel round the area organizing the life of the churches. In one of the churches he noticed a young man of good physique, handsome features, and spirited personality, and put him under the charge of the bishop, whom he also calls elder; Clement's interchangeable use of the terms creates some problems for the history of church government, but whatever the conditions in Asia Minor at the end of the first century there is evidence that into the third century in Alexandria the bishop was elected from among the elders. The bishop took the young man home, brought him up and led him to baptism; the language at this point is full of technical terms from the Mysteries. He then thought his duty finished. But the young man fell into bad company, and like a powerful horse which has moved off course he got the bit between his teeth and could not be checked (a typical image of Clement's, with reminiscences of Plato *Phaedr.* 246B; 254C); he became leader of a gang of highwaymen. Now it happened that John had occasion to revisit the church. He called on the bishop to "repay the deposit." On learning what had happened he rebuked the bishop, called for a horse, and rode off to the highwaymen's headquarters where he confronted the renegade. The old man's devotion moved the robber chief, and the promise of Christ's forgiveness brought him back to the church. There followed a period of prayer and fasting, and words of attractive power, like the Song of the Sirens in Homer's *Odyssey* (12,184), but leading to life not death. John did not leave until he had brought the young man to the point where he could leave him as bishop of the church, in the knowledge, we may assume, that he would shepherd the souls of others more faithfully than his had been guarded.

At this point some lines are missing: the story is complete, but we do not know how Clement linked it with his peroration. When we rejoin him it is to a vision of the hosts of heaven; and the Savior opening the gate of eternal life to the man who, endowed with riches, has repented his past, listened to the guidance of Christian disciples, and used his riches for good works. Clement ends with a classic doxology. "If a man keeps his gaze fixed on salvation, yearns for it, demands it, shamelessly, violently, he shall receive true purification and unchanging life from the good Father who is in heaven, to whom through his Son Jesus Christ, the Lord of living and dead, and through the Holy Spirit, be glory, honor, might and eternal majesty now and from generation to generation and from age to age. Amen" (42).

II   Salvation for the Rich?

Salvation for the Rich? is a minor work. But it is a late and mature work, written after *Miscellanies,* or at least well after the third book. It is important as an example of popular preaching and of the treatment of a knotty ethical problem. Clement's approach is typical of the man, and, as we might expect, does not vary essentially from what we find elsewhere. We can single out the following points.

First, Clement is not a revolutionary, gunning for the rich. Nor is he a toady licking their boots. He has almost certainly encountered the problem of the rich Christian not in general or theoretical terms but through individual church members or aspirants to church membership. And though he speaks in general terms we can trace a particular, individual, and personal concern behind his words.

Second, it is not easy to draw a general social and economic theory from the pages of the gospels without fear of contradiction, as theorists have found across the centuries. Insofar as it is possible at all it would be more radical than Clement proposes. Clement's social theory is in fact Stoic rather than Christian.

Third, Clement has in fact a middle-class approach, and just as on the educated side he must find a place for Greek philosophy within the church, so socially he must find a place for possessions. Clement's approach is liberal, and as we of the twentieth century know, liberals can with justice be seen both as the vanguard of progress and as obstacles to progress. Clement is of those who kept the church from radicalism for good or bad.

Fourth, in order to do this he has had to go against the plain meaning of some words in the gospel. It is possible to do this in two ways. It is possible to treat the words of Jesus as referring to the individual before him only and to refuse to generalize from them. It is possible to reject the literal meaning of the words and to interpret them symbolically. It is typical of Clement that he chooses the latter. He is plainly wrong to do so. Worse, the tendency to interpret words spiritually rather than literally waters down the sheer harsh, heroic, material, this-worldly aspect of the gospel; in the end it waters down the Incarnation.

Fifth, Clement's thinking weaves together a number of strands, here principally four. There is the New Testament, of which he has a close, detailed, and assimilated knowledge. His interpretations are occasionally fantastic, but in general we can only be deeply impressed by the depth of his knowledge and understanding. There is his beloved Plato, never far from his mind. Plato has contributed less to the thought of this treatise than usual, but he has considerably influenced the expression and imagery. There are, as we have seen, the Stoics, a pervasive influence at this time, not least among the Platonists; after all Clement grew up in the reign of Marcus Aurelius. And there are the Gnostics, and Clement is anxious to bring the best of their thinking to Christian use.

Finally, we may note that this is a piece of fine writing. It is nearly always clear; when it is not, it is because Clement has pushed the desire for antithesis too hard. It makes effective use of quotations and literary allusions, from prose and poetry, sacred and secular sources. It is well-ordered, with the story of St. John and the robber as a climactic call to repentance. It uses relevant imagery in metaphor and simile without overdoing it; we feel that we are exploring a garden, not a hothouse. There are striking phrases and memorable epigrams, including some unobtrusive wordplay and one very powerful oxymoron. But what is most impressive about the style is that it persuades us of Clement's own convictions: when he is eager to convict the reason, it is simple and direct; when he wishes to communicate his passionate concern, the style rises and the language grows richer and more overwhelming. Behind the style lies the man, sane and balanced, and at the same time eager, generous, concerned, enthusiastic.

[178]

CHAPTER 7

Lost Works

EUSEBIUS lists Clement's works as follows (*HE* 6,13): *Miscellanies* in eight books; *Outlines* in eight books; *Exhortation to the Greeks; The Tutor; Salvation for the Rich?; On the Passover; On Fasting; On Evil-Speaking; Exhortation to Endurance* or *To the Newly Baptized; Against the Judaizers* or *The Rule of the Church.* In addition to these we know of three other works: *On Providence* in two books; *On the Prophet Amos; On First Principles;* and naturally his *Letters* were preserved.

Of these fourteen works, as we have seen, only four survive with any degree of completeness. Of the others, some are mere names. Of the books *On Fasting* and *On Evil-Speaking* and the one recorded by Palladius *On the Prophet Amos* no trace or fragment remains beyond the title.

To these we may add others which he mentions in his own writing: *On Marriage; On Continence; On Resurrection; On Prophecy; On the Soul; On the Birth of Man; On Transmigration of Souls; On the Devil; On the uniqueness of God, proclaimed by law, prophets and gospel; Against Heresies; On Prayer; On the Origin of the World; On the Examination of Dogmas.* We can be fairly certain that many, perhaps most, of these were books he vaguely thought of writing but never got around to. Some may refer to parts of his work as we have seen it, or part of some lost work, under another title. But it is possible that some represent work which was completed but has not survived.

I   On First Principles

A serious loss is the book *On First Principles.* This was a work of Clement's maturity. When he wrote *Miscellanies* he had it in mind to write such a work (3,3,13; 3,3,21), but he had not yet executed his purpose. By the time he wrote the little treatise *Salvation for the Rich?* he had finished it, and refers his hearers to the larger work, which he calls *An Exposition on First Principles and Theology*, for an allegorical explanation of the hidden meaning of the camel passing through a strait and narrow way (itself an interesting conflation of two gospel-passages: *Mk.* 10,25; *Mt.* 7,14). This is all we know. But we have Origen's work *On First Principles*. Origen had followed Clement in publishing a volume of *Miscellanies*. Miscellaneous it certainly was; he quoted from Plato and the Platonist Numenius, from the Stoics Cornutus and Chaeremon, from the Neo-Pythagoreans; he discussed a number of passages in Paul's letters; he turned to allegorical interpretation of *Daniel*. In the treatise *On First Principles* Origen claimed to be liberated from bondage to Greek philosophy; but he did not renounce his learning. *On First Principles* was an attempt to present a comprehensive Christian philosophy, an expression of the rule of faith. Origen divides the treatise into four: God, The World, Man, and Scripture. He is fundamentally concerned with freewill, evil and redemption, and in the first three books discusses these in terms of God, the World, and Man. The fourth book deals with Christian education, and, in particular, the need to treat Scripture allegorically.

We are not here concerned with Origen's peculiar and individual views; they were original and important. But some of his admirers have argued for the novelty and originality of producing such a work at all. I cannot think so. Clement's work is lost, and we know little enough about it, but we know that he treated allegorical interpretation systematically, as did Origen, and it is likely that Origen patterned his work on that of the older man, while incorporating his own interpretation and understanding of the themes. Clement has sometimes seemed a slight figure by the side of Origen; this could be merely because we have lost his major work.

II   The Rule of the Church

Almost equally regrettable is the loss of *The Rule of the Church*. The alternative title, *Against the Judaizers*, suggests that this might have been a notable defense of liberal Christianity, and perhaps the most important of all Clement's works to the understanding of his mind. This must remain the speculation of a pipedream. As it is, we must be content with a solitary extract preserved by Nicephorus of Constantinople in the fifteenth century. The extract is entirely characteristic of Clement, though it adds nothing new to our knowledge of him. It interprets the Old Testament passage about the building of the Temple by the Son of David (2 *Kings* 8,27; 2 *Chron.* 6,18) in terms of an allegory of the Incarnation and of the dwelling of Christ with the faithful. There are typical cross-references to 1 *Peter* 2,5 and to *John* 2,19–21.

III   Outlines

Outlines was what we would today call *An Introduction to the New Testament*—as Eusebius puts it, "not passing over the disputed books—I mean *Jude* and the rest of the 'catholic' letters, and *Barnabas* and what is called *The Revelation of Peter*." It is to *Outlines* that we owe the attribution of *Hebrews* to Paul, an attribution which few scholars today would accept, and one which Clement ascribes to Pantaenus, a sure sign that there was no tradition of Pauline authorship. Most of the citations preserved are slight, and consist of comments on individual verses of the New Testament, of varying helpfulness by our standards. Thus on 1 *Corinthians* 11,10 Clement suggests that the angels who are not to see are the righteous and virtuous who might be scandalized by what they saw: the "real" angels would see through any covering. On 2 *Corinthians* 6,12 he rightly, or at least reasonably, explains "in your bowels" as "in your love towards God." In the passage of *Galatians* in which Paul declares that he "withstood Cephas to his face" Clement cannot have it that the two great apostles fell out, and maintains that it must have been "another man of the same name." The "angels" of the churches in *Revelation* are elders.

A substantial fragment, dealing with parts of 1 *Peter, Jude,* 1 *John,* and 2 *John,* has come down to us in a Latin version by Cassiodorus under the title *Adumbrations of Clement.* There is little, however, that calls for our notice. It is mostly paraphrase, sane and sensible, with close attention to the original, and with occasional cross-references to the gospel-writers and to Paul; we note again that Clement attributes *Hebrews* to Paul. There are also a few references to the Old Testament, but generally these are already implicit in the text on which he is commenting. Perhaps the only non-scriptural reference is to the apocryphal *Acts of John*; we must remember that the canon of the New

Testament was by no means finalized. There is no tendency to refer to classical philosophy. Clement is more interested in the permanent message of these writings than in their temporal occasion. He comments on the authorship of *Jude*, simply because Jude describes himself as "slave of Jesus Christ and brother of James"; Jude might have written "brother of Jesus Christ" but Jesus had become for him Lord. On John himself Clement has no comment, but he does discuss the destination of his second letter. This is a familiar crux. The letter begins, "The elder to the lady elect and her children." Clement describes this as written to, or for, a group of virgins, and treats Elect (*Eclecta*) as the Christian name of a woman from Babylon, indicating her election to the church. In general Clement is not interested in the background to these writings.

In these passages there are no extravagant interpretations. Typical comment will be found on 1 *John* 3,1: "The world does not recognize us, because it did not recognize him." "By the world," comments Clement, "he means those who live materialistically in luxury." He means a little more than that, but it will do. Unfortunately, we lack most of the commentary on the fourth chapter of this letter, which is the great exposition of human love. At one point only does Clement's peculiar theology flash out. This is on 2,3: "In this we know that we have known him, if we keep his commandments." The verse is irresistible to Clement's Christian gnosticism, and his words are preserved in Greek as well as in Latin (though wrongly attributed to Clement of Rome): "The gnostic (*intellector*) on all occasions fulfills the works of virtue; but to fulfill the works of virtue does not always make you a gnostic."

Photius, the Byzantine patriarch and lexicographer, says (*Bibliotheca* 109) that there were irreligious and fabulous passages in *Outlines* as well as orthodox interpretations. Photius spells out his criticisms. Clement introduces irrelevant and alien ideas. He reduces the Son to a created being. He speculates on reincarnation and the existence of many universes before Adam. He produces Eve from Adam "shamefully and godlessly"; Photius does not satisfy the curiosity he has been careful to arouse. Clement evidently was regarded as a kind of former-day Bultmann: he made myths not merely of the angels copulating with the daughters of men, but of the Incarnation. In fact he is said to have speculatively identified two Words, of which only the lesser, and not even that in any real sense, was revealed to men. There is no trace of these eccentricities of interpretation in the passages which survive to us. No doubt it was these irreligious and fabulous passages which led to the suppression of this important work.

IV   To the Newly Baptized

Eusebius in his Church History (6,13) mentions a work by Clement entitled *Exhortation to Endurance or To the Newly Baptized*. In the Escorial Library in Madrid there is a fourteenth century manuscript containing miscellaneous theological citations. One of these is headed "Precepts from Climent," but the author appears in the contents table as Clement. The thought of the passage is much what we should expect from our Clement, and the allusion to the lighthouse commanding the harbor at Alexandria places it; it is a reasonable conjecture that the extract is taken from the work mentioned by Eusebius. The passage is so attractive that it is worth quoting it in full:

"Practise quietness in thought and action, in speech and movement. Avoid precipitancy and impetuosity. This is the way to help your mind to remain firm, instead of being agitated and weakened by your precipitancy, inadequate in the range of its understanding, dark in its vision. It will not be subject to gluttony, or a fervor of anger, or the other passions; it will not be a ready prey to these. Your mind must rise above the passions; it must sit high on a quiet throne and turn its gaze to God. Never be open to sharp temper in fits of anger, never be lazy in reasoning, never be overhesitant in movement, so that your quietness may be beautified by a pleasing rhythm, and your demeanor may be seen to be divine and holy. Guard against the outward signs of arrogance, a haughty demeanor, head held high, footstep elevated and delicate.

"See that your words are gentle and your greetings warm to all that you meet. Show respect to women, and keep your eyes on the ground. Be circumspect in all your talk. Make sure that your answers are helpful, geared in to the need of your listeners, audible but no louder, not so faint that those present cannot hear it, nor deafening in its projection. Be on your guard against ever saying anything ill-considered and ill-thought out. Don't interrupt off-hand another man's argument with your own. Take your turn in listening and conversing with a fair share of speech and silence. Be glad to learn, and unstinting in teaching. Never hide wisdom from others in a grudging spirit; don't be too shy to instruct others. Obey elders as if they were your father. Respect God's servants. Be in the lead in wisdom and virtue. Don't be quarrelsome with your friends, don't be rude to them, or try to make fools of them. Be firm in renouncing lies, sharp practice and violence. Meet arrogance and violence with silence, gently and nobly.

"Let all your thoughts and all your actions be devoted to God. Dedicate your whole life to Christ. Frequently turn your soul to God, and let your thinking rely on the power of Christ, as if it were in some harbor by the divine light of the Savior away from the surge of talk and action. In the daytime freely communicate the fruits of your thinking to men, but most of all, night and day alike, to God. Don't let an excess of sleep overpower you and detain you from your prayers and hymns to God; long sleep is in partnership with death. Ally yourself constantly with Christ who makes the divine beam shine from heaven; let Christ be your lasting, unending joy.

"Do not relax your soul's tension by indulging in rich food and drink. Realize that it is enough to meet the body's needs. Don't dash to the table before dinnertime has arrived. Let your dinner be bread, and let the vegetable products of earth and the fruits of trees be set before you. Go to your meal as if you do not want to stay there;[1] don't show yourself half crazy with gluttony. Don't eat meat or insist on wine, except under doctor's orders. Substitute for the pleasure to be had from these, joy in divine thoughts and hymns, provided for you by wisdom from God. Let meditation on heaven be your constant guide to heaven.

"Drop all your material anxieties. Be confident in expectations directed towards God. He will provide your necessities, enough food to keep life going, clothing for your body, and shelter from the cold of winter. The whole earth is your king's and all that grows on it, and he looks after his servants' bodies with extreme care as being shrines and temples to himself. So don't be afraid of extreme illness or the approach of old age (to which you must sooner or later look forward). When we wholeheartedly fulfill his commandments we shall no longer be ill.

[184]

"In this knowledge prepare your soul stoutly to face illness. Be tough, like an athlete, who is ready to face a hard time of it with his powers unshaken. Do not let your soul be crushed by pain, whether illness lies heavily upon you or some other disaster hits you. Show your quality. Meet hardship with resolution. Give thanks to God even in the middle of your difficulties. His thoughts are wiser than men, and difficult or rather impossible for men to discern. Pity those who are in distress. Pray for God's help for human beings; God will listen to the request of his friend and will bring help to those in distress, desiring to make his power known to men, with the purpose that when they have attained true knowledge, they will return to God and enjoy eternal bliss, when the Son of God appears and restores good things to those who are his own."

The first thing that we notice about this passage is that it stands in the tradition of the Pastoral Epistles. This is natural, for they too were written with the practical needs of an established church in mind. In particular we catch a number of echoes of the first letter to Timothy. "Do not rebuke an elder, but entreat him as a father" (1 *Tim.* 5,1); "in supplications and prayers night and day" (1 *Tim.* 5,5); "a little wine for your stomach's sake" (1 *Tim.* 5,23). Apart from these there are a number of other allusions to Paul's letters, especially to the fifth chapter of *Ephesians*, and the thought that our bodies are limbs of Christ and temples of the Holy Spirit is found in Paul (1 *Cor.* 3,16-7). The note of joy is strongly reminiscent of *Philippians*. Curiously, there is little reference to the gospels, though Clement clearly has Jesus's "Do not be anxious for the morrow" (*Mt.* 6,34) in his mind, and the thought of the disciples as God's friends comes from *John* (15,13-5). There is one excellent reference to the opening of *Psalm* 24: "The earth is the Lord's, and the fullness thereof." Once again we are aware of Clement's assimilated knowledge of the scriptures, and especially the New Testament.

The extract is little dominated by Greek philosophy. At one point Clement uses the word "great-souled" (here rendered "noble"). This is used by Aristotle to describe the crown of the virtues (*NE* 4,1123 A 34ff.) and the similarities and differences are alike so marked that we may think that Clement is making a deliberate comparison. Thus Aristotle's great-souled man, like

Clement's convert, does not make hasty movements or speak shrilly, is deliberate in speech, courageous and steadfast in action, frank in praise and criticism, indifferent to external goods, happy to help others. But, unlike Clement's convert, he is haughty, and is ashamed to receive help from others. Further, there is an essential and profound difference, in that Aristotle's hero is self-centered. Aristotle's ideal is *autarkeia*, self-sufficiency. But Clement's hero is God-centered and dependent on God.

There is one clear piece of Stoicism. This is the reference to the "tension" in the soul. The term was originally applied to muscular activity, and so to that activity of the inner personality which is the real object of life. Diogenes the "Dog," founder of the Cynic sect, is recorded as saying that no labor is noble unless its object is tension in the soul. Later Stoic writers[2] speak of the tension in the universe which makes possible its unceasing activity, and tension in the soul as being the impact of the divine fire on the soul stirring it to action. So all movement of soul and body is explained in terms of spiritual tension, and the soul's strength is defined as a proper tension in decision and action. As a metaphor it is obvious enough; we condemn "slackness," and speak of a person as being "under strain." But "tenseness" is today regarded as undesirable as well as slackness, whereas the Stoics saw tenseness as a condition of action, as Clement has accepted their analysis. The mastery of the passions is similarly Stoic, as is the injunction to simple living.

The attraction of the passage lies in its account of the Christian gentleman. The term is apt. Clement's ideal Christian is a *gentle* man. The opening note is quietude, based on prayerful reflection. The readiness alike to teach and learn is notable. One recalls Chaucer's Oxenford Clerk

And gladly wolde he lerne and gladly teche

or Goldsmith's Vicar of Wakefield, who was always ready to engage strangers in conversation, since either they would learn from him or he from them. Indeed, the Vicar has something of Clement's ideal about him. Delightful too is the warning not to interrupt; conversation is dialogue, not monologue—either way. Clement does not follow the Greek proverb: "You have two ears and one tongue. Why not listen twice as much as you talk?"

[186]

He believes in fair shares. We notice the somewhat Puritanical attitude to women with a Victorian respectfulness; the fellowship between men and women which characterized the early church is a thing of the past. Respect for fathers is assumed, and transferred to fathers in God. Simple living, vegetarianism, and a normal but undogmatic teetotalism—this, as a Stoic writer says, does no one any harm, and whether or not it is virtue, it is certainly economy. The stress on not fearing illness is striking; we are reminded of the disastrous plagues which swept the Empire in Marcus Aurelius's reign; we rarely feel the hand of death so near. The Christian will of course show an active concern for others. But above all he will be God-centered, Christ's ally. And in all the note of joy sounds; Christ is the Christian's "lasting, unending joy."

V   On the Passover

The work *On the Passover* calls for little comment. If we may trust Eusebius (*HE* 6,13,9), it was not a work of great originality. Clement was moved to write by his contemporaries in order to preserve for posterity the views of Melito, Irenaeus, and some others. But it was a subject to appeal to Clement with his strong sense of analogy and typology; he could hardly fail to see Jesus as the Paschal Lamb. In fact in a passage which we may legitimately see as climactic, he says that when the archetype is absent the image receives equal honor, but in the presence of the truth the image receives its light from the truth. For the rest the citations appear a trifle miscellaneous. This was a commissioned work, however appropriate, and Clement may have been constrained to fill out some passages with extraneous matter. One wonders in what context he produced the curious information that you can strike sparks out of the bones of lioncubs, as out of flints, or even that gentle exercise is good for leprosy. But one can forgive a deal of irrelevance for one flashing epigram: "The man who knows himself is the home and throne of the Lord."

VI   On Providence

Another lost work was entitled *On Providence*. We know little enough about it, but there is a brief extract, wrongly attributed to Clement of Rome in a compilation by one Anastasius in the Ambrosian Library in Milan. It refers to the fullness of life enjoyed by Brahmins living in the fresh air of the mountains, and attributes death and disease to excess and deficiency of the natural elements. We have already noted Clement's familiarity with Indian thought, perhaps through Pantaenus (*Str.* 1,15,68; 115,72; 3,7,60). We can deduce that Clement would advocate simple living, as he does elsewhere, in dependence on the providence of God.

Other extracts show a strong philosophical bent. Thus, in the case of God, God is his own substance, spirit, eternal, without beginning, incorporeal, indefinable, the cause of all that is, giving substance to the universe. Nature is the true reality of the universe, the depth of its being (to borrow a phrase from Paul Tillich); it is the growth (the Greek word for "nature" means "growth") towards true being, and this is implanted by the providence of God. We can analyse substances into those which are what they are, like stones; those with powers of growth, plants; those with "soul" and powers of perception, animals; those with "soul," powers of perception and of ratiocination, human beings. Man is thus, under God, at the summit of the pyramid of being, with an immaterial soul and a mind which is the image of God; Clement's interpretation of the *Genesis* story is to be noted. The whole analysis follows Aristotle closely. Another passage deals with the will. However firmly Clement believes in Providence he does not find it incompatible with freewill. Will is a natural power reaching out for its natural object. Will is a natural outreach appropriate to the nature of a rational being. Will is the free movement of a mind which is its own master. Clement here uses the noun *autexousiotes* for "freedom of will," it is not certainly attested elsewhere.

Another passage which may come from this work is discussed under "Fragments of Unknown Origin" below.

VII *Letters*

We may well imagine that Clement had a sizeable correspondence. Of this we have little trace. But in 1960 Morton Smith discovered in the monastery of Mar Saba near Jerusalem the manuscript of a letter. In its present form it is an eighteenth-century copy, written in the flyleaf of a seventeenth-century book; the original, in manner and in matter, seems clearly to have been written by Clement. The recipient was one Theodore, and the author is warning him against heresy. The warning is a curious one: it illustrates well Clement's peculiar combination of Gnosticism and anti-Gnosticism. The Carpocratians were a Gnostic sect. It is evident that Theodore was attracted by the claim of the Carpocratians to possess a secret gospel associated with the name of Mark. Clement rebuts the claim and goes on to assert that the church at Alexandria possesses a genuine secret gospel associated with the name of Mark, produced after Mark had written the familiar gospel in Rome and settled in Alexandria. He cites some passages to show the differences between the text of the secret gospel and the received text; the full secret might be revealed only to those initiated into "the Greater Mysteries" at Alexandria.

The other fragments of letters—there are only three—show a strong pastoral and practical sense. One suggests that a righteous man will not expect service, but that it will be a mark of grace to offer him service. A second maintains that in the kingdom of heaven there is no more desire, since desire arises from lack, and in that kingdom all good things are present. The third runs, "The Father has the power to make nobody poor. But if he took away the act of benefit to another, no one would think to feel sympathy. As it is, it is for the sake of one another that some are rich and some poor, so that there may be room for benefaction." This is dangerously close to the position of the evangelicals of the late eighteenth and early nineteenth centuries, and the Sunday School manuals which inculcated deference to the paternalism of the upper classes, and Wilberforce's treatise enjoining on the upper classes precisely that paternalism. It is dangerously close to the Islamic practice of maintaining beggars so that the righteous may have someone on whom to practise the virtue of almsgiving. Clement, we see again, was no revolutionary. If he sought change, he was a gradualist working within the status quo. Yet these brief extracts do show an awareness of the person to whom he is writing and a clear desire for the living out of the Christian life in the fullest sense.

VIII   *Fragments of Unknown Origin*

Finally, we must mention nearly thirty citations from Clement where the exact source is either not known or assigned wrongly to an extant work. They are generally short, and it would be difficult to draw out a coherent picture from them. The longest of these passages, which we owe to Maximus the Confessor in the seventh century, is certainly philosophical, and I should not myself hesitate to assign it to the work *On Providence*. It is an answer to the question "How does God know the world?", a question which implies that only a corporeal being could perceive corporeal reality. The answer given is that God knows material entities as acts of his will, seeing that he made the world by an act of his will. The words are not explicitly assigned to Clement, but are said to be a general view of Pantaenus's circle, among whom Clement is explicitly named. It is likely that they were taken from Clement, who perhaps attributed the answer to Pantaenus.

Some passages show allegorical or typological interpretation: of the tree in which the birds nest (*Matthew* 13,32) as the Church; of the image of God as a dove (*Luke* 3,22) as indicating the simplicity and gentleness of the new revelation of the spirit; of the seven lamps in *Revelation* as seven spirits.

There is the characteristic epigrammatic expression of good sense. "The justification of the faithful does not lie in negative refusal to do wrong but in positive purity of intention." "The test of a man's character is the company he keeps." (But was not Jesus accused of keeping company with publicans and sinners? And did not that lovable old hippie Diogenes the Dog say "The Sun visits cesspools without becoming defiled"?) "Truth is the property of those few who can discover it and hold it firm for contemplation through a long period of examination and practice." "Prayer is true priesthood and true sacrifice."

The most interesting of all these miscellaneous passages comes from a collection of religious sayings in a manuscript in Paris. In it Clement suggests that Christian piety is a kind of knowledge, or science, appropriate to its theme. If you want to become an orator, you study writings on oratory. If you want to become a doctor, you study writings on medicine. You would not study writings on medicine to become an orator, or on oratory to become a doctor. If you want to become a Christian, you should concentrate exclusively on Christian writings. There are three things of extraordinary interest in this passage. The first is the argument that piety is a form of knowledge. This is derived from Socrates, who claimed that all the virtues were forms of knowledge. It seems a highly intellectualist view for a Christian to take, but as we have seen, Clement does not mean ratiocinative knowledge in a narrow sense; a husband is scripturally said to "know" his wife. The second is the analogy with professional skill or craftsmanship. This also is taken directly from Socrates. The third is the astonishing conclusion to an argument based on Greek philosophy that the would-be Christian should concentrate exclusively on Christian writings. Plainly Clement does not mean that Plato, for example, has nothing to say to the Christian. When then does he mean? He could mean that Plato (and other authors) may prepare the mind to receive Christ, but the rest must be left to Christian writers. He could mean that Greek culture is dangerous to the catechumen unless mediated through a Christian mind like his own. Or he could mean that to come to Christ we must soak ourselves in the Christian witnesses, but that once we have received Christ we can find profit in non-Christian authors read in the light of Christ.

CHAPTER 8

Clement's Achievement

Conclusion

IN his masterly book *Christ and Culture* H. Richard Niebuhr identified five main attitudes which Christians have taken towards secular culture. The first emphasizes the opposition between Christ and culture. The second claims a fundamental agreement between Christ and culture. In the third ("Christ above culture"), Christ is seen as the fulfillment of cultural aspirations, at once continuous and discontinuous with the culture that has gone before. The fourth sees "Christ and Culture in Paradox," a dualist view in which man lives in two worlds and has responsibilities to both. The final attitude is conversionist; Christ is seen as the transformer of culture. In this debate Clement clearly belongs to the third group, of which he is the supreme representative.[1] "There is only one river of truth, but a lot of streams disgorge their waters into it" (*Str.* 1,5,29).

He has, as Montdésert says, an "audacious optimism, his confidence in the power and authority of truth." But the Logos, who reveals truth, also "loves concealment." Hence, allegorical interpretation.[2] Yet this, alien to our temper, springs from the assumption that there is a pattern in the universe, and that if you cut through the universe at different points you will find the same pattern. So too with Clement's rich use of imagery; it comes from a total view of life. Even his characteristic wordplay is linked to a belief that word and object are part of a single pattern.

Clement in his use of language appears at his most modern and at his most profound. He insists that we cannot speak of God as he is (*Str.* 2,16; 5,17). We can speak about God; we are not naming him, but pointing the mind in the right direction; we may think of One, or light, or reality—and go beyond that. A whole philosophy of religious language might be built on

Clement's assertion that essential discourse is to say "God is the Lord of all" (*Str.* 6,17).

Clement's philosophy of life centers on God, who is one and beyond one (*Paed.* 1,8,71); it looks backward to the Middle Platonism of Maximus of Tyre and Albinus, and forward to the Neo-Platonism of Plotinus. His theology is based firmly on the Logos, as the revelation of God. He found in Philo woven together the Jewish Memra, the Word by which God speaks and it is done, and the Greek teaching of the Reason behind the universe, and he Christianized Philo; he declared that the Logos was revealed in Jesus (*Protr.* 1,7). It is astonishing that Clement was accused of denigrating the Son; it was a juster charge that he identified the Son too closely with the Father. But Clement's theology is not a systematic construct; it is an expression of experience.

The world is good; Clement will have nothing of Gnostic dualism; evil is not a substance. But man is fallen, and God becomes man so that man may become God (*Protr.* 8,4; *Str.* 7,101,4). Clement has a warm, joyous, healthy picture of human life as he portrays the Christian gentleman in the last two books of *The Tutor* and the fragment from *To the Newly Baptized.* From faith to fulfillment there are two roads, one moral and one intellectual, love and knowledge. Ultimately they are one; knowledge is the perfection of love (*Str.* 4,7,54), love the perfection of knowledge. The ultimate aim is knowledge of God. To know oneself is to know God; to know God is to become like God (*Paed.* 3,1).[3] The true Gnostic has his fulfillment in the eternal vision of God.

As a man Clement's sanity attracts us. For many this was an age of anxiety. Already in the reign of Marcus Aurelius the frontier dams of empire were leaking, straining. The emperor himself had been a pensive, wistful, ineffective agnostic. Contrast the warm humanity of Clement with his insistence that joy is the keynote of the church and gladness of the Christian gnostic (*Str.* 7,101). Charles Bigg said of him: "No later writer has so serene and hopeful a view of human nature."[4]

Clement is the real founder of a Christian philosophy of religion. The Neo-Platonists were to come to their philosophical commitment in three stages—purification, initiation, vision. The Christian Platonist before them offers a parallel scheme. It was a remarkable achievement to conceive it, still more to go so far towards executing it. Adolf Harnack assessed it justly. He called it "the boldest literary experiment in the history of the church," "the first attempt to use Holy Scripture and the church tradition —together with the assumption that Christ, as the Reason of the world, is the source of all truth—as the basis of a presentation of Christianity, which at once addresses itself to the cultured by satisfying the scientific demand for a philosophical ethic and theory of the world, and at the same time reveals to the believer the rich content of his faith."[5]

Notes and References

Chapter One

1. This section reduplicates some of what I have written in an unpublished work *The First Christian Cities*.

2. The best guide to the Pre-Platonics is G. S. Kirk and J. E. Raven *The Presocratic Philosophers* (Cambridge, 1957). G. S. Kirk *Heraclitus: The Cosmic Fragments* (Cambridge, 1954) takes a different view of the philosophy of flux. On Parmenides see now the learned but controversial L. Taran *Parmenides* (Princeton, 1965).

3. Plato's evidence is unreliable. See the introduction to J. Ferguson *Socrates: A Source Book* (London, 1970). This presents the later evidence, which is ambiguous because the writers had access to other records contemporary with Socrates, but at the same time are forcing Socrates into their molds.

4. For all this see conveniently J. Ferguson "Epicureanism under the Roman Empire" in the Festschrift for Joseph Vogt (forthcoming).

5. George Herbert "The Elixer."

6. The most important primary sources are conveniently available in English in R. M. Grant (ed.) *Gnosticism: An Anthology* (London: Collins, 1961). J. Doresse *The Secret Books of the Egyptian Gnostics* (New York, 1960) summarizes, rather cursorily, unpublished finds. The two most useful secondary studies available in English are Hans Jonas *The Gnostic Religion* (Boston: Beacon Press, sec. ed., 1963) and R. M. Grant *Gnosticism and Early Christianity* (New York: Harper & Row, sec. ed., 1966). For Valentinus see F. M. M. Sagnard *La Gnose Valentinienne* (Paris, 1947).

7. This whole account is based on Jonas *op. cit.* c.8.

Chapter Two

1. J. Ferguson "Sun, Line and Cave Again" *Classical Quarterly* N.S.13 (1963) 188 ff. for the purpose of the way of illusion.

2. N. W. de Witt *Epicurus and his Philosophy* (Minneapolis, 1954); Lucian *Alexander or The False Prophet*.

Chapter Three

1. For some of the basic ideas see J. Ferguson *Moral Values in the Ancient World* (London, 1938). For concepts of love see A. Nygren *Agape and Eros* (E. T. London, 1953); J. Burnaby *Amor Dei* (London, 1938); M. C. D'Arcy *The Mind and Heart of Love* (London, 1945); C. S. Lewis *The Four Loves* (London, 1960).

2. See further J. Barbel *Christos Angelos* (Bonn, 1941).

3. See further. R. Storrs *Ad Pyrrham* (London: Oxford University Press, 1959).

4. I owe some references in this passage to an unpublished thesis by Mr. John Herbert.

Chapter Four

1. This is a controversial view, though it seems to be the only view which makes sense of the evidence. The matter has elicited much argument. See E. de Faye *Clément d'Alexandrie* (Paris, 1898); C. Heussi "Die Stromateis des Clemens Alexandrinus und ihr Verhältnis zum Protreptikos und Paedagogos" *Z. f. Wiss. Theol.* 45 (1902) 465 ff.; F. Prat "Projets littéraires de Clément d'Alexandrie" *Rech. sci. rel.* 15 (1925) 234 ff.; J. Munck *Untersuchungen über Klemens von Alexandria* (Stuttgart, 1933); G. Lazzati *Introduzione allo studio di Clemente Alessandrino* (Milan, 1939); F. Quatember *Die Christliche Lebeshaltung des Klemens von Alexandria* (Vienna, 1947).

2. See A. J. Festugière *La Révélation d'Hermès Trismégiste* (Paris, 1944) 1, 23–24.

3. The first four chapters are excellently discussed in the first chapter of P. Camelot's *Foi et Gnose* (Paris, 1944); the whole book in P. K. Prümm "Glaube und Erkenntnis im zweiten Buch der Stromata des Klemens von Alexandrea" *Scholastik* 12 (1937) 17–57.

4. J. Ferguson "Justice and Love" in *Studies in Christian Social Commitment* (Independent Press, 1954).

5. *Alexandrian Christianity* (London, 1954) p. 25.

6. *op. cit.*, p. 34.

Chapter Five

1. For a fuller exploration of this theme (without special reference to Clement) see J. Ferguson *The Place of Suffering* (James Clarke, 1972.

2. Völker's attempt to dismiss Clement's *via negativa* as not integral to his thought seems to be misguided; this passage is completely coherent with what surrounds it.

3. For another ingenious interpretation see A. Platt "Plato *Republic* 614 B" *Classical Review* 25 (1911) 13–4.

Chapter Six

1. *Astathos.* MS *Eustathos* Wil.
2. Epict. fr. 57; Stob. 1,17,3; Plut. *Sto. rep.* 7,4; Sen. *QN* 2,6,4–6; Stob. 2,7,56,5.

Chapter Seven

1. J. Ferguson "Athens and Jerusalem" *Rel. St.* 8 (1972) 1–13.
2. For the background see J. Tate "The Beginnings of Greek Allegory" *Classical Review* 41 (1927) 214 ff.; "Plato and Allegorical Interpretation" *Classical Quarterly* 23 (1929) 142 ff.; 24 (1930) 1 ff.
3. H. Merki *Omoiosis Theoi Von der platonischen Angliechung an Gott zur Gottähnlichkeit bei Gregor von Nyssa (Paradosis* 7) (Freiburg in der Schweiz, 1952) is a magisterial survey.
4. *The Christian Platonists of Alexandria* p. 72.
5. *Dogmengeschichte* 2,324.

Selected Bibliography

The following bibliography is selective only. For those wishing more detailed information, consult the works of Lilla and Méhat or Osborn.

PRIMARY SOURCES

BUTTERWORTH, G. W. *Clement of Alexandria* (Loeb). London, 1919. Contains selections with Greek text and English translation.

CASEY, R. P. *The* Excerpta ex Theodoto of *Clement of Alexandria* (Studies and Documents 1) London, 1934.

HORT, F. J. H. and MAYOR, J. B. *Clement of Alexandria, Miscellanies Book VII.* This is learned and judicious.

STÄHLIN, O. *Die griechischen christlichen Schriftsteller der ersten drei Jahrhundert. Vols.* 12, 52 (15), 17, 39. Leipzig, 1905–60. The soundest edition.

WILSON, W. *Clement of Alexandria.* (Ante-Nicene Christian Library vols. 4 and 12). Edinburgh, 1882–84. The only complete English translation, and it is coyly Latin at some points. Individual works are gradually appearing in the "Sources chrétiennes" series (Paris: various dates) with Greek text, French translation and useful notes. These editions are outstanding.

SECONDARY SOURCES

BARDY, G. *Clément d'Alexandrie.* Paris, 1926.

BIGG, C. *The Christian Platonists of Alexandria.* Oxford, 1913.

CHADWICK, H. *Early Christian Thought and the Classical Tradition.* Oxford. 1966.

COGNAT, J. *Clément d'Alexandrie: Sa doctrine et sa polémique.* Paris, 1959.

DE FAYE, E. *Clément d'Alexandrie.* Paris, 1906. The best of all books on Clement.

LAZZATI, G. *Introduzione allo studio di Clementi Alessandrino.* Milan, 1939.

LILLA, S. R. A. *Clement of Alexandria: A Study in Christian Platonism and Gnosticism.* Oxford, 1971. A learned study, concerned with particular problems.

MOLLAND, E. *The Conception of the Gospel in the Alexandrian Theology.* Oslo, 1938.

MONDÉSERT, C. *Clément d'Alexandrie*. Paris, 1944.

OSBORN, E. F. *The Philosophy of Clement of Alexandria*. Cambridge, 1957. The most useful recent general work on Clement in English.

POHLENZ, M. *Klemens von Alexandreia und sein hellenisches Christentum*. Göttingen, 1943.

TOLLINTON, R. B. *Clement of Alexandria*. 2 vols. London, 1914. This is still the best study in English.

VÖLKER, W. *Die Wahre Gnostiker nach Clemens Alexandrinus*. Berlin, 1952. The best of all studies of Clement's thought.

Index

Abraham, 95, 111, 116, 127, 140, 145
abstinence, 129, 131
Academy, 33
Achamoth, 42
Acts of John, 181
Acts of the Apostles, 128
action(s), 69, 106, 112, 124, 135, 138, 153, 173
Adam, 117, 127, 145, 159, 182
adornment, 88-90, 91, 98, 99
Aeons, 41, 102, 103, 123, 158-59
Aeschylus, 57, 125; *Agememnon*, 149; *Prometheus Bound*, 57, 65, 115
Africa, martyrs of, 134; Roman rule of, 24, 26
agapan, 77
agape, 9, 71, 127, 130, 146, 175; *see also* love
agricultural imagery, 81, 86, 87, 102, 107, 110, 133, 135, 144, 154
Agrippinus, 15
Albinus, 34, 78, 193
Alexander, bishop of Jerusalem, 16; of Abonuteichos, 55; of Aphrodisias, 35; the Great, 20, 143, 155; Tiberius Julius, 22
Alexandria, 13-16, 19, 20-24, 30, 34-35, 57, 84, 92, 93, 99; church at, 27-28, 165-66, 176, 189
allegorical interpretation, 18, 28, 43, 73, 82, 86. 99, 111, 114. 124, 131, 141-42, 161, 180, 181, 190, 192
Ambrose, 89
Amos, 57-58

Anacharsis, 115
Anaxagoras, 55, 168
Anaxarchus, 112
Anaximander, 55
Androcydes, 149
animal imagery, 59, 60, 61-62, 102; symbolism, 141
anthropomorphism, 18
Antinous, 51
Antiphon, 149
Antisthenes, 32, 56
Antonines, 79
Antoninus Pius, 26
apatheia. See freedom from passion
Apelles, 90
Apocalypse of Elijah, 60
Apocalypse of Peter, 162
Apocrypha, 18, 28
Apollinides, 101
Apollo, 118
Apollos, 22
Apologists, 148
aporia (aporein). See doubt
Apostolic Canons, The, 23
Aratus the Stoic, 56
Archelaus, 153
Aristarchus, 114
Aristippus, 84
Aristocles of Messana, 35
Ariston of Chios, 85
Aristophanes, 89
Aristotelian philosophy, 31, 34-35, 49, 114-15, 124, 127
Aristotle, 34-35, 44, 47, 55, 80, 101, 121, 125, 128, 141, 143, 148, 153,

Aristotle (*Continued*)
156-57, 185, 188; *De Interpretatione*, 156; fr., 147; *Metaphysics*, 119; *N.E.*, 125, 185; *Part. An.*, 83
Arrian, 108
art and sculpture, 51-54, 61
Artificer (Demiurge), 158-59
Artorius, 80
asceticism, 128
ascetic sects, 130, 131
Aspasius, 35
assumption, 121
astronomy, 145
ataraxia. See freedom from disturbance
Athenagoras, 14; *Supplication for the Christians*, 14; *Leg.*, 148
Athens, 13, 14, 31, 33-34, 35, 63, 66, 72, 116
athletics imagery, 24, 60, 122, 149, 151, 167, 175
atomic theory, 31
Atomists, 55
Augustine of Hippo, 44, 53; *Confessions*, 53, 67
Aulus Gellius, *N.A.*, 107
Augustus, 20, 25
Aurelius, Marcus, 14, 26, 36, 99-100, 134, 178, 187, 193
autarky. See self-sufficiency
autexousiotes. See freedom of will

Bacchylides, 79, 101
Balaam, 95
barbaros, 120
baptism, 27, 121, 125, 159, 161
Bardesanes, 14
Bardy, G., 15
Basilides, 18, 121, 123, 128, 129, 137, 139, 140
Basilidians, 153
Basil of Caesarea, 54
baths, evils of, 94; use of, 96
beauty, natural, 85, 91; spiritual, 91; true, 89-90, 91
behavior, Christian, 96-100, 183-87, 193
Being, ultimate, 59
Bigg, Charles, 7, 193

Bion, 149
Blake, William, 39
Bousset, W., 157-58
Brahmins, 188
Buddha, 114
Buddhism, 15
Bultmann, R., 182

Caesar, Julius, 117
Caligula, 22
Callimachus, 57
Camelot, P. R., 7, 120
cannibalism, pagan charges of, 29, 48
Carpocrates, 129
Carpocratians, 86, 129-30, 189
Casey, R. P., 160
Cassianus, Julius, 130
Cassiodorus, *Adumbrations of Clement*, 181
Catechetical School, 15
categories of Aristotle, 156
causality, 157
Cecilia, 46
Celsus, 129-30, 164
Cenchreae, 72
Chadwick, H., 130, 131
Chaeremon, 180
character, 69, 106
Charidemus, 153
Charlesworth, M. P., *The Lost Province*, 25
chariot imagery, 33, 59, 65, 97, 101, 125, 172, 176
Chaucer, Oxenford Clerk in, 186
Chesterton, G. K., 50, 175
Christ, mystical body of, 75
Christian behavior, 183-85; character of ideal, 151-52; community, 82-83; desire for heaven, 18, 23; symbols, 141; worship, 80, 84, 105
Christianity and Epicureanism, 36, 84; and true Gnostic, 148; appeal of, to underprivileged, 164-65; in conflict with Rome, 29-31; official religion of Rome, 26; reaching Alexandria, 22; spread of, under Rome, 25, 164-65; state of, 14, 27-29, 94-95

Index

[205]

Index

Index